**Only a Born Again will enter into Heaven
Are you ready?**

Other Books by Hélèné Fulton

Witchcraft in the Church

Get Sanctified in 365 days. The Ultimate Devotional for men and women

Beware of Pagan Traditions & False Religions?

The Complete Deliverance Manual?

Only a Born Again will enter into Heaven
Are you ready?

Hélèné Fulton

Michael Bradley

Light the World Ministries
2014

Copyright © 2014 by Hélènè Fulton
All rights reserved. This book or any portion thereof may not be reproduced or used in any manner whatsoever without the express written permission of the publisher except for the use of brief quotations in a book review or scholarly journal.

First Printing: 2014

ISBN 978-0-620-59499-8

Published by Light the World Ministries

www.lighttheworldministries.co.za
E-mail churchoffice@lighttheworldministries.co.za

Ordering Information:
Special discounts are available on quantity purchases by corporations, associations, educators, and others. For details, contact the publisher at the above listed address.
Bookings for Public speaking or Seminars etc.:
E-mail churchoffice@lighttheworldministries.co.za

Bookstores and wholesalers: Please contact
Light the World Ministries on e-mail
churchoffice@lighttheworldministries.co.za for all orders

Dedication

For all the unconditional love, guidance and teachings, all glory to:

God the Father
God the Son
God the Holy Spirit

To my loving husband Robert thank you for all your support, patience, love and help in the ministry.

Thank you to Chris Bradley for continuing the work of his brother and my dear brother in Christ, Michael Bradley who played a big role in my walk with the Lord.

Tanja Davey – Thank you for the design of the cover. You are a true inspiration on listening to the voice of the Holy Spirit.

Leeanne Naicker – Thank you for all the help with the editing on this book and thank you that I know that I can always count on you.

Contents

Contents ix
Foreword xiii
Preface xv
Chapter 1: Born Again 17
Chapter 2: Water Baptism 25
Chapter 3: God's (Moral & Commandments) Laws .. 31
Chapter 3: Who is the Holy Spirit 53
Chapter 5: How to hear God's voice 65
Chapter 6: Full Surrender 79
Chapter 7: Sanctification 124
Chapter 8: God is the Potter, we are the Clay 148
Chapter 9: Seeking After the Lord with All of Your Heart 165
Chapter 10: Living a Good and Righteous Life before the Lord 205
Chapter 11: Worshiping the Lord 235
Chapter 12: MINDSET - BE Transformed by the Renewing of Your Mind 253
Chapter 13: You Are What You Think 269
Chapter 14: Death and Life Are in the Power of the Tongue 285
Chapter 15: In the World – But Not of the World ... 305
Chapter 16: God is No Respecter of Persons 313

Chapter 17: The 9 Fruits of the Holy Spirit..............324

Chapter 18: The Power of Love 349

Chapter 19: Letting Go of your Past 382

Chapter 20: Be Anxious for Nothing 393

Chapter 21: Godliness with Contentment is Great Gain...404

Chapter 22: Slave to None – Servant to All.............422

Chapter 23: Be Slow to Anger..438

Chapter 24: Pride will come before the Fall............448

Chapter 25: Choose Your Friends Carefully 481

Chapter 26 Fasting...493

Chapter 26 Tithe..494

References 505

Foreword

I became born again at the age of 9 years when an Evangelist visited the Orthodox (NG) church I was attending.

From that day on I had a lot of questions that could not be answered by our minister.

I was attacked both physically and spiritually and could not understand why. More on this and my testimony in my book Witchcraft in the Church.

I started to ask God the questions and God started to answer me through His Spirit. I knew that the answers could not come from myself as how would I possibly know such advance things.

I found that this is the case with many people that become born again regardless of their age.

If you become born again it is impossible to remain in a church that are not born again as your spirit will not get the food it needs to grow.

This book is written to help every born again believer regardless of how many years you have been born again.

This book guarantees you a closer more intimate relationship with Father God.

This book explains what it is to be born again as well as how to fully surrender to God. This book also explains the sanctification process step by step.

If you have any questions that were not covered in this book, feel free to contact me.

God has directed me to write this book so if you do not agree with anything feel free to take it up with God Himself.

If you are involve in any form of the occult and want help to get out. We will gladly assist you with the love of Christ.

Preface

The greatest gift in our life time is the gift of Salvation and it is a gift that has been freely given to us by our Father God through His Son Jesus Christ. Once you have given your heart to the Lord, you are Born Again!!!

You start walking down the winding narrow road that leads to a closer relationship with God ultimately leading to eternity in Heaven. The new journey with Christ means a lot more introspection, learning and growing as a new believer in Christ.

This book offers the key steps to establishing an intimate relationship with God.

Once you make the decision to get closer to God and seek Him earnestly and with passion, you will see the fruits of the Holy Spirit unleashed in your life. We all long to have the peace that passeth all understanding, to feel free from all burdens and have someone else do all the worrying and take care of things for us, well there is - His name is Jesus! And this is exactly what this book offers you. You will learn about sanctification, what it means and what you need to do to start this process in your life.

You will learn about the fruits of the Holy Spirit and how to unleash these in your life.

One of the most profound verses in the bible is that of God being the Potter and we being the clay. Allow yourself to be molded and shaped by the hands of God Himself through this book. God has no favourites, regardless of how big or small our sins may be - He loves us all unconditionally!!!

He is waiting for each of us to dig deep and seek him passionately so that He can show us His everlasting love. Allow yourself to be awakened spiritually and surrender your all to God and He will transform and renew your thoughts, your mind and your life! If you want to know God like never before and walk with Him, then this book is a must read. Don't allow yourself to remain in the past, be bold and be strong for the Lord thy God is with thee... After all the Lord did say that we shall see and do even greater things even if we have faith as small as a mustard seed.

So allow the Holy Spirit to lead and transform your life!

Leeanne Naicker

Chapter 1: Born Again

The New Birth

3 There was a man of the Pharisees named Nicodemus, a ruler of the Jews. 2 This man came to Jesus by night and said to Him, "Rabbi, we know that You are a teacher come from God; for no one can do these signs that You do unless God is with him." ³ Jesus answered and said to him, **"Most assuredly, I say to you, unless one is born again, he cannot see the kingdom of God."** ⁴ Nicodemus said to Him, "How can a man be born when he is old? Can he enter a second time into his mother's womb and be born?" ⁵ Jesus answered, **"Most assuredly, I say to you, unless one is born of water and the Spirit, he cannot enter the kingdom of God.** ⁶ That which is born of the flesh is flesh, and that which is born of the Spirit is spirit. ⁷ Do not marvel that I said to you, 'You must be born again.' ⁸ The wind blows where it wishes, and you hear the sound of it, but cannot tell where it comes from and where it goes. So is everyone who is born of the Spirit." ⁹ Nicodemus answered and said to Him, "How can these things be?" ¹⁰ Jesus answered and said to him, "Are you the teacher of Israel, and do not know these things? ¹¹ Most assuredly, I say to you, We speak what We know and testify what We have seen, and you do not receive Our witness. ¹² If I have told you earthly things and you do not believe, how will you believe if I tell you heavenly things? ¹³ No one has ascended to heaven but He who came down from heaven, *that is,* the Son of Man who is in heaven. ¹⁴ And as Moses lifted up the serpent in the wilderness, even so must the Son of Man be lifted up, ¹⁵ that whoever believes in Him should not perish but have eternal life. ¹⁶ **For God so loved the world that He gave His only begotten Son, that whoever believes in Him should not perish but have everlasting life.**

[17] For God did not send His Son into the world to condemn the world, but that the world through Him might be saved.
[18] "He who believes in Him is not condemned; but he who does not believe is condemned already, because he has not believed in the name of the only begotten Son of God. [19] And this is the condemnation, **that the light has come into the world, and men loved darkness rather than light, because their deeds were evil.** [20] For everyone practicing evil hates the light and does not come to the light, lest his deeds should be exposed. [21] But he who does the truth comes to the light, that his deeds may be clearly seen, that they have been done in God."

John 3:1-21

Nicodemus was a theological professor and a member in parliament, he paid his tithe from all his income, he fasted two days a week, he prayed two hours a day. But look at what Jesus is asking Nicodemus in verse 10. *"Are you the teacher of Israel, and do not know these things?*

Even in today's modern world with millions of preachers about 95% of them are not born again and probably does not even know what it means. This is scary as they are the teachers of the gospel.

It is very easy to say that I believe the Bible. It is very easy to say I know the Bible. It is even easier to say I'm a Christian but are you really a Christian? Are you 100% sure that you will enter the kingdom of God (Heaven) when your physical body dies.
You might be a very good person doing wonderful deeds for your fellow man but have you really been born again!

Are you a new person in Jesus Christ?

Are you willing to deny yourself and give yourself completely over to Jesus Christ? Are you willing to let Jesus Christ control your life?

Jesus did not say you ought to be born again He said **you have to be** born again if you want to enter the kingdom of God.

What Jesus was saying is that it is easy to say I'm a Christian but it is different matter to really know Jesus Christ.

You cannot just do the things to show people you're a Christian; you need to know Jesus Christ Himself. Jesus said this because he knows your heart. Yes Jesus Christ knows every person's heart. He knows you say you love Him but He knows that your heart belongs to business or pleasure or even to Satan.

All the sins you're doing each day comes from within. It starts from the heart and once it reaches the mind you're already making plans to fulfill that desire. That is why God said guard your heart in His word (the Bible).

[23] Keep thy heart with all diligence; for out of it are the issues of life.

Proverbs 4:23 (KJ)

There's a lot of good people supporting the under privilege, but some people are doing it to be seen by others. God looks at what's inside your heart. Even if man lived in paradise, he'll still have an evil heart.

You can only change this if you give your heart to God to control completely.

Never please people please God.
Born again means to be "born from above."
Nicodemus had a real need. He was hungry to change and he needed a change of his heart - a spiritual transformation.
New birth, being born again, is an act of God whereby eternal life is imparted to the person who believes indicates that "born again" also carries the idea "to become children of God" through trust in the name of Jesus Christ.

[17] Therefore, if anyone *is* in Christ, *he is* a new creation; old things have passed away; behold, all things have become new.

2 Corinthians 5:17

[5] not by works of righteousness which we have done, but according to His mercy He saved us, through the washing of regeneration and renewing of the Holy Spirit,

Titus 3:5

[3] Blessed *be* the God and Father of our Lord Jesus Christ, who according to His abundant mercy has begotten us again to a living hope through the resurrection of Jesus Christ from the dead

1 Peter 1:3

[29] If you know that He is righteous, you know that everyone who practices righteousness is born of Him.

1 John 2:29

[9] Whoever has been born of God does not sin, for His seed remains in him; and he cannot sin, because he has been born of God.

1 John 3:9

[7] Beloved, let us love one another, for love is of God; and everyone who loves is born of God and knows God.

1 John 4:7

5 Whoever believes that Jesus is the Christ is born of God, and everyone who loves Him who begot also loves him who is begotten of Him. [2] By this we know that we love the children of God, when we love God and keep His commandments. [3] For this is the love of God, that we keep His commandments. And His commandments are not burdensome. [4] For **whatever is born of God overcomes the world. And this is the victory that has overcome the world—our faith.**

1 John 5:1-4

[18] We know that whoever is born of God does not sin; but he who has been born of God keeps himself, and the wicked one does not touch him.

1 John 5:18

[12] But as many as received Him, to them He gave the right to become children of God, to those who believe in His name: [13] who were born, not of blood, nor of the will of the flesh, nor of the will of man, but of God.

John 1:12-13

Why do you need to be born again?

2 And you *He made alive,* who were dead in trespasses and sins,

Ephesians 2:1

To the Romans in Romans 3:23, the Apostle wrote, *for all have sinned and fall short of the glory of God,* So, a person needs to be born again in order to have their sins forgiven and have a relationship with God.

²³ for all have sinned and fall short of the glory of God

Romans 3:23

How does that come to be?

⁸ For by grace you have been saved through faith, and that not of yourselves; *it is* the gift of God, ⁹ not of works, lest anyone should boast.

Ephesians 2:8-9

When a person is "saved," he/she has been born again, spiritually renewed, and is now a child of God by right of new birth. Trusting in Jesus Christ, the One who paid the penalty of sin when He died on the cross, is what it means to be "born again" spiritually.

¹⁷ Therefore, if anyone *is* in Christ, *he is* a new creation; old things have passed away; behold, all things have become new.

2 Corinthians 5:17

If you have never trusted in the Lord Jesus Christ as your Savior, how can you hear the Holy Spirit as He speaks to you? How will you hear the Holy Spirit when He warns you of danger?

Do you have what it takes to be a born again Christian?

Do you want a personal relationship with Jesus?

Don't say the prayer just you want "fire protection".

Become born again because you want to with all your heart.

Will you pray the prayer of repentance and become a new creation in Jesus Christ today?

[12] But as many as received Him, to them He gave the right to become children of God, to those who believe in His name: [13] who were born, not of blood, nor of the will of the flesh, nor of the will of man, but of God.

John 1:12-13

If you are tired of living a life without meaning in a materialistic world that lacks compassion and love, a world that has chosen mammon as it's god and that will sacrifice anything and anybody to achieve its ultimate goal: "financial freedom", then please consider the alternative.

Jesus Christ is waiting for you every single day to open up your heart to Him and to invite Him into your life. If you prayed this prayer with a sincere and a true heart - then you can be assured that the Lord has prepared a place for you in heaven.

Once you are ready to take the next step the following prayer will be your ticket to Eternity:

The Prayer that will change Your Eternal Destiny

"Father, I thank You that Jesus died for me. I confess I have broken Your laws. Forgive my sins. I receive the pardon right now. Lord Jesus, come into my life. Give me a new heart with new desires. And by Your Spirit, give me the power to live a life that is pleasing to You. Father please fill me with the Holy Spirit. Thank you for forgiving me as You have promised. Thank You for the gift of eternal Life."

Congratulations and welcome to the family of God. No matter what you've done in your life, you've received a full pardon in God's eyes. That's how easy it is for you.
But it was not free - it cost God the life of His beloved Son, Jesus Christ in your place. Just thank Him for loving you so much.

Write this date in your Bible as this is the date the new you were born.

Chapter 2: Water Baptism

The English word "Baptism" comes from the Greek word "Baptizo", which means to, dip under, immerse, and whelm that is, to cover wholly with fluid. So this cannot include sprinkling a few drops of water on a baby's forehead.

You need to get baptised because Jesus was baptised and He **left an example for us to follow** in His steps.

John Baptizes Jesus

13 Then Jesus came from Galilee to John at the Jordan to be baptized by him. 14 And John *tried to* prevent Him, saying, "I need to be baptized by You, and are You coming to me?" 15 But Jesus answered and said to him, "Permit *it to be so* now, for thus it is fitting for us to fulfill all righteousness." Then he allowed Him. 16 When He had been baptized, Jesus came up immediately from the water; and behold, the heavens were opened to Him, and He saw the Spirit of God descending like a dove and alighting upon Him. 17 And suddenly a voice *came* from heaven, saying, "This is My beloved Son, in whom I am well pleased."

Matthew 3:13-17

Jesus was baptised to "fulfil" or "complete" all righteousness by being **obedient** to His Father's (God) will. He was not baptised because He was a forgiven sinner, for He had no sin. He was always righteous. If Jesus was not baptised, He would have disobeyed His Father's will and would no longer have been righteous.

Obedience pleases God and brings the blessing of God.

21 For He made Him who knew no sin *to be* sin for us, that we might become the righteousness of God in Him.

2 Corinthians 5:21

Christians are also righteous and so like Christ are baptised to fulfil or complete all righteousness, by an act of obedience.

It is a commandment of God in scripture and children of God desire to obey God.

[15] And He said to them, "Go into all the world and preach the gospel to every creature. [16] He who believes and is baptized will be saved; but he who does not believe will be condemned.
Mark 16:15-16

Do you love God? Look what the Bible tells us.

[15] "If you love Me, keep My commandments.
John 14:15

Are there any special conditions you need to fulfil before you can be baptised?

[35] Then Philip opened his mouth, and beginning at this Scripture, preached Jesus to him. [36] Now as they went down the road, they came to some water. And the eunuch said, "See, *here is* water. What hinders me from being baptized?"

³⁷ Then Philip said, "If you believe with all your heart, you may." And he answered and said, "I believe that Jesus Christ is the Son of God."
³⁸ So he commanded the chariot to stand still. And both Philip and the eunuch went down into the water, and he baptized him.
³⁹ Now when they came up out of the water, the Spirit of the Lord caught Philip away, so that the eunuch saw him no more; and he went on his way rejoicing.

Acts 8:35-39

When the Ethiopian eunuch asked the evangelist Phillip: "What hinders me from being baptized?" "

The Evangelist answered and said: "If you believe with all your heart, you may."

And he answered and said, "I believe that Jesus Christ is the Son of God."

⁹ that if you confess with your mouth the Lord Jesus and believe in your heart that God has raised Him from the dead, you will be saved.

Romans 10:9

Once you are saved, you are ready for baptism. There is no special spiritual level you have to reach to prepare yourself for baptism. When you are saved you are re-born with God's righteousness and there is nothing else you can do to prepare yourself for baptism.

Water baptism is a symbolic burial, by which the new born again Christian publicly declares they have died, and are now beginning a new life, in Christ.

Water baptism outwardly demonstrates what has happened inwardly. Water baptism helps you to grasp the reality of the spiritual truth that the old "you" has died.

Water baptism is only as important as the person being baptized believes it to be. Water baptism is their confession, and a public commitment.

You die to the old you when you accept Jesus Christ as your Lord and Savior. So some people see baptism as a burial to that old self. When they come out from under the water they come out as a new person.

But unless the person really believes they died, there is no need for a burial.

It is not something you do to impress God or your pastor, but something to impress on our mind what happened to us inwardly. Water baptism is for your benefit not God's.

[38] Then Peter said to them, "Repent, and let every one of you be baptized in the name of Jesus Christ for the remission of sins; and you shall receive the gift of the Holy Spirit.

Acts 2:38

Peter is not giving a new way for water baptism but is instructing these disciples in the authority of the name of Jesus Christ that since they have repented and been forgiven of their sins, they must now obey God and get baptised.

[41] Then those who gladly received his word were baptized; and that day about three thousand souls were added *to them.*

Acts 2:41

Some Christians have struggled to receive the infilling of the Holy Spirit, because in their hearts they have determined to disobey God and not get baptised by immersion.

⁴⁷ "Can anyone forbid water, that these should not be baptized who have received the Holy Spirit just as we *have?*" ⁴⁸ And he commanded them to be baptized in the name of the Lord. Then they asked him to stay a few days.

Acts 10:47-48

Peter used his authority in the name of Jesus Christ to order them to be baptised and was not giving new instructions for water baptism.

We baptize people through our authority in Jesus Christ in the name of the Father and the Son and the Holy Spirit.

Why was Jesus baptized in water? He was, and is, our pattern. And, in a sense, He was, at that point, dying to His past life.

He was beginning His public ministry.

Jesus was declaring that He was dead to any selfishness and existed solely to do the will of Father God.

Must you be baptized to be saved? No. Once you have accepted Jesus Christ as your Lord and Saviour, you are saved.

⁴³ And Jesus said to him, "Assuredly, I say to you, today you will be with Me in Paradise."

Luke 23:43

Jesus told this criminal that he will be with Him. This man was not baptized.

³⁸ He who believes in Me, as the Scripture has said, out of his heart will flow rivers of living water." ³⁹ But this He spoke concerning the Spirit, whom those believing in Him would receive; for the Holy Spirit was not yet *given,* because Jesus was not yet glorified.

John 7:38-39

¹⁷ And these signs will follow those who believe: In My name they will cast out demons; they will speak with new tongues

Mark 16:17

The household of Cornelius became believers, received the Holy Spirit, and began speaking in tongues, **before** being baptized in water.

According to Jesus receiving the Holy Spirit happens *only* to those who are believers, and they are therefore saved.

So, these believers were born again and ready for Heaven, before they were baptized in water.

If any of you want to be baptized and you are staying in Gauteng feel free to contact us on the e-mail provided in the front of this book.

Chapter 3: God's (Moral & Commandments) Laws

[17] "Do not think that I came to destroy the Law or the Prophets. I did not come to destroy but to fulfill. [18] For assuredly, I say to you, till heaven and earth pass away, one jot or one tittle will by no means pass from the law till all is fulfilled. [19] Whoever therefore breaks one of the least of these commandments, and teaches men so, shall be called least in the kingdom of heaven; but whoever does and teaches *them,* he shall be called great in the kingdom of heaven.
Matthew 5:17-19

When a lawyer asked Jesus Christ:

[36] "Teacher, which *is* the great commandment in the law?"
[37] Jesus said to him, "'You shall love the LORD your God with all your heart, with all your soul, and with all your mind.' [38] This is *the* first and great commandment. [39] And *the* second *is* like it: 'You shall love your neighbor as yourself.' [40] On these two commandments hang all the Law and the Prophets."
Matthew 22:36-40

[3] "You shall have no other gods before Me.
[4] "You shall not make for yourself a carved image—any likeness *of anything* that *is* in heaven above, or that *is* in the earth beneath, or that *is* in the water under the earth; [5] you shall not bow down to them nor serve them. For I, the LORD your God, *am* a jealous God, visiting the iniquity of the fathers upon the children to the third and fourth *generations* of those who hate Me, [6] but showing mercy to thousands, to those who love Me and keep My commandments.
[7] "You shall not take the name of the LORD your God in vain, for the LORD will not hold *him* guiltless who takes His name in vain.

⁸ "Remember the Sabbath day, to keep it holy. ⁹ Six days you shall labor and do all your work, ¹⁰ but the seventh day *is* the Sabbath of the LORD your God. *In it* you shall do no work: you, nor your son, nor your daughter, nor your male servant, nor your female servant, nor your cattle, nor your stranger who *is* within your gates. ¹¹ For *in* six days the LORD made the heavens and the earth, the sea, and all that *is* in them, and rested the seventh day. Therefore the LORD blessed the Sabbath day and hallowed it.

¹² "Honor your father and your mother, that your days may be long upon the land which the LORD your God is giving you.

¹³ "You shall not murder.

¹⁴ "You shall not commit adultery.

¹⁵ "You shall not steal.

¹⁶ "You shall not bear false witness against your neighbor.

¹⁷ "You shall not covet your neighbor's house; you shall not covet your neighbor's wife, nor his male servant, nor his female servant, nor his ox, nor his donkey, nor anything that *is* your neighbor's."

Exodus 20:3-17

⁷ 'You shall have no other gods before Me.

⁸ 'You shall not make for yourself a carved image—any likeness *of anything* that *is* in heaven above, or that *is* in the earth beneath, or that *is* in the water under the earth; ⁹ you shall not bow down to them nor serve them. For I, the LORD your God, *am* a jealous God, visiting the iniquity of the fathers upon the children to the third and fourth *generations* of those who hate Me, ¹⁰ but showing mercy to thousands, to those who love Me and keep My commandments.

¹¹ 'You shall not take the name of the LORD your God in vain, for the LORD will not hold *him* guiltless who takes His name in vain.

¹² 'Observe the Sabbath day, to keep it holy, as the LORD your God commanded you. ¹³ Six days you shall labor and do all your work, ¹⁴ but the seventh day *is* the Sabbath of the LORD your God. *In it* you shall do no work: you, nor your son, nor your

daughter, nor your male servant, nor your female servant, nor your ox, nor your donkey, nor any of your cattle, nor your stranger who *is* within your gates, that your male servant and your female servant may rest as well as you. [15] And remember that you were a slave in the land of Egypt, and the LORD your God brought you out from there by a mighty hand and by an outstretched arm; therefore the LORD your God commanded you to keep the Sabbath day.

[16] 'Honor your father and your mother, as the LORD your God has commanded you, that your days may be long, and that it may be well with you in the land which the LORD your God is giving you.

[17] 'You shall not murder.

[18] 'You shall not commit adultery.

[19] 'You shall not steal.

[20] 'You shall not bear false witness against your neighbor.

[21] 'You shall not covet your neighbor's wife; and you shall not desire your neighbor's house, his field, his male servant, his female servant, his ox, his donkey, or anything that *is* your neighbor's.'

[22] "These words the LORD spoke to all your assembly, in the mountain from the midst of the fire, the cloud, and the thick darkness, with a loud voice; and He added no more. And He wrote them on two tablets of stone and gave them to me.

Deuteronomy 5:7-22

I have heard some preachers preach that you cannot sin because you are under grace. I think they did not get the memo from God.

You are saved by grace. Grace does not give you a free to sin card.

17 And it is easier for heaven and earth to pass away than for one tittle of the law to fail.

Luke 16:17

We still have to obey all God's Moral Laws and Commandments.

15 "If you love Me, keep My commandments.

John 14:15

The old Mosaic Law versus the new Law of Grace

The laws of the Old Testament as describe in the book of Leviticus were fulfilled through Jesus Christ when He was crucified. His death as the perfect Lamb of God served as the propitiation needed to redeem all who would believe in Him. No need to sacrifice a goat or lamb or anything else prescribed in the book of Leviticus when Jesus Himself met all the conditions for us.

But in contrast, the moral laws of the Old Testament are as applicable today as ever.

Remember what Jesus said in Matthew 5:17-19.

17 "Do not think that I came to destroy the Law or the Prophets. I did not come to destroy but to fulfill. 18 For assuredly, I say to you, till heaven and earth pass away, one jot or one tittle will by no means pass from the law till all is fulfilled. 19 Whoever therefore breaks one of the least of these commandments, and teaches men so, shall be called least in the kingdom of heaven; but whoever does and teaches *them,* he shall be called great in the kingdom of heaven.

Matthew 5:17-19

You are responsible to know and follow these guidelines, not by your own strength, but by the Holy Spirit that lives inside of us.

As you study God's Word (The Bible both Old and New Testament), you will come to know God's Commandments and Moral laws. God will enable you to follow them.

Remember it is not going to be easy as our flesh (human body) has a sinful nature.

[20] Therefore by the deeds of the law no flesh will be justified in His sight, for by the law *is* the knowledge of sin.
Romans 3:20

[19] for the law made nothing perfect; on the other hand, *there is the* bringing in of a better hope, through which we draw near to God.
Hebrews 7:19

[15] John bore witness of Him and cried out, saying, "This was He of whom I said, 'He who comes after me is preferred before me, for He was before me.'"
[16] And of His fullness we have all received, and grace for grace.
[17] For the law was given through Moses, *but* grace and truth came through Jesus Christ.
John 1:15-17

²⁸ For he is not a Jew who *is one* outwardly, nor *is* circumcision that which *is* outward in the flesh; ²⁹ but *he is* a Jew who *is one* inwardly; and **circumcision *is that* of the heart, in the Spirit**, not in the letter; whose praise *is* not from men but from God.

Romans 2:28-29

The verse above also answers any questions you might have on circumcision.

²³ "Woe to you, scribes and Pharisees, hypocrites! For you pay tithe of mint and anise and cummin, and have neglected the weightier *matters* of the law: **justice and mercy and faith**. These you ought to have done, without leaving the others undone. ²⁴ Blind guides, who strain out a gnat and swallow a camel!

Matthew 23:23-24

⁴⁴ Then He said to them, "These *are* the words which I spoke to you while I was still with you, that **all things must be fulfilled which were written in the Law of Moses and *the* Prophets and *the* Psalms concerning Me.**" ⁴⁵ And He opened their understanding, that they might comprehend the Scriptures.

Luke 24:44-45

The Law exposes our guilt & points us to the cross

¹⁷ And this I say, *that* the law, which was four hundred and thirty years later, cannot annul the covenant that was confirmed before by God in Christ, that it should make the promise of no effect. ¹⁸ For if the inheritance *is* of the law, *it is* no longer of promise; but God gave *it* to Abraham by promise.

Purpose of the Law

¹⁹ What purpose then *does* the law *serve?* It was added because of transgressions, till the Seed should come to whom the promise was made; *and it was* appointed through angels by the

hand of a mediator. [20] Now a mediator does not *mediate* for one *only,* but God is one.

[21] *Is* the law then against the promises of God? Certainly not! For if there had been a law given which could have given life, truly righteousness would have been by the law. [22] But the Scripture has confined all under sin, that the promise by faith in Jesus Christ might be given to those who believe. [23] But **before faith came, we were kept under guard by the law, kept for the faith which would afterward be revealed.** [24] **Therefore the law was our tutor** *to bring us* **to Christ**, that we might be justified by faith. [25] But after faith has come, we are no longer under a tutor.

Galatians 3:17-25

⁷ What shall we say then? *Is* the law sin? Certainly not! On the contrary, I would not have known sin except through the law. For I would not have known covetousness unless the law had said, "You shall not covet."

Romans 7:7

¹² Therefore **the law *is* holy, and the commandment holy and just and good.**

Law Cannot Save from Sin

¹³ Has then what is good become death to me? Certainly not! But sin, that it might appear sin, was producing death in me through what is good, so that sin through the commandment might become exceedingly sinful.

Romans 7:12-13

¹⁹ Now we know that whatever the law says, it says to those who are under the law, that every mouth may be stopped, and **all the world may become guilty before God.** ²⁰ Therefore by the deeds of the law no flesh will be justified in His sight, for **by the law *is* the knowledge of sin.**

God's Righteousness Through Faith

²¹ But now **the righteousness of God apart from the law is revealed**, being witnessed by the Law and the Prophets, ²² even **the righteousness of God, through faith** in Jesus Christ, to all and on all who believe. For there is no difference; ²³ **for all have sinned and fall short of the glory of God,** ²⁴ **being justified freely by His grace through the redemption that is in Christ Jesus,** ²⁵ whom God set forth *as* a propitiation by His blood, through faith, to demonstrate His righteousness, because in His forbearance God had passed over the sins that were previously committed, ²⁶ to demonstrate at the present time His righteousness, **that He might be just and the justifier of the one who has faith in Jesus.**

Boasting Excluded

[27] Where *is* boasting then? It is excluded. By what law? Of works? No, but by the law of faith. [28] Therefore we conclude that a man is justified by faith apart from the deeds of the law. [29] Or *is He* the God of the Jews only? *Is He* not also the God of the Gentiles? Yes, of the Gentiles also, [30] since *there is* one God who will justify the circumcised by faith and the uncircumcised through faith. [31] Do we then make void **the law through faith**? Certainly not! On the contrary, we establish the law.

Romans 3:19-31

The Promise Granted Through Faith

[13] For the promise that he would be the heir of the world *was* not to Abraham or to his seed through the law, but through the righteousness of faith. [14] For if those who are of the law *are* heirs, faith is made void and the promise made of no effect, [15] because **the law brings about wrath**; for where there is no law *there is* no transgression.
[16] Therefore *it is* of faith that *it might be* according to grace, so that the promise might be sure to all the seed, not only to those who are of the law, but also to those who are of the faith of Abraham, who is the father of us all

Romans 4:13-16

Death in Adam, Life in Christ

[12] Therefore, just as through one man sin entered the world, and death through sin, and thus death spread to all men, because **all sinned**— [13] (For until the law sin was in the world, but sin is not imputed when there is no law. [14] Nevertheless death reigned from Adam to Moses, even over those who had not sinned according to the likeness of the transgression of Adam, who is a type of Him who was to come. [15] But the free gift *is* not like the offense. For if by the one man's offense many died, much more **the grace of God** and the **gift by the grace of the one Man, Jesus Christ**, abounded to many.

Romans 5:12-15

²² And according to the law almost all things are purified with blood, and without shedding of blood there is no remission.
Hebrews 9:22

¹⁸ Therefore, as through one man's offense *judgment came* to all men, resulting in condemnation, **even so through one Man's righteous act** *the free gift came* **to all men, resulting in justification of life.** ¹⁹ For as by one man's disobedience many were made sinners, so also by one Man's obedience many will be made righteous.
²⁰ Moreover **the law entered that the offense might abound**. But where sin abounded, grace abounded much more, ²¹ so that as sin reigned in death, even so grace might reign through righteousness to eternal life through Jesus Christ our Lord.
Romans 5:18-21

Freed from the Law
7 Or do you not know, brethren (for I speak to those who know the law), that the law has dominion over a man as long as he lives? ² For the woman who has a husband is bound by the law to *her* husband as long as he lives. But if the husband dies, she is released from the law of *her* husband. ³ So then if, while *her* husband lives, she marries another man, she will be called an adulteress; but if her husband dies, she is free from that law, so that she is no adulteress, though she has married another man.
⁴ Therefore, my brethren, you also have become dead to the law through the body of Christ, that you may be married to another—to Him who was raised from the dead, that we should bear fruit to God. ⁵ For when we were in the flesh, the sinful passions which were aroused by the law were at work in our members to bear fruit to death.

⁶ But now we have been delivered from the law, having died to what we were held by, so
that we should serve in the newness of the Spirit and not *in* the oldness of the letter.

Sin's Advantage in the Law
⁷ What shall we say then? *Is* the law sin? Certainly not! On the contrary, I would not have known sin except through the law. For I would not have known covetousness unless the law had said, "You shall not covet." ⁸ But sin, taking opportunity by the commandment, produced in me all *manner of evil* desire. For apart from the law sin *was* dead. ⁹ I was alive once without the law, but when the commandment came, sin revived and I died. ¹⁰ And the commandment, which *was* to *bring* life, I found to *bring* death. ¹¹ For sin, taking occasion by the commandment, deceived me, and by it killed *me.* ¹² **Therefore the law *is* holy, and the commandment holy and just and good.**

Law Cannot Save from Sin
¹³ Has then what is good become death to me? Certainly not! **But sin, that it might appear sin, was producing death in me through what is good, so that sin through the commandment might become exceedingly sinful.** ¹⁴ For we know that the law is spiritual, but I am carnal, sold under sin. ¹⁵ For what I am doing, I do not understand. For what I will to do, that I do not practice; but what I hate, that I do. ¹⁶ If, then, I do what I will not to do, **I agree with the law that *it is* good.** ¹⁷ But now, *it is* no longer I who do it, but sin that dwells in me. ¹⁸ For I know that in me (that is, in my flesh) nothing good dwells; for **to will is present with me, but *how* to perform what is good I do not find.** ¹⁹ For the good that I will *to do,* I do not do; but the evil I will not *to do,* that I practice. ²⁰ Now if I do what I will not *to do,* it is no longer I who do it, but sin that dwells in me.
²¹ I find then a law, that evil is present with me, the one who wills to do good. ²² For **I delight in the law of God according to the inward man.** ²³ But I see another law in my members,

warring against the law of my mind, and bringing me into captivity to the law of sin which is in my members. [24] O wretched man that I am! Who will deliver me from this body of death? [25] I thank God—through Jesus Christ our Lord!
So then, with the mind I myself serve the law of God, but with the flesh the law of sin.

Romans 7:1-25

Free from Indwelling Sin
8 *There is* therefore now no condemnation to those who are in Christ Jesus, who do not walk according to the flesh, but according to the Spirit. [2] For the law of the Spirit of life in Christ Jesus has made me free from the law of sin and death. [3] For what the law could not do in that it was weak through the flesh, God *did* by sending His own Son in the likeness of sinful flesh, on account of sin: He condemned sin in the flesh, [4] **that the righteous requirement of the law might be fulfilled in us who do not walk according to the flesh but according to the Spirit.** [5] **For those who live according to the flesh set their minds on the things of the flesh, but those** *who live* **according to the Spirit, the things of the Spirit.** [6] For to be carnally minded *is* death, but to be spiritually minded *is* life and peace. [7] Because the carnal mind *is* enmity against God; for it is not subject to the law of God, nor indeed can be. [8] So then, those who are in the flesh cannot please God.
[9] **But you are not in the flesh but in the Spirit**, if indeed the Spirit of God dwells in you. **Now if anyone does not have the Spirit of Christ, he is not His.**

Romans 8:1-9

It is clear from the verses above that if we are born again and in line with God that God through the Holy Spirit will convict us of what we are doing wrong. If we are not born again, how can we have the Holy Spirit in us? You get the Holy Spirit when you are born again as then you invite Him to come live inside of you. Now Romans 8 verse 9 clearly states that if you do not have the Spirit of Christ you are not a child of God.

[13] And do not present your members *as* instruments of unrighteousness to sin, but **present yourselves to God as being alive from the dead**, and your members *as* instruments of righteousness to God. [14] For sin shall not have dominion over you, for **you are not under law but under grace.**

From Slaves of Sin to Slaves of God
[15] What then? Shall we sin because we are not **under law but under grace**? Certainly not! [16] **Do you not know that to whom you present yourselves slaves to obey, you are that one's slaves whom you obey, whether of sin** *leading* **to death, or of obedience** *leading* **to righteousness?**
Romans 6:13-16

Yes we are under grace like so many preachers preach but they forget to also read verse 15 and 16 to you.

If you are a child of God then you should not keep yourself busy with fortune telling, rebellion and all the things I mention in my book Witchcraft in the Church.

Present Condition of Israel
[30] What shall we say then? That Gentiles, who did not pursue righteousness, have attained to righteousness, even the righteousness of faith; [31] but Israel, pursuing the law of righteousness, has not attained to **the law of righteousness**. [32] Why? Because ***they did* not *seek it* by faith**, but as it were, **by the works of the law**. For they stumbled at that stumbling stone. [33] As it is written:
"Behold, I lay in Zion a stumbling stone and rock of offense, And whoever believes on Him will not be put to shame."
Romans 9:30-33

[3] For they being ignorant of God's righteousness, and seeking to establish their own righteousness, have not submitted to the righteousness of God. [4] For Christ *is* the end of **the law for righteousness** to everyone who believes.
[5] For Moses writes about the righteousness which is of the law, "The man who does those things shall live by them."
Romans 10:3-5

The Law of Love (*agapao* - God's love)

[37] Jesus said to him, "**You shall love the L**ᴏʀᴅ **your God with all your heart, with all your soul, and with all your mind.**' [38] This is *the* first and great commandment. [39] And *the* second *is* like it: '**You shall love your neighbor as yourself.**'
Matthew 22:37-39

Love Your Neighbor
[8] Owe no one anything except to love one another, for he who loves another has fulfilled the law. [9] For the commandments, "You shall not commit adultery," "You shall not murder," "You shall not steal," "You shall not bear false witness," "You shall not covet," and if *there is* any other commandment, are *all* summed up in this saying, namely, "You shall love your neighbor as

yourself." [10] Love does no harm to a neighbor; therefore **love *is* the fulfillment of the law.**

Romans 13:8-10

The source of this "agapao" love is God -- through the Holy Spirit in us. Ordinary human affection or "phileo" love does not meet God's standard.

You cannot love your neighbour if you do not love yourself.

You can only love yourself if you truly love God because He created you. In His eyes He created you good and in His likeness (image).

So if you complain about your looks then you are saying God did not do a good job when He created you.

If you became fat that is not God's doing that is your own doing. Do something about it.

What we do in life has consequences. You cannot blame anyone but yourself for what happen to you when you do something that you should not have done.

If you drink too much and as a result of the amount of alcohol in your blood, have an accident that dis figures you that are your own doing.

If you are racist then how can you call yourself a child of God? Did God not tell you to love your neighbour? And believe me God did not mean neighbour as in the person living next to you.

¹⁴ For all the law is fulfilled in one word, *even* in this: "You shall love your neighbor as yourself." ¹⁵ But if you bite and devour one another, beware lest you be consumed by one another!

Walking in the Spirit

¹⁶ I say then: Walk in the Spirit, and you shall not fulfill the lust of the flesh. ¹⁷ For the flesh lusts against the Spirit, and the Spirit against the flesh; and these are contrary to one another, so that you do not do the things that you wish. ¹⁸ But if you are led by the Spirit, you are not under the law.

¹⁹ Now the works of the flesh are evident, which are: adultery, fornication, uncleanness, lewdness, ²⁰ idolatry, sorcery, hatred, contentions, jealousies, outbursts of wrath, selfish ambitions, dissensions, heresies, ²¹ envy, murders, drunkenness, revelries, and the like; of which I tell you beforehand, just as I also told *you* in time past, **that those who practice such things will not inherit the kingdom of God.**

²² But the fruit of the Spirit is love, joy, peace, longsuffering, kindness, goodness, faithfulness, ²³ gentleness, self-control. Against such there is no law. ²⁴ And those *who are* Christ's have crucified the flesh with its passions and desires.

Galatians 5:14-24

Bear and Share the Burdens

6 Brethren, if a man is overtaken in any trespass, you who *are* spiritual restore such a one in a spirit of gentleness, considering yourself lest you also be tempted. ² Bear one another's burdens, and so fulfill the law of Christ.

Galatians 6:1-2

Glorify God in Body and Spirit
¹² All things are lawful for me, but all things are not helpful. All things are lawful for me, but I will not be brought under the power of any.

1 Corinthians 6:12

This is only true for those who have been joined to Jesus Christ through the cross and are led by the Holy Spirit to follow His ways. They are no longer "under" the judgment of the law but live by God's wonderful grace. It's not true for those who reject His Word and Spirit!

Dead to Sin, Alive to God
6 What shall we say then? Shall we continue in sin that grace may abound? ² Certainly not! How shall we who **died to sin** live any longer in it? ³ Or do you not know that as many of us as were baptized into Christ Jesus were baptized into His death? ⁴ Therefore we were buried with Him through baptism into death, that **just as Christ was raised from the dead** by the glory of the Father, even **so we also should walk in newness of life**.

Romans 6:1-4

Stand firm in God's grace; don't return to legal bondage"

Justification by Faith
3 O foolish Galatians! Who has bewitched you that you should not obey the truth, before whose eyes Jesus Christ was clearly portrayed among you as crucified? ² This only I want to learn from you: Did you receive the Spirit by the works of the law, or by the hearing of faith? ³ Are you so foolish? **Having begun in the Spirit, are you now being made perfect by the flesh?** ⁴ Have you suffered so many things in vain—if indeed *it was* in vain? ⁵ Therefore He who supplies the Spirit to you and works miracles among you, *does He do it* by the works of the law, or by the

hearing of faith?— ⁶ just as Abraham "believed God, and it was accounted to him for righteousness." ⁷ Therefore know that *only* those who are of faith are sons of Abraham. ⁸ And the Scripture, foreseeing that God would justify the Gentiles by faith, preached the gospel to Abraham beforehand, *saying,* "In you all the nations shall be blessed." ⁹ So then those who *are* of faith are blessed with believing Abraham.

The Law Brings a Curse
¹⁰ For **as many as are of the works of the law are under the curse**; for it is written, "Cursed *is* everyone who does not continue in all things which are written in the book of the law, to do them." ¹¹ But that no one is justified by the law in the sight of God *is* evident, for "the just shall live by faith." ¹² Yet the law is not of faith, but "the man who does them shall live by them." ¹³ Christ has redeemed us from the curse of the law, having become a curse for us (for it is written, "Cursed *is* everyone who hangs on a tree"), ¹⁴ that the blessing of Abraham might come upon the Gentiles in Christ Jesus, that we might receive the promise of the Spirit through faith.

Galatians 3:1-14

⁴ But when the fullness of the time had come, God sent forth His Son, born of a woman, born under the law, ⁵ **to redeem those who were under the law**, that we might receive the adoption as sons.
⁶ And because you are sons, God has sent forth the Spirit of His Son into your hearts, crying out, "Abba, Father!" ⁷ Therefore you are no longer a slave but a son, and if a son, then an heir of God through Christ.

Galatians 4:4-7

¹³ For not even those who are circumcised keep the law, but they desire to have you circumcised that they may boast in your flesh. ¹⁴ But God forbid that I should boast except in the cross of

our Lord Jesus Christ, by whom the world has been crucified to me, and I to the world.

Galatians 6:13-14

Christ Our Peace

[14] For **He Himself is our peace, who has made both one, and has broken down the middle wall of separation,** [15] having abolished in His flesh the enmity, *that is,* the law of commandments *contained* in ordinances, so as **to create in Himself one new man *from* the two,** *thus* making peace, [16] and that He might reconcile them both to God in one body through the cross, thereby putting to death the enmity. [17] And He came and preached peace to you who were afar off and to those who were near. [18] For through Him we both have access by one Spirit to the Father.

Ephesians 2:14-18

[5] circumcised the eighth day, of the stock of Israel, *of* the tribe of Benjamin, a Hebrew of the Hebrews; concerning the law, a Pharisee; [6] concerning zeal, persecuting the church; concerning the righteousness which is in the law, blameless.
[7] But what things were gain to me, these I have counted loss for Christ. [8] Yet indeed I also count all things loss for the excellence of the knowledge of Christ Jesus my Lord, for whom I have suffered the loss of all things, and count them as rubbish, that I may gain Christ [9] and be found in Him, not having my own righteousness, which *is* from the law, but that which *is* through faith in Christ, the righteousness which is from God by faith;
[10] that I may know Him and the power of His resurrection, and the fellowship of His sufferings, being conformed to His death, [11] if, by any means, I may attain to the resurrection from the dead.

Philippians 3:5-11

Pressing Toward the Goal

¹² Not that I have already attained, or am already perfected; but I press on, that I may lay hold of that for which Christ Jesus has also laid hold of me.

Philippians 3:12

⁸ But we know that the law *is* good if one uses it lawfully, ⁹ knowing this: that the law is not made for a righteous person, but for *the* lawless and insubordinate, for *the* ungodly and for sinners, for *the* unholy and profane, for murderers of fathers and murderers of mothers, for manslayers, ¹⁰ for fornicators, for sodomites, for kidnappers, for liars, for perjurers, and if there is any other thing that is contrary to sound doctrine, ¹¹ according to the glorious gospel of the blessed God which was committed to my trust.

1 Timothy 1:8-11

Animal Sacrifices Insufficient
10 For the law, having a shadow of the good things to come, *and* not the very image of the things, can never with these same sacrifices, which they offer continually year by year, make those who approach perfect. ² For then would they not have ceased to be offered? For the worshipers, once purified, would have had no more consciousness of sins.

Hebrews 10:1-2

⁸ Previously saying, "Sacrifice and offering, burnt offerings, and *offerings* for sin You did not desire, nor had pleasure *in them*" (which are offered according to the law), ⁹ then He said, "Behold, I have come to do Your will, O God." He takes away the first that He may establish the second. ¹⁰ By that will we have been sanctified through the offering of the body of Jesus Christ once *for all*.

Hebrews 10:8-10

⁷ Do they not blaspheme that noble name by which you are called?

⁸ If you really fulfill *the* royal law according to the Scripture, "You shall love your neighbor as yourself," you do well; ⁹ but if you show partiality, you commit sin, and are convicted by the law as transgressors. ¹⁰ For **whoever shall keep the whole law, and yet stumble in one *point*, he is guilty of all.** ¹¹ For He who said, "Do not commit adultery," also said, "Do not murder." Now if you do not commit adultery, but you do murder, you have become a transgressor of the law. ¹² So speak and so do as those who will be judged by the law of liberty.

¹³ For judgment is without mercy to the one who has shown no mercy. Mercy triumphs over judgment.

James 2:7-13

So Remember…

8 *There is* therefore now **no condemnation to those who are in Christ Jesus**, who do not walk according to the flesh, but according to the Spirit. ² For **the law of the Spirit of life in Christ Jesus has made me free from the law of sin and death.**

Romans 8:1-2

Chapter 3: Who is the Holy Spirit

The Holy Spirit is a divine person without a human body. The Holy Spirit is a disembodied, intangible and invisible reality.

The Holy Spirit is the third person of the Godhead (trinity as some put it) and is as much God as the Father and Jesus Christ the Son are. He is not just an influence or attitude. The Holy Spirit is truly God, a divine personality. Therefor you can never referred to the Holy Spirit as "it" or as a "force".

[3] But Peter said, "Ananias, why has Satan filled your heart to lie to the Holy Spirit and keep back *part* of the price of the land for yourself? [4] While it remained, was it not your own? And after it was sold, was it not in your own control? Why have you conceived this thing in your heart? You have not lied to men but to God."

Act 5:3-4

[16] And I will pray the Father, and He will give you another Helper, that He may abide with you forever— [17] the Spirit of truth, whom the world cannot receive, because it neither sees Him nor knows Him; but you know Him, for He dwells with you and will be in you. [18] I will not leave you orphans; I will come to you.

John 14:16-18

26 But the Helper, the Holy Spirit, whom the Father will send in My name, He will teach you all things, and bring to your remembrance all things that I said to you.
John 14:26

7 Nevertheless I tell you the truth. It is to your advantage that I go away; for if I do not go away, the Helper will not come to you; but if I depart, I will send Him to you.
John 16:7

The Holy Spirit came to live inside of every born again believer and is every born again believers best friend. We know from scripture that the Holy Spirit was very important to Jesus Christ's ministry while he was here on earth.

7 but made Himself of no reputation, taking the form of a bondservant, and coming in the likeness of men.
Philippians 2:7

When Jesus left Heaven became a man, totally dependent on the Holy Spirit for power to perform healing and miracles.

1 In the beginning God created the heavens and the earth. 2 The earth was without form, and void; and darkness was on the face of the deep. And the Spirit of God was hovering over the face of the waters.
3 Then God said, "Let there be light"; and there was light.
Genesis 1:1-3

Let's think about it for a while. What was this light if:

[14] Then God said, "Let there be lights in the firmament of the heavens to divide the day from the night; and let them be for

signs and seasons, and for days and years; ¹⁵ and let them be for lights in the firmament of the heavens to give light on the earth"; and it was so. ¹⁶ Then God made two great lights: the greater light to rule the day, and the lesser light to rule the night. *He made* the stars also. ¹⁷ God set them in the firmament of the heavens to give light on the earth, ¹⁸ and to rule over the day and over the night, and to divide the light from the darkness. And God saw that *it was* good. ¹⁹ So the evening and the morning were the fourth day.

Genesis 1:14-19

The stars, sun and moon was only created on the fourth day.

1 In the beginning was the Word, and the Word was with God, and the Word was God. ² He was in the beginning with God. ³ All things were made through Him, and without Him nothing was made that was made. ⁴ In Him was life, and the life was the light of men. ⁵ And the light shines in the darkness, and the darkness did not comprehend it.

John 1:1-5

In Genesis 1:1

¹ In the beginning God created the heavens and the earth.   **God the Father**

In Genesis 1:2

² The earth was without form, and void; and darkness *was* on the face of the deep. And the Spirit of God was hovering over the face of the waters.   **God the Holy Spirit**

In Genesis 1:3

³ Then God said, "Let there be light"; and there was light. **God the Son** known to men as Yeshua (Jesus

Christ) or (the Light and the Word of God). In *Hebrew* Yeshua means Salvation!

⁶ Jesus said to him, "I am the way, the truth, and the life. No one comes to the Father except through Me.

John 14:6

⁷ For there are three that bear witness in heaven: the Father, the Word, and the Holy Spirit; and these three are one.

1 John 5:7

¹³ Then Jesus came from Galilee to John at the Jordan to be baptized by him. ¹⁴ And John *tried to* prevent Him, saying, "I need to be baptized by You, and are You coming to me?"
¹⁵ But Jesus answered and said to him, "Permit *it to be so* now, for thus it is fitting for us to fulfill all righteousness." Then he allowed Him.
¹⁶ When He had been baptized, Jesus came up immediately from the water; and behold, the heavens were opened to Him, and He saw the Spirit of God descending like a dove and alighting upon Him. ¹⁷ And suddenly a voice *came* from heaven, saying, "This is My beloved Son, in whom I am well pleased."
³⁸ how God anointed Jesus of Nazareth with the Holy Spirit and with power, who went about doing good and healing all who were oppressed by the devil, for God was with Him.

Act 10:38

Jesus Christ's ministry continue on earth today through His children who receive the power and ability of the Holy Spirit as He did when He was on the earth.

⁴⁹ Behold, I send the Promise of My Father upon you; but tarry in the city of Jerusalem until you are endued with power from on high."

Luke 24:49

Dunamis (power) in Greek means inherent power capable of reproducing itself from which we get our English word 'dynamo.'

⁸ But you shall receive power when the Holy Spirit has come upon you; and you shall be witnesses to Me in Jerusalem, and in all Judea and Samaria, and to the end of the earth."

Acts 1:8

Jesus Christ is God's gift to the sinner. The Holy Spirit is God's gift to His children.

¹⁷ the Spirit of truth, whom the world cannot receive, because it neither sees Him nor knows Him; but you know Him, for He dwells with you and will be in you.

John 14:17

⁵ So He came to a city of Samaria which is called Sychar, near the plot of ground that Jacob gave to his son Joseph. ⁶ Now Jacob's well was there. Jesus therefore, being wearied from *His* journey, sat thus by the well. It was about the sixth hour.
⁷ A woman of Samaria came to draw water. Jesus said to her, "Give Me a drink." ⁸ For His disciples had gone away into the city to buy food.

⁹ Then the woman of Samaria said to Him, "How is it that You, being a Jew, ask a drink from me, a Samaritan woman?" For Jews have no dealings with Samaritans.
¹⁰ Jesus answered and said to her, "If you knew the gift of God, and who it is who says to you, 'Give Me a drink,' you would have asked Him, and He would have given you living water."
¹¹ The woman said to Him, "Sir, You have nothing to draw with, and the well is deep. Where then do You get that living water? ¹² Are You greater than our father Jacob, who gave us the well, and drank from it himself, as well as his sons and his livestock?"
¹³ Jesus answered and said to her, "Whoever drinks of this water will thirst again, ¹⁴ but whoever drinks of the water that I shall give him will never thirst. But the water that I shall give him will become in him a fountain of water springing up into everlasting life."

John 4:5-14

³⁷ On the last day, that great *day* of the feast, Jesus stood and cried out, saying, "If anyone thirsts, let him come to Me and drink. ³⁸ He who believes in Me, as the Scripture has said, out of his heart will flow rivers of living water." ³⁹ But this He spoke concerning the Spirit, whom those believing in Him would receive; for the Holy Spirit was not yet *given,* because Jesus was not yet glorified.

John 7:37-39

It is through salvation in which the believer's well becomes so full of water that it begins to overflow and turns into rivers of living water. Jesus is making a direct reference to the Holy Spirit in verse 39. A river has obviously much more water than a well and so the Bible calls this second experience being filled with the Holy Spirit.

What is the "sign" of the infilling of the Holy Spirit?

19 And it happened, while Apollos was at Corinth, that Paul, having passed through the upper regions, came to Ephesus. And finding some disciples ² he said to them, "Did you receive the Holy Spirit when you believed?"
So they said to him, "We have not so much as heard whether there is a Holy Spirit."

Acts 19:1-2

⁵ When they heard *this,* they were baptized in the name of the Lord Jesus. ⁶ And when Paul had laid hands on them, the Holy Spirit came upon them, and they spoke with tongues and prophesied.

Acts 19:5-6

⁴⁴ While Peter was still speaking these words, the Holy Spirit fell upon all those who heard the word. ⁴⁵ And those of the circumcision who believed were astonished, as many as came with Peter, because the gift of the Holy Spirit had been poured out on the Gentiles also. ⁴⁶ For they heard them speak with tongues and magnify God.
Then Peter answered, ⁴⁷ "Can anyone forbid water, that these should not be baptized who have received the Holy Spirit just as we *have?"*

Acts 10:44-47

2 When the Day of Pentecost had fully come, they were all with one accord in one place. ² And suddenly there came a sound from heaven, as of a rushing mighty wind, and it filled the whole house where they were sitting. ³ Then there appeared to them divided tongues, as of fire, and *one* sat upon each of them. ⁴ And they were all filled with the Holy Spirit and began to speak with

other tongues, as the Spirit gave them utterance.

Acts 2:1-4

² For he who speaks in a tongue does not speak to men but to God, for no one understands *him;* however, in the spirit he speaks mysteries.

1 Corinthians 14:2

Tongues is you direct, supernatural communication with Almighty God on a closed frequency that the devil cannot understand. Speaking in your home language is speaking from your mind; speaking in tongues is speaking from your spirit by the Holy Spirit within you the mysteries and divine secrets of God.

⁴ He who speaks in a tongue edifies himself, but he who prophesies edifies the church.

1 Corinthians 14: 4

Speaking in tongues edifies and builds us up it recharges your spirit with God's supernatural power and ability.

Don't worry if you did not start speaking in tongues when you became born again. Keep asking God for this gift and when God sees you are ready He will give it to you.

I have found that many people are scared to open their mouth and start talking because our human nature wants to analyse everything. We want to understand what we are saying. Let God through the Holy Spirit do the work in you. Speaking in tongues is the Holy Spirit at work when we do not have the words to adequately express what we feel in our hearts.

²⁶ Likewise the Spirit also helps in our weaknesses. For we do not know what we should pray for as we ought, but the Spirit Himself makes intercession for us with groanings which cannot be uttered.

Romans 8:26

How can I receive the infilling of the Holy Spirit?

³⁸ Then Peter said to them, "Repent, and let every one of you be baptized in the name of Jesus Christ for the remission of sins; and you shall receive the gift of the Holy Spirit. ³⁹ For the promise is to you and to your children, and to all who are afar off, as many as the Lord our God will call."

Acts 2:38-39

The Holy Spirit is God's free gift to all His children and there is nothing we can do to work for or earn the Holy Spirit.

⁹ "So I say to you, ask, and it will be given to you; seek, and you will find; knock, and it will be opened to you. ¹⁰ For everyone who asks receives, and he who seeks finds, and to him who knocks it will be opened. ¹¹ If a son asks for bread from any father among you, will he give him a stone? Or if *he asks* for a fish, will he give him a serpent instead of a fish? ¹² Or if he asks for an egg, will he offer him a scorpion? ¹³ If you then, being evil, know how to give good gifts to your children, how much more will *your* heavenly Father give the Holy Spirit to those who ask Him!"

Luke 11:9-13

The Holy Spirit will give you words or strange sounds to utter, but you will have to yield your tongue and vocal organs to the Holy Spirit, and in total cooperation begin to speak them out. Don't let your mind get in the way by analysing the words.

¹⁹ Do not quench the Spirit.
1 Thessalonians 5:19

³⁷ On the last day, that great *day* of the feast, Jesus stood and cried out, saying, "If anyone thirsts, let him come to Me and drink. ³⁸ He who believes in Me, as the Scripture has said, out of his heart will flow rivers of living water." ³⁹ But this He spoke concerning the Spirit, whom those believing in Him would receive; for the Holy Spirit was not yet *given,* because Jesus was not yet glorified.
John 7:37-39

Jesus said being filled with the Holy Spirit is as simple as drinking a glass of spiritual water.

¹⁴ For if I pray in a tongue, my spirit prays, but my understanding is unfruitful. ¹⁵ What is *the conclusion* then? I will pray with the spirit, and I will also pray with the understanding. I will sing with the spirit, and I will also sing with the understanding.
1 Corinthians 14:14-15

We as born again Christians should pray in tongues and in our home language, in the privacy of our room or home every day. We can also pray in tongues in our car or at any available opportunity when you won't disturb other people. We should attend at least one good prayer meeting a week where our praying can be stimulated by the enthusiastic praying of other more mature Christians. We should also worship God in tongues in the worship service at the appropriate time, but never interrupt the speaker in service by praying out aloud in tongues.

Prayer

Breathe on me, Holy Spirit. Pour out Your shining glory. Baptize me with power. Manifest Your presence with fire. I have been a scattered person. Gather me into Your one-ness. Send a mighty wind and bursts of flame. Let me hear and see and feel. And let me speak with new tongues, the languages of my heavenly home.

Heavenly Father, I want to experience all that You have in store for me in Christ Jesus. I am sorry for my pride that may have kept me from experiencing any part of the life in the Spirit. I do repent of this pride and I ask You to reveal Your life and love to me. I want You to take over my guidance and be my Master. I don't know all that this means now, but I trust You to teach me. Father, I ask You to baptize me in Your Holy Spirit. I want all You have suffered to give me. O, Lord Jesus, I empty myself of all that I thought I knew if it stands in Your way of baptizing me in your Spirit. Pour out your power upon me so that I might live a life worthy of Your name. I thank You Father; I do now receive all of Jesus; I thank You Jesus, I do now receive all of Your Holy Spirit; I thank you Holy Spirit that You have made all this possible by Your faithful love. I thankfully pray in Jesus' name. Amen.

Prayer to receive a fresh infilling of the Holy Spirit.

My Heavenly Father, I am your child and I believe in my heart that Jesus has been raised from the dead and I have confessed Him as my Lord. Jesus said, "How much more shall your Heavenly Father give the Holy Spirit to those that ask Him." I ask You now in the name of Jesus to fill me with the Holy Spirit. I step into the fullness and power that I desire in the name of Jesus. I confess that I am a Spirit-filled Christian. As I yield my vocal organs, I expect to speak in tongues for the Spirit gives me utterance in the name of Jesus. Praise the Lord!

Chapter 5: How to hear God's voice

God wants to bless you abundantly but He cannot do this if you do not have a personal relationship with Him.

If you are not fully for and with God you are working for the devil. Shocking isn't it.

The Parable of the Sower
[4] And when a great multitude had gathered, and they had come to Him from every city, He spoke by a parable: [5] "A sower went out to sow his seed. And as he sowed, some fell by the wayside; and it was trampled down, and the birds of the air devoured it. [6] Some fell on rock; and as soon as it sprang up, it withered away because it lacked moisture. [7] And some fell among thorns, and the thorns sprang up with it and choked it. [8] But others fell on good ground, sprang up, and yielded a crop a hundredfold." When He had said these things He cried, "He who has ears to hear, let him hear!"

The Purpose of Parables
[9] Then His disciples asked Him, saying, "What does this parable mean?"
[10] And He said, "To you it has been given to know the mysteries of the kingdom of God, but to the rest *it is given* in parables, that
'Seeing they may not see,
And hearing they may not understand.'

The Parable of the Sower Explained
[11] "Now the parable is this: The seed is the word of God. [12] Those by the wayside are the ones who hear; then the devil comes and takes away the word out of their hearts, lest they should believe and be saved. [13] But the ones on the rock *are those* who, when

they hear, receive the word with joy; and these have no root, who believe for a while and in time of temptation fall away. ¹⁴ Now the ones *that* fell among thorns are those who, when they have heard, go out and are choked with cares, riches, and pleasures of life, and bring no fruit to maturity. ¹⁵ But the ones *that* fell on the good ground are those who, having heard the word with a noble and good heart, keep *it* and bear fruit with patience.

Luke 8:4-15

Christians speak to God all the time. God still speaks to His children.

God wants to have a personal relationship with you. Without a personal relationship there is no communication. God still talk to us the problem is we do not listen.

Just like you need a reception for you mobile phone to take calls, you got to be tuned in, in order to hear God speak. Sometimes the signal on your mobile phone is not so clear, you have a lot of static and noise, sometimes it sounds like the person on the other side is stuttering, you keep walking around to different spots until you can hear the person clearly. When we are out of line with God we will not hear when God speak to us.

God wants to communicate with you by His Word the Bible.

How can I hear God speak to me?

Cultivate an open mind.

⁵ "A sower went out to sow his seed. And as he sowed, some fell by the wayside; and it was trampled down, and the birds of the air devoured it.

Luke 8:5

¹² Those by the wayside are the ones who hear; then the devil comes and takes away the word out of their hearts, lest they should believe and be saved.

Luke 8:12

When you've got a closed mind, God is not going to get through.

On every farm, in every field there's a footpath that the farmer would walk down. As he went he would sow the seed out onto the land that was tilled.

Let's look at some of the characteristics of a footpath. Firstly, they're hardened because of constant traffic of people walking up and down. The soil is compacted and it's not fertile and it is hard and a footpath is narrow.

Do you know anybody like that? They're closed minded, narrow minded, hard hearted. They're not even open to the possibility that God might speak to them.

Many of us are like that. We are so hard that we have already decided that we are going to do it our way that we are not even willing to give God a change. We've decided that we do not want to hear from God. Some even have so much pride in them that they think that they don't need God. Some even think that they are gods themselves. I have even heard a person tell me that we are all gods.

Does this sound familiar:
I can take this decision on my own.
I can past this test without asking God for help.
I can handle it on my own.
I can resolve it, solve, fix or handle it myself.
I can resolve this conflict.
I can handle my kids on my own
I can get this job on my own

Anytime you do not ask God through pray about something, you're saying, "I don't need God in this".

All of the above are called pride.

Fear of what God might say to us. What if I pray and ask God and God tells me to do something I don't want to do? He might tell me something hard, He might tell me to do something unpopular, He might tell me to do something I think I can't do or I don't want to do. So I'm afraid I'll lose my freedom. I'm afraid I'll lose my fun. I'm afraid I'll lose my fulfilment in life. I'm afraid I'll lose my family or friends. So I close my mind and basically say no thanks, to God.

When you've been hurt and hold on to those hurtful memories, it causes you to close your mind to God.

You start saying things like:

Why did God allow this?

Why did this happen to me?
How can God allow this if He is such a loving and powerful God?

God has given us free will. People will do bad things that might hurt you. Not everything that happens to us is God's will.

Bitterness only prolongs the pain.

Some people blames God for what happens to them and others even blames satan because they think that they're OK as long as they do not blame God.

Even if you blame satan for what people did to you, if you keep thinking about it and keep wondering about it and keep wanting answers why it happened to you, you are harboring bitterness!!! As a result, you close our mind.

God is the only person who can heal, never turn away from God.

Doers—Not Hearers Only
[21] Therefore lay aside all filthiness and overflow of wickedness, and receive with meekness the implanted word, which is able to save your souls.

The first step is to open your mind and let God in.

[6] Some fell on rock; and as soon as it sprang up, it withered away because it lacked moisture.

Luke 8:6

¹³ But the ones on the rock *are those* who, when they hear, receive the word with joy; and these have no root, who believe for a while and in time of temptation fall away.

Luke 8:13

Make time to hear God. Plan quite time with God into your schedule just like you make time for everything else.

If you only give God your leftover time you will miss out on what God wants to say to you.

Just as the hardened path represents the closed mind, the shallow soil represents a superficial mind. It's shallow.

When Jesus Christ talks about rocky soil here He's not talking about soil with a bunch of rocks in it as much of the Middle East and particularly in Israel, much of Israel is built on bedrock of. Jesus is saying this represents the superficial type of hearer who hears the word of God. This is the people that get all excited about it but it doesn't last. When the heat is on and when the problems come they will wither and fall away. Read the Word of God (the Bible) and then meditate on it to give it time to sink in.

God can't talk to us unless we make the time to spend with Him.

⁷ And some fell among thorns, and the thorns sprang up with it and choked it.

Luke 8:7

¹⁴ Now the ones *that* fell among thorns are those who, when they have heard, go out and are choked with cares, riches, and pleasures of life, and bring no fruit to maturity.

Luke 8:14

When your mind is crowded with thoughts about the bills that needs to be paid, children, and all the daily worries that comes with raising a family we cannot hear God when He speaks to us. You need to become quiet, put aside all of these things and just focus on God.
Make time to spend with God away from noise.
You can be so busy making money that you don't have time for God. You can be so busy making a living that you don't really live. Don't just get up and go to work. Be joyful in the Lord.

Although God gave us the fun in the world and the senses to enjoy it, we should not be too busy having fun that we forget about God. Sit down and make a list every time that you are too busy to read your Bible. Just put the "thing" that kept you busy and the date and time and pretty soon you will see what is keeping you away from God.

Just like in the parable, weed will start growing in your spiritual life if you stop going to church, reading your Bible, stop listening to Christian music and the only thing that you can do to fix this is to get back on your knees and ask God for forgiveness and get back in line with God. Start reading your Bible in the morning and evenings and pray in the morning and evenings.

Be willing to listen to God and to do what God tells you to do.

Prayer for Restoration
Father I come to You with my body, soul and spirit. Father please Hide Your face from my sins and blot out all my iniquities. Father create in me a clean heart. Father renew a steadfast spirit within me. I pray this in Jesus Christ's name. Amen

[14] For God may speak in one way, or in another,
Yet man does not perceive it.
Job 33:14

I have seen the looks on people's faces when I say God told me....Yes I speak to God all the time and God speaks back to me through the Holy Spirit.

A number of years ago there was a Time magazine that came out with the headlines that said, "God is dead". The next day the reporters lined up at Billy Graham's home and said, Is God dead, Dr. Graham? He said: "Are you kidding? I just talked to Him."

God is not limited to a single way to talk to us. God spoke once through a burning bush. God spoke one time through a cloud. He often speaks through angels. One time He spoke through a pillar of fire. Another time He even spoke to Balaam through a donkey.
Some of the most common ways God speaks to us.

God speaks through the Bible

¹⁶ All Scripture *is* given by inspiration of God, and *is* profitable for doctrine, for reproof, for correction, for instruction in righteousness

2 Timothy 3:16

The Bible is the living Word of God. So many people tell me that God does not speak to them. If you are one of the people that never hear God speak to you then I have only one question for you. Do you spend quality time reading the Bible?

God speaks to us through His teachers

Their Conversion
¹³ For this reason we also thank God without ceasing, because when you received the word of God which you heard from us, you welcomed *it* not *as* the word of men, but as it is in truth, the word of God, which also effectively works in you who believe.

1 Thessalonians 2:13

Ever attended a church service and it felt like the preacher's sermon was speaking to you directly. Well it was God speaking to you through his servant.

God speaks through you too. How many times have a friend come to you for advice or you've said something that was a real turning point in a person's life.

You were speaking and afterwards you though where did that come from?

That was God working through you.

[13] These things we also speak, not in words which man's wisdom teaches but which the Holy Spirit teaches, comparing spiritual things with spiritual.

1 Corinthians 2:13

The more teachings you hear the more God can talk to you.

Most Christians are experiencing spiritual anorexia. The only Bible they ever get is for 30 minutes on Sunday morning, the rest of the week they have no more teaching in their lives. That's if they do attend church every Sunday.

Yes you can even listen to some of the good teachers on TV. I can recommend the following:
- Joyce Meyer
- John Hagee
- Mathew Hagee
- Kenneth Copeland
- Perry Stone
- Mark Dristoll
- Marilyn and Sarah
- T D Jakes

Just to name a few.

God speaks through [1]impressions and dreams and visions.

---

[1] an idea, feeling, or opinion about something or someone, esp. one formed without conscious thought or on the basis of little evidence.

¹⁵ In a dream, in a vision of the night,
When deep sleep falls upon men,
While slumbering on their beds,
¹⁶ Then He opens the ears of men,
And seals their instruction.

Job 33:15-16

⁶ Then He said,
"Hear now My words:
If there is a prophet among you,
I, the LORD, make Myself known to him in a vision;
I speak to him in a dream.
⁷ Not so with My servant Moses;
He *is* faithful in all My house.
⁸ I speak with him face to face,
Even plainly, and not in dark sayings;
And he sees the form of the LORD.
Why then were you not afraid
To speak against My servant Moses?"
⁹ So the anger of the LORD was aroused against them, and He departed.

Numbers 12:6-9

²⁶ But the Helper, the Holy Spirit, whom the Father will send in My name, He will teach you all things, and bring to your remembrance all things that I said to you.

John 14:26

God gives us ideas, wisdom and knowledge. But be sure to avoid the rationalist and the mystic when you think of impressions.

The rationalist denies that God ever speaks to us through the mind or impressions like visions, dreams and prophecy. The rationalist will tell you that God only speaks through the Bible and never gives you any impressions. These people miss out on God's comfort, care, concern, and guidance.

The mystic thinks that every impression they get is from God. The mystic who thinks that every impression they get is from God tends to make a lot of stupid mistakes and they often embarrass themselves, and they become troublemakers. These people do not have a good foundation of the Word of God and they are "lone rangers" because they do not want to be accountable to anyone.

God will not give you an impression that contradicts His revealed will through His Word.

When learning to hear God's voice always remembers that there are 3 voices. God's voice, the devils voice and your own voice
God's Voice
Your own voice
The devils voice

Ask God for a spirit of discernment to be able to know when it is Him speaking to you.

I always tell my spiritual children that if God tells you to plant a seed of R100. Then your own voice will tell you No R100 is too much have you seen the person's rings or car? You can use the money better yourself. Then the devil will tell you yes besides you still need to buy bread and milk and a chocolate for yourself.

About 2 years back I was standing with a friend in ²Checkers and we were standing in front of the Mayonnaise. I heard God say take a bottle of Mayonnaise. I knew that we were not going to make anything that requires Mayonnaise, so just to confirm I ask her and she also confirmed that we don't need Mayonnaise. When we arrive back home, her husband that was cooking for us asked where is the Mayonnaise? We were shocked. The bigger shock was when her husband said but I ask God to tell you to bring Mayonnaise.

You see what happened here. God did tell me to bring Mayonnaise. But I chose to give in to not listen and to top it off even asked her for confirmation.

> ³⁰ Blows that hurt cleanse away evil,
> As *do* stripes the inner depths of the heart
> **Proverbs 20:30**

Sometimes God will use the pain of rejection, loss, prison, a storm to slow you down or to get your attention.

In the case of the disobedient Jonah, God used a fish to swallow him.

> ¹⁷ Now the LORD had prepared a great fish to swallow Jonah. And Jonah was in the belly of the fish three days and three nights.
> **Jonah 1:17**

Pain is Gods megaphone!

---

² A groceries store in South Africa

Prayer Points

O Spirit of life that raised up Jesus Christ from the dead, breathe life into my prayer altar

O Spirit of life that raised up Jesus Christ from the dead, breathe life into my dream life

O Spirit of life that raised up Jesus Christ from the dead, breathe life into my marriage

O Spirit of life that raised up Jesus Christ from the dead, breathe life into my calling

O Spirit of life that raised up Jesus Christ from the dead, breathe life into my finances

O Spirit of life that raised up Jesus Christ from the dead, breathe life into my every organ in my body

Every strongman throwing a spiritual blanket over my eyes in the spirit, be consumed by the fire of the Lord in Jesus Christ' name.

Spirit of the Living God, open my eyes to see in the spirit in Jesus Christ' name.

O Lord, open my ears to hear Your voice clearly in Jesus Christ' name.

Thank you Lord for answering my prayers.

Chapter 6: Full Surrender

Now that I you are saved, what do you do next? What is the next step in your new walk with the Lord?

If there is one theme that you will see repeated over and over again in many of our chapters is the extreme importance that each and every Christian turn their entire lives over to God the Father for Him to fully handle.

If you have just made Jesus your Savior, there is one more thing you must do. **You must now make Jesus the Lord over your life.** Jesus must now become both your Lord and Savior, not just your Savior.

You must now make the second biggest decision that you will ever make in this life. The first biggest decision is whether or not you will accept Jesus as your personal Savior through His sacrificial death on the cross. Now that you have done that, you have become truly saved and born again.

However, you are now faced with the second biggest decision that you will ever make in this life. And that decision is – who is going to run the rest of your life from now on – you or God?

As you will see in the Scripture verses I will list below, the Bible makes it very clear as to who should be guiding your steps in this life – and that Person is God the Father through the Holy Spirit!

This decision as to who will be running your life from now onwards will determine the course your life will take. If you decide to run your own life and call all of your own shots, then your life is going to take a completely different course as to the one it would take if you would turn your entire life over to God the Father for Him to fully handle.

The Bible specifically tells us that if we choose to follow our own way and path in this life – then that path will eventually lead to death. In other words, you will have forever wasted your one and only opportunity to find out exactly what you were created for, and what your true divine destiny was going to be in the Lord.

The Bible makes it very clear that good works will not get us into heaven. We can only be saved by grace through our faith in Jesus Christ and His sacrificial death on the cross. However, once we are saved, God the Father expects us to do something with what time we still have left down here on this earth. He now wants all of us to come and **"work"** for Him.

The Bible tells us that God will be **"rewarding"** us for the good works that we will do for Him while living down here on this earth. Again, these good works cannot get us saved, but they can get us the bigger and better rewards once we enter into heaven. Some of the verses I will list below specifically tell us that God will be rewarding us **"according to our labors"** for Him in this life. In other words, good works for the Lord will be highly rewarded once we cross over and enter into heaven.

However, there is one slight catch to all of this. If we choose to run our own lives instead of turning the reigns of our life over to God the Father, then we will not be embarking on the real path that God would like us to travel on – and any works that we end up doing while traveling on our own path will in no way be as highly rewarded as the works that are done operating in God's perfect will for our lives.

This life is but for a moment, a blink of an eye compared to the eternal time frame that is operating up in heaven. We will spend the rest of eternity with God and Jesus once we enter into heaven.

So ask yourself – do you want to work for yourself and the small rewards that you can get down here that will all perish the minute you die and cross over – or do you want to work for God the Father, do His perfect will for your life, accomplish what He wants you to accomplish in this life, and then receive His full and final just rewards that will last forever once you enter into heaven?

The rewards that God will bestow upon you for faithfully working for Him down here on this earth will be heavenly rewards that will last you for all of eternity. All of the things that you try and accomplish on your own, out of your own flesh, will in no way be rewarded anywhere near to what they would have been had you been operating under God's perfect will for your life.

So what does your natural, common sense and intelligence tells you would be the wisest decision as to who should be running your life? You – with your limited powers, limited intelligence, and limited strength – or God the Father, who is all-powerful, all-knowing, and all-perfect? Since God is all-powerful and all-knowing, this means He knows much better than you do what you should be doing with your life, what mountains you should be seeking to climb, and what goals and aspirations you should be striving after in this life.

Since God's knowledge is absolutely perfect on all matters – this means He will know you better than you could ever know yourself. He knows what your real strengths and weaknesses are better than you could ever know for yourself, since your knowledge is limited and imperfect – including what you think you know about yourself.

Only God knows what you were really created to be in this life.
Only God knows what you would really be best at.
Only God knows what your true divine calling should be in this life.
Only God knows who you should marry and what jobs you should be taking in this life.

And since God is all-powerful and there is nothing that He cannot do or accomplish – then this means He can also anoint you with His divine power for whatever He will be calling you to do for Him in this life.

So not only do you get God's perfect knowledge and wisdom guiding you in this life as to exactly what you should be striving for – but you will also have His divine power flowing through you so that you can be very good at the jobs and tasks that He will be calling you to do for Him.

But if you decide to choose your own way and call all of your own shots, then God will not be anointing you with His divine power or guiding you every step of your way – and you will then be forced to try and find your own way, all without any of God's help, power, or guidance. As a result, when it is all finally said and done, you will have become a failure in God since you will have chosen to travel down your own path rather than the path God already had set out for you long before you were even born through your mother's womb!

Bottom line – you have to look at the real "big picture." The real big picture is not only what happens in this life, but also what happens in the next life. The next life in heaven is nothing but a continuation of this life that we are living down here on this earth. But there is one main difference. This life on earth is but for a very short period of time. The life we will be living up in heaven will be forever – with no more crossovers into any other realms.

We should thus be living this life for what will be recorded up in heaven – not for what will be recorded down here. Any trophies, medals, money, or material possessions that we might be able to acquire down here will not be crossing over with us when we enter into heaven. There are only three things that will be crossing over with us when we enter into heaven:

- Ourselves
- Our saved family members and friends

- And all of the good works that we will do for God operating under His perfect will for our life

Nothing else will be crossing over! That is why you have to look at the complete big picture, not just a small part of it, which is our earthly existence.

As you will see in the following Scripture verses, you have to become both saved and surrendered if you really want to enter into the real walk with the Lord. Christians are obviously saved, but many of them are not operating under this full surrender with the Lord. As a result, they have married the wrong people and are thus living in miserable marriages or have gone through multiple divorces. They have chased after the wrong jobs in their life and thus have no real sense of fulfilment or accomplishment in their lives.

The only way that you can find what your true divine destiny is going to be in this life, who your true soul mate should be, and what you were really born to be in this life, is by entering into God the Father's perfect will for your life. There is absolutely no other way! The center of God's perfect will for your life is the safest and most fulfilling realm that you will ever enter into in this life!

Stepping out into God's perfect will for your life where He is now guiding and leading your life in the direction that He will want it go in is like stepping from the dugout out onto the real field where the real action of life is really at. Too many of God's people are trying to play the game of life from the stands, and this is all because they are refusing to turn the reigns of their life over to Him God) for Him to fully handle.

Study the Scripture verses in this chapter very, very carefully. These verses are giving you major, and I mean major revelation from God the Father on the second most important decision that you will ever make in your life.

Who you will be choosing to run your life – you or God – will make or break what time you still have left down here on this earth. You only have one shot, one opportunity, and one window in which to leave your mark in this world. Let God the Father, through the Holy Spirit, guide you into the most incredible realm you can imagine this side of heaven – the realm of God's perfect will for your life!

I will break the Scripture verses down under the appropriate captions below so you can fully grasp what God is trying to tell you in these very powerful verses. I will then end this chapter by showing you how to enter into this full surrender with the Lord, and how to maintain it for the rest of your earthly life if you decide you want to do this with the Lord.

Choose This Day Who You Will Serve

These first set of verses will all hit the nail right on the head. The very first verse from Joshua is one of the most classic statements ever made on the full surrender that God is looking for from each one of us. Joshua is a perfect example of someone who lived his entire life right in the Lord. He fully followed God all the days of his life and was completely successful in accomplishing all of the missions that God had set him out on.

Joshua is a powerful role model for all Christians to follow by the way that he lived his life for God. His story is a perfect example for all Christians on how to properly follow God and the call that He can place on your life. As a final testament to this man's story, God saw fit to name one of the books of the Bible after him – **"The Book of Joshua."**

In this first verse, Joshua says to choose this day whom you will serve. He says as far as he and his household are concerned, they will be serving the Lord. Joshua knew that he had to make a choice on how to live his life – either by serving himself and his own wants and desires – or to fully serve God the Father. As a result of making the correct decision as to who should be running his life, he became one of the most successful men in the Bible with everything that he accomplished for God.

He was the first one to lead the Israelites from the desert into the Promised Land to begin to conquer and gain possession of the specific lands that God wanted them to have. Joshua ended his life making the statement that God had not failed to give him every ounce of land that his foot had stepped on. God was able to do this for him because he was willing to fully follow God every step of the way.

The second verse then goes one step further to explain that each person has to make this choice for themselves as to who they are going to serve and follow in this life. This second verse specifically says that you cannot serve two masters – that you cannot try and serve both God and mammon. The word "mammon" means wealth and riches.

Jesus Himself makes some very radical, intense statements on this issue. He says that those who are not with Him are against Him, and that He has not come to bring peace, but division! He specifically states that He has come with a sword to set a man against his own father and a daughter against her own mother.

In other words, Jesus is drawing a major battle line in the sand. What He means by setting a son against his father or a daughter against her own mother is that each person must choose to serve and follow Him, and Him alone. And if you choose to serve and follow anyone else in this life – then you are going directly against Him. God has to be Number 1 in your life. He will not accept a second or third position next to your family and friends.

Here are 10 very powerful verses all showing us that we are to only serve and follow the Lord in this life.

¹⁵ And if it seems evil to you to serve the Lord, **choose for yourselves this day whom you will serve**, whether the gods which your fathers served that *were* on the other side of the River, or the gods of the Amorites, in whose land you dwell. **But as for me and my house, we will serve the Lord.**"

Joshua 24:15

You Cannot Serve God and Riches
²⁴ "**No one can serve two masters**; for either he will hate the one and love the other, or else he will be loyal to the one and despise the other. **You cannot serve God and ³mammon.**

Matthew 6:24

²⁶ **If anyone serves Me, let him follow Me;** and where I am, there My servant will be also. If anyone serves Me, him *My Father will honor.*

John 12:26

²⁹ But Peter and the *other* apostles answered and said: "**We ought to obey God rather than men.**

Acts 5:29

⁴ Delight yourself also in the Lord,
And He shall give you the desires of your heart.
⁵ **Commit your way to the Lord,
Trust also in Him,**
And He shall bring *it* to pass.
⁶ He shall bring forth your righteousness as the light,
And your justice as the noonday.
⁷ Rest in the Lord, and wait patiently for Him;

---

³ worldly gain personified as a false god

Do not fret because of him who prospers in his way,
Because of the man who brings wicked schemes to pass.
Psalm 37:4-7

[14] But as for me, I trust in You, O Lord;
I say, "You *are* my God."
[15] **My times *are* in Your hand**;
Deliver me from the hand of my enemies,
And from those who persecute me.
Psalm 31:14

[30] He who is not with Me is against Me, and he who does not gather with Me scatters abroad.
Matthew 12:30

[49] "I came to send fire on the earth, and how I wish it were already kindled! [50] But I have a baptism to be baptized with, and how distressed I am till it is accomplished! [51] **Do *you* suppose that I came to give peace on earth? I tell you, not at all, but rather division.** [52] For from now on five in one house will be divided: three against two, and two against three.
Luke 12:49

[34] "Do not think that I came to bring peace on earth. I did not come to bring peace but a sword. [35] For I have come to 'set a man against his father, a daughter against her mother, and a daughter-in-law against her mother-in-law'; [36] and 'a man's enemies *will be* those of his *own* household.' [37] He who loves father or mother more than Me is not worthy of Me. And he who loves son or daughter more than Me is not worthy of Me. [38] And he who does not take his cross and follow after Me is not worthy of Me. [39] He who finds his life will lose it, and he who loses his life for My sake will find it.

A Cup of Cold Water

⁴⁰ "He who receives you receives Me, and he who receives Me receives Him who sent Me.

Matthew 10:40

³³ So likewise, whoever of you does not forsake all that he has cannot be My disciple.

Luke 14:33

Notice that Jesus says that unless you are willing to take up your cross and follow Him – that you will not be worthy of Him! What does Jesus mean when He says to take up your cross? What does the cross represent? What happened when Jesus went to the cross? He died a **maximum death.** The cross thus represents a maximum death for all of us.

When you enter into this full surrender with God the Father – you are putting everything in your life to a **maximum death** in reference to yourself, since God will now be the One to control the direction your life will now be taking. You are **putting to death** all of your wants, all of your desires, and what you think you should be doing with your life since you have now turned the reigns of your life over to God the Father for Him to fully handle.

What did Jesus really do when He went to the cross to die for all of our sins? He fully surrendered His entire being and His entire life over to God the Father in order to complete God's perfect will for His life down here on this earth. It was God's perfect will that He go to the cross to die for all of us – and Jesus was willing to fully surrender every part of His being and every part of His earthly life to God the Father to complete that divine call.

This is why Jesus says in one of the previous verses that unless you are willing to **"forsake all"** – you cannot truly become one of His disciples. **Forsaking all means that you are willing to fully surrender every aspect of your life over to God the Father and go with His perfect will and plan for your life rather than your own.**

Notice the specific wording in some of the above verses, all showing that the only way to live this life is under a full and complete surrender with God the Father:

1. We will serve the Lord
2. Commit your way to the Lord
3. My times are in Your Hand
4. No one can serve two masters
5. If anyone serves Me – let him follow Me
6. We ought to obey God rather than men
7. He who is not with Me is against Me

All of the above verses are definitely showing us that the only way to truly **"find"** our life in this life is to fully commit to serving the Lord and going with His perfect will for what He wants to do with our life. There is no other way in this life to find true, inner happiness and fulfillment other than living and operating in the center of God's perfect will for your life. And the only way this can be done is by completely surrendering every aspect of your being and every aspect of your life over to God the Father.

Doing the Will of God

These next set of verses will perfectly connect to all of the ones listed before. Once you fully surrender every aspect of your being and life over God the Father for Him to fully handle – then the next thing God will do is to let you know exactly what it is He wants you to do for Him in this life. Your job now, after entering into this full surrender with Him, is to seek to do His specific will for your life.

When you really cut into this part of your walk with the Lord – what God is basically looking for from each one of us is that we take our lives one day at a time – and in each one of these days that we accomplish, to the best of our abilities, what He wants us to accomplish for that specific day. In other words, do what God wants you to do on a daily basis. Do the best and be the best that you can at the jobs and tasks that God will be calling you to do for Him on a daily basis.

In these next set of verses, you will see specific words telling us that we must seek to do the will of God the Father and not our own will – and that we are to seek to finish the work that He has laid out before us.

[21] "Not everyone who says to Me, 'Lord, Lord,' shall enter the kingdom of heaven, but he who does the will of My Father in heaven.

Matthew 7:21

[34] Jesus said to them, "**My food is to do the will of Him who sent Me, and to finish His work.**
John 4:34

[30] I can of Myself do nothing. As I hear, I judge; and My judgment is righteous, because **I do not seek My own will but the will of the Father who sent Me.**
John 5:30

[20] Now may the God of peace who brought up our Lord Jesus from the dead, that great Shepherd of the sheep, through the blood of the everlasting covenant, [21] **make you complete in every good work to do His will, working in you what is well pleasing in His sight**, through Jesus Christ, to whom *be* glory forever and ever. Amen.
Hebrews 13:20

[8] Therefore do not be ashamed of the testimony of our Lord, nor of me His prisoner, but share with me in the sufferings for the gospel according to the power of God, [9] who has saved us and **called *us* with a holy calling, not according to our works, but according to His own purpose and grace** which was given to us in Christ Jesus before time began,
2 Timothy 1:8-9

[22] And when He had removed him, He raised up for them David as king, to whom also He gave testimony and said, 'I have found David the *son* of Jesse, a man after My *own* heart, **who will do all My will.**'
Acts 13:22

[35] Then I will raise up for Myself a faithful priest ***who* shall do according to what *is* in My heart and in My mind.** I will build him a sure house, and he shall walk before My anointed forever.
1 Samuel 2:35

All of these verses are telling us, without any other possible interpretation, that we are to seek to do the will of God for our lives, and that we are to follow God, and God alone, as to what it is we should be striving after in this life.

The verse above from Acts 13:22 is God the Father talking about King David. King David was the greatest king that Israel has ever had. Notice that God saw that David would be a man that would follow after **"all"** of His will – not just some or part of His will. This was one of the main keys as to why David became the greatest king that Israel has ever had.

Notice the verse from 2 Timothy 1:8 states that we have a **"holy calling"** from the Lord, but that this holy calling is for God's purpose for our lives, not for our own purpose, which will now lead us right into the next topic.

God Has A Perfect Plan and Destiny For Your Life

Once you are willing to completely surrender your entire life over to the God the Father for Him to fully handle, then what will happen next is that God will be setting you up to follow the specific path that He will want you to follow in Him – and in that path will be your call, your purpose, your duties, and the tasks that you will now be seeking to accomplish for Him. **God now has a set plan and a set future for your life**.

One of the verses listed below states that **"where there is no vision,"** the people will perish. What I believe this verse is trying to tell us is that unless you know what your purpose is in this life, what you created for, and what it is you should be striving after – then you will aimlessly wander throughout your entire life never accomplishing anything of any real worth, and never fulfilling the divine destiny to which God has called you. This is also why some people jump from one type of job to another, not really finding that specific job for them. They did not know God in the matter.

Your life will **"perish"** right before your very eyes because you had never sought to do God's perfect will for your life. You thus will have forever lost and wasted the one and only chance you had to do something of any consequence in this life with what little time you had to do it in.

Here are 5 very good verses showing us that we all have a holy calling from the Lord, and that our days have been **"determined and fashioned"** to do something specific for the Lord.

¹⁸ Where *there is* no revelation (vision), the people cast off restraint;
But happy *is* he who keeps the law.

Proverbs 29:18

¹¹ For I know the thoughts that I think toward you, says the LORD, thoughts of peace and not of evil, **to give you a future and a hope.**

Jeremiah 29:11

¹⁶ Your eyes saw my substance, being yet unformed.
And in Your book they all were written,
The days fashioned for me,
When *as yet there were* none of them.

Psalm 139:16

⁵ Since **his days** *are* **determined,**
The number of his months *is* **with You;**
You have appointed his limits, so that he cannot pass.

Job 14:5

²⁸ And we know that all things work together for good to those who love God, **to those who are the called according to** *His* **purpose.**

Romans 8:28

¹⁴ "For many are called, but few *are* chosen."

Matthew 22:14

Notice the verse from Psalm 139:16 is literally telling us that God knows exactly what He wants to do with our lives before we have even been formed in our mother's womb! It says that before we have even been born, God already has our days **"fashioned"** out for us. The next verse from Job 14:5 says that all of our days are **"determined"** by the Lord.

These two powerful words – **"determined and fashioned"** – are both telling us that God has our entire lives perfectly planned out for us if we are willing to enter into His perfect will for our life. But the last verse, where it is stating that many are called but few are chosen, is sadly telling us that most people will never enter into God's perfect will for their lives. I believe this verse is not talking about our salvation, but about our calls in God. I believe this verse is showing us that God is **"calling"** many to come and work for Him, but most are turning Him down for various reasons. Most people would rather control their own destinies rather than turn the reigns of their life over to God the Father for Him to fully handle. As a result, they will never find what their true divine destinies would have been in the Lord in this lifetime.

God Will Guide Your Steps in This Life

After coming into this full surrender with the Lord where He is now in full control of your life – two things will now start to occur. God will immediately place you on the path that He will want you to follow in Him. And on that path will be your call or calls, your jobs, and exactly what He will want you to do for Him for the rest of your earthly life.

The second thing that will occur is that God will then start to guide your steps so that you can get to where you need to go to so you can fully accomplish everything that He will want you to accomplish for Him. If God is going to call you to be a great musician, a great Bible teacher, a great evangelist, a great doctor, or a great policeman – then He is also going to have to guide your steps so that you can make it to the tops of these types of mountains.

These calls will not fruit out overnight. You will have to work and sweat to make it into these types of calls or whatever it is God is calling you to do for Him. This is where the real adventure of life is really at – in the climbing to the tops of these types of mountains. So not only do you get God's best for your life as to what your divine destiny is going to be in Him – but you will also be getting God's guidance on a daily basis so that you can reach these kinds of specific goals.

If God is going to call you to be a great evangelist, but does not guide your steps on a daily basis on how to get there, then you will never make it on your own.

You can only get to the top of your personal mountain in your call with God only if God is anointing you and leading you to be able to climb that mountain. Otherwise you will never make it on your own. Jesus specifically says that without Him we can do absolutely nothing.

Many people have decided, without consulting God first, what mountains and goals they should be striving after in this life. They then might make it halfway up their mountain, but then all of a sudden it happens – everything breaks down and they fall completely back down to the bottom of the mountain, literally losing everything they had built up in climbing halfway up that mountain.

The Bible says that unless God builds the **"house"** of our lives – we will labor in vain trying to do it all on our own. There are many Christians who are now living defeated and broken lives as a result of broken dreams – all because they were trying to do it all on their own without any of God's help, guidance, or power to get them there.

Again, study these next set of verses very, very carefully. These are major, foundational verses in which to ground on in your walk with the Lord. The first verse will specifically tell you that it is the job of the Holy Spirit Himself to guide your steps in this life.

The Bible tells us that the steps of a good man are **"ordered"** by the Lord, and that it is not in man to try and direct his own steps in this life. And that if he does try to direct his own steps in this life that its way will eventually lead to death!

These are major power verses burn these major power verses into your memory bank. Get it settled once and for all in your mind and in your spirit that God will lead you and direct your steps in this life. This job now belongs to Him, and Him alone. This job does not belong to you, your best friends, or your parents!

¹⁴ For as many as are led by the Spirit of God, these are sons of God.

Romans 8:14

²³ The steps of a *good* man are ordered by the L<small>ORD</small>,
And He delights in his way

Psalm 37:23

²³ O L<small>ORD</small>, I know the way of man *is* not in himself;
It is not in man who walks to direct his own steps.

Jeremiah 10:23

¹² There is a way *that seems* right to a man,
But its end *is* the way of death.

Proverbs 14:12

²⁴ A man's steps *are* of the L<small>ORD</small>;
How then can a man understand his own way?

Proverbs 20:24

⁹ A man's heart plans his way,
But the L<small>ORD</small> directs his steps.

Proverbs 16:9

¹³³ Direct my steps by Your word,
And let no iniquity have dominion over me.

Psalm 119:133

5 Therefore be imitators of God as dear children.

Ephesians 5:1

²⁷ My sheep hear My voice, and I know them, and they follow Me.

John 10:27

⁵ Trust in the LORD with all your heart,
And lean not on your own understanding;
⁶ In all your ways acknowledge Him,
And **He shall direct your paths.**

Proverbs 3:5

23 The LORD *is* my shepherd;
I shall not want.
² He makes me to lie down in green pastures;
He leads me beside the still waters.
³ He restores my soul;
He leads me in the paths of righteousness
For His name's sake.

Psalm 23:1-3

¹⁷ Thus says the LORD, your Redeemer,
The Holy One of Israel:
"I *am* the LORD your God,
Who teaches you to profit,
Who leads you by the way you should go.

Isaiah 48:17

⁴ Show me Your ways, O LORD;
Teach me Your paths.
⁵ **Lead me in Your truth and teach me**,
For You *are* the God of my salvation;
On You I wait all the day.

Psalm 25:4

⁸ I will instruct you and teach you in the way you should go;
I will guide you with My eye

Psalm 32:8

¹¹ Teach me Your way, O LORD,

And **lead me in a smooth path, because of my enemies.**
Psalm 27:11

[11] **The LORD will guide you continually,**
And satisfy your soul in drought,
And strengthen your bones;
You shall be like a watered garden,
And like a spring of water, whose waters do not fail.
Isaiah 58:11

[14] For this *is* God,
Our God forever and ever;
He will be our guide
Even **to death.**
Psalm 48:14

[12] Moreover You led them by day with a cloudy pillar,
And by night with a pillar of fire,
To give them light on the road
Which they should travel.
Nehemiah 9:12

[6] All we **like sheep have gone astray;**
We have turned, every one, to his own way;
And the LORD has laid on Him the iniquity of us all.
Isaiah 53:6

[32] "Therefore you shall be careful to do as the LORD your God has commanded you; **you shall not turn aside to the right hand or to the left.**
Deuteronomy 5:32

Notice the last verse is telling us that once we embark on the path that God now has us set up on, that we are not to change course by attempting to turn to the right or to the left. The Bible says that the road God will now place us on is a **"straight"** and narrow road. There is no turning back once you enter in on the path of God's perfect will for your life.

In the second last verse, it specifically tells us that if we seek to go after our own way in this life, that we are looked upon by God as sheep that have gone astray.

All of these verses are extremely powerful. Notice the specific words that I will now number and bold for you, once again to hammer home the point that it is God's job to fully guide your steps in this life.

1. **Led by the Spirit of God**
2. **The steps of a good man are ordered by the Lord**
3. **It is not in man who walks to direct his own steps**
4. **A way which seems right to a man ... its end is the way of death**
5. **A man's steps are of the Lord**
6. **The Lord directs his steps**
7. **Direct my steps by Your Word**
8. **Be followers of God as dear children**
9. **My sheep hear My voice ... and they follow Me**
10. **He shall direct your paths**
11. **He leads me by still waters**
12. **He leads me in the paths of righteousness**
13. **Leads you by the way you should go**
14. **Lead me in your truth**
15. **I will guide you with My eye**
16. **Lead me in a smooth path**

17. The Lord will guide you continually
18. He will be our guide even to death
19. Led them by day … to give them light on the road which they should travel

When you read all of these key phrases one after the other, there is no question that the only way for each and every Christian to live this earthly life is under a full and complete surrender with God the Father – with God leading your life every step of the way on a daily basis through the Holy Spirit. There is no other way in which to live this life. I do not think God the Father could have made it any clearer than by the way that He has worded all of the above Scripture verses.

The Consequences of Not Fully Following God

One of the most dramatic examples of one group of people who followed God **"fully"** and another group who did not were the Israelites who were tested by God the Father in the desert after being rescued from the Egyptians in the story of Moses.

Near the beginning of the 40 year wilderness experience, they were all getting ready to go into the Promised Land to reap their big reward in God. However, before they went in, they sent in twelve spies to see what their enemies looked like and what they would encounter once they crossed over to possess the land from some of these evil people. When the spies came back, ten of them came back with a bad report. They said the enemies were too big and that their kingdoms were too well fortified.

Mind you, the Israelites had just seen one of the greatest displays of God's power that the world has ever seen when He threw 10 whopper plagues at the Pharaoh to set them free. Not to mentioned the parting of the Sea. Yet, just as they were getting ready to cross over into their Promised Land, they started questioning and doubting that God could take these enemies out for them, even though God had just got done delivering them from an entire Egyptian nation several years earlier!

When God sees their lack of faith and belief in Him that He could conquer these lands for them, He threw up His hands and said that was going to be it. He pronounced a severe judgment on them, telling them that all of the men 20 years of age and older would not enter into the Promised Land due to their lack of faith and belief in Him to be able to accomplish this mission for them, and because they had not **"wholly followed God."**

However, God then states that He will allow Joshua, Caleb and all the men under 20 years of age to go in there to conquer and possess the land – all because they had a **"different spirit"** in them and because they would be willing to **"follow God fully."**

This story is a perfect poster story for one group of people who were willing to follow God fully, and another group of people who were not. As a result, the one group that was willing to follow God fully got to go into the Promised Land, while the other group did not! Those are the consequences of not having enough faith and belief in God the Father and not being willing to fully follow Him in this life.

So many Christians have missed out on entering into their Promised Land this side of heaven – all because they failed to fully follow God and take the path that He wanted them to take in this life!

Here are two very powerful Scripture verses describing the above scenario.

[11] **'Surely none of the men who came up from Egypt, from twenty years old and above, shall see the land of which I swore to Abraham, Isaac, and Jacob, because they have not wholly followed Me,** [12] except Caleb the son of Jephunneh, the Kenizzite, and Joshua the son of Nun, for they have wholly followed the LORD.' [13] So the LORD's anger was aroused against Israel, and He made them wander in the wilderness forty years, until all the generation that had done evil in the sight of the LORD was gone.

Numbers 32:11-13

[20] Then the LORD said: "I have pardoned, according to your word; [21] but truly, as I live, all the earth shall be filled with the glory of the LORD— [22] because all these men who have seen My glory and the signs which I did in Egypt and in the wilderness, and have put Me to the test now these ten times, and have not heeded My voice, [23] they certainly shall not see the land of which I swore to their fathers, nor shall any of those who rejected Me see it. [24] **But My servant Caleb, because he has a different spirit in him and has followed Me fully**, I will bring into the land where he went, and his descendants shall inherit it.

Numbers 14:20-24

These two verses are giving all Christians major revelation on what God is looking for from each one of us. He is looking for those who will "**follow Him fully.**"

Being willing to fully follow God means that you are willing to enter into this full surrender with Him where He will be the One who will fully guide your steps in this life – not you or anyone else. I do not even get dressed in the morning without asking God what He wants me to wear for that day.

Here are two more good verses showing the negative consequences of not being willing to fully follow God in this life.

30 **"Woe to the rebellious children," says the Lord,**
"Who take counsel, but not of Me,
And who devise plans, but not of My Spirit,
That they may add sin to sin;
² Who walk to go down to Egypt,
And **have not asked My advice**,
To strengthen themselves in the strength of Pharaoh,
And to trust in the shadow of Egypt!
³ Therefore the strength of Pharaoh
Shall be your shame,
And trust in the shadow of Egypt
Shall be *your* humiliation.

Isaiah 30:1-3

¹⁹ **If you are willing and obedient,**
You shall eat the good of the land;
²⁰ **But if you refuse and rebel,**
You shall be devoured by the sword";
For the mouth of the Lord has spoken.

Isaiah 1:19-20

All four of these verses are as clear as they can be. Choose God and His divine path for your life, and you will find true, inner happiness and fulfillment in this life.

Choose your way or anyone else's way – and you will reap absolutely nothing in this life as far as God is concerned when it is all finally said and done.

God Will Reward Those Who Will Fully Follow Him

For those who are willing to fully follow God in this life and operate in this full surrender with Him, there are some incredible blessings and rewards that God can bestow upon you – not only in this life, but also in the next life as well.

Here are 6 very good verses all stating that Jesus will be rewarding us for the good works that we are willing to do for Him while down here on this earth.

Again, these good works will not get us into heaven, as the Bible is very clear that it is only by grace through faith in Jesus that we can receive eternal salvation. But God and Jesus will be rewarding us to some degree for the works that we are willing to do for Them down here.

The Bible does not tell us exactly what these rewards will be – but if we are dealing with a God of maximum intensity, then you can bet that these rewards are going to be something very special and will definitely surpass any rewards that we can receive down here on this earth.

Notice in 5 out of the 6 verses that it says that God and Jesus will be specifically rewarding us for our **"works and labor"** that we are willing to do for Them.

²⁶ For what profit is it to a man if he gains the whole world, and loses his own soul? Or what will a man give in exchange for his soul? ²⁷ **For the Son of Man will come in the glory of His Father with His angels, and then He will reward each according to his works.**
Matthew 16:26-27

⁸ Now he who plants and he who waters are one, **and each one will receive his own reward according to his own labor.**
1 Corinthians 3:8

¹² "And behold, I am coming quickly, **and My reward *is* with Me, to give to every one according to his work.**
Revelation 22:12

²³ I will kill her children with death, and all the churches shall know that I am He who searches the minds and hearts. **And I will give to each one of you according to your works.**
Revelation 2:23

²⁷ For the Son of Man will come in the glory of His Father with His angels, and then **He will reward each according to his works.**
Matthew 16:27

²⁹ And everyone who has left houses or brothers or sisters or father or mother or wife or children or lands, **for My name's sake, shall receive a hundredfold, and inherit eternal life.**
Matthew 19:29

Depending on what God may call you to do for Him in this life – some may be forced to leave family, friends, cities, states/provinces, or possibly even their own countries. If they receive this kind of extra heavy call from the Lord, notice the last verse says that God will be rewarding those who are willing to take on these types of extra-heavy calls with a hundredfold type reward and blessing.

Again, the Bible does not tell us what this hundredfold reward and blessing may be. But my guess is that it will be one, big, whopper, intense reward due to the extreme sacrifices these people will be making in order to accomplish the divine missions that God will send them out on.

Bottom line – any earthly wealth by way of money, possessions, and fame that is acquired by doing our own thing and calling all of our own shots in this life will all completely disappear the second we physically die and depart from this life. We will take absolutely nothing that we have earned, made, or acquired into the next life.

Jesus Himself could not have said it any better when He says in one of the above verses that what good will it do a man if he gains the whole world in the area of material wealth and possessions, but loses his own soul in the process of acquiring all of that wealth. It will have all been for nothing when that person comes to the end of his/her life, and he/she is forced to face up to his/her own mortality and comes to the full realization that all of the earthly wealth that he/she was able to acquire and accumulate will all die and perish right alongside his/her physical body when he/she finally dies and leaves this world.

None of that earthly wealth will be passing over with him/her into the next life.

Many wealthy people do not come to this revelation until they are literally on their deathbeds. They then all of a sudden "see" that they had their priorities all wrong in this life, and they had chased after all the wrong things in this life.

The Bible makes it very clear that if we choose to do our own thing and follow our own way in this life – that our way will eventually lead to death. For those who are not born again Christians, it will mean the death of their souls by not making it into heaven. For those who are born again Christians, it will mean the loss of being able to receive some really big intense rewards from God once we enter into heaven to be with Him for all of eternity.

Everyone Will Face God For A Personal Judgment

These next 3 verses will show us that each and everyone of us will have to face the Lord for a personal judgment when we die and cross over.

These verses will tell us that everything that we have done in this life, all the good with all of the bad, will come before the Lord for judgment and scrutiny. There will not be one thing that will be hidden from Him, no matter how secret we may think it is this side of heaven.

The last verse I will list from Ecclesiastes states that **"every work"** that we have done will be brought before God for judgment. There are only two types of work that God will be judging – those that are done in the perfect will of God for our lives, and those that are done operating out of our own wills.

Which works do you think will be the more highly rewarded and the more approved of by our Lord once we cross over to meet Him face to face – the works that were done in His name, for His sake, and in His perfect will for our lives – or the works that were done solely for ourselves and for our own self-gratification?

These next 3 verses are a very sobering reminder of what is going to happen to each and everyone of us when we die and cross over. This is why you must get all of your priorities set straight and live your life for what will be recorded up in heaven, not for what will perish down here the minute you die and cross over.

[13] Let us hear the conclusion of the whole matter:
Fear God and keep His commandments,
For this is man's all.
[14] **For God will bring every work into judgment,**
Including every secret thing,
Whether good or evil.
Ecclesiastes 12:13-14

[13] And there is no creature hidden from His sight, but all things *are* naked and open to the eyes of Him to whom we *must give* account.
Hebrews 4:13

[10] For we must all appear **before the judgment seat of Christ, that each one may receive the things** *done* **in the body, according to what he has done, whether good or bad.**
2 Corinthians 5:10

Knowing what all of these Scripture verses are trying to tell you – who do you want to live your life for?

Yourself and your own goals and aspirations, knowing full well that none of your fleshly accomplishments will be highly rewarded by God once you enter into heaven. Or do you want to live for God and His call for your life – knowing that everything that you do for Him operating under His perfect will for your life will be very highly rewarded once you enter into heaven?

Each person must make their own personal choice on this matter. You must choose this day whom you will serve – yourself or God. There is no middle area or neutral grounds on this issue. This is an all-or-nothing proclamation being made by the Lord to each and every born again believer. After you get saved, this will now become the biggest and most important decision that you will ever make in this life.

How to Enter Into a Full Surrender with the Lord

Before you really enter into this full surrender with the Lord, you really need to think about this and really chew on the ramifications that making this full surrender will entail. This will be the most life-altering decision that you will ever make in this life. If you turn your life over to the Lord for Him to completely handle – your life will take a completely different course as versus the one your life would take if you would decide to control your own destiny and call all of your own shots.

Once you make this full surrender with the Lord, there is no turning back, no matter what hell, life, or the devil may try and throw your way. You can obviously always bail out on God anytime you want to; as He will never force you to stay loyal to Him and fully serve Him. You are free to go anytime you want.

However, once you have the knowledge of what this full surrender is really all about, and then you decide to embark on this adventure with God, and you then bail out on Him some years down the road – God is going to judge you much more severely when you die and cross over to face Him for your own personal judgment as versus another Christian who really did not have much knowledge on this part of the walk with Him. To whom much is given, much more will be expected!

Jesus Himself has stated that you are better off never having known the truth than having known the truth, and then turning back to your old ways. Once you receive knowledge from God as to what He wants you to do with your life and how He wants you to handle it – then He will expect you to do something with that knowledge and implement it into your life.

The Bible says that faith without any type of works will be dead.
Even though God will always let you bail out on Him anytime you want to in your walk with Him, you must make this decision for yourself as to whom you will choose to serve and follow in this life – yourself or God.
If you decide to fully serve God and fully surrender your entire life over to Him, then you must set your face like flint, draw your battle line in the sand, and march forward determined that you will stay true,

loyal, and faithful to God for the rest of your earthly life – no matter what the cost – and no matter what life, hell, or the devil tries to throw your way to try and knock you off course. **This is a full surrender to the death!**

That is why I say there is no turning back once you decide to make this decision to fully surrender your entire life to the Lord and follow His perfect will for your life. You will be held accountable for the knowledge that you now have about this part of your walk with God the Father.

If after really thinking and meditating on all of this, you decide that there is no other way to live your life, and that you truly want to enter into this full surrender with the Lord – it now becomes very easy to do. You do not have to get all worked up into any type of major prevailing or travailing. This is simply a conscience decision that you will make with your own intellect operating out of your own free will with the Lord.

Here are two short, simple prayers getting straight to the point with God on this decision. The first prayer will be the one that you will do to make the initial full surrender with Him. The second prayer will be the one that you should do at least once or twice a year for the rest of your life so you can let God know that you mean serious business with Him as to who should be running your life – and that you will continue to let Him have the reigns of your life to the day you literally die. One last thing. When I say making a full surrender to God, I mean making a full and complete surrender. You can hold nothing back. Some Christians only surrender certain parts of their life to God, but not other parts. If you do not make a full and complete surrender of everything in your life to God the Father – then you will partially handcuff Him in being able to work full force in your life.

To make sure that you fully surrender everything over to the Lord, you must surrender 4 specific things over to Him. The apostle Paul says we have 3 parts to our beings – body, soul, and spirit. He then says we are to have all three parts of our being **"completely sanctified"** in the Lord. The only way that can happen is if we are willing to completely surrender all three parts of our being to the Lord for Him to sanctify.

Here is the verse from Paul that is specifically telling us to do this:

[23] Now may the God of peace Himself **sanctify you completely; and may your whole spirit, soul, and body be preserved blameless at the coming of our Lord Jesus Christ.**
                                                               1 Thessalonians 5:23

For the people that does not know. You are a spirit (lowercase as only the Holy Spirit is spelled with a capital S) you have a soul and you live in a body.

In addition to these three parts of our being, God now wants one more thing from us – and that is our **"entire life."** And when I say entire life, I mean everything in our life – past, present, and future.

Some Christians may surrender their job lives over to God, but not the choice as to who they should marry.

They then marry the wrong person as a result of making this decision all on their own, and as a result, they end up throwing a spanner into the course that their life had been taking in the Lord, and they sometimes are completely knocked off the course that God had initially set them up on.

This is why the Bible tells us that God has to be the One to build the house that you are attempting to build in this life. One wrong move on your part could cause the whole house to completely unravel and fall apart.

A chain is only as strong as each of the individual links.

One weak or broken link can cause the whole chain to completely unravel!

Marrying the wrong person or taking the wrong job could cause you to lose valuable years on the mountain you are attempting to climb in God due to having to deal with the serious consequences of making that wrong choice. This is why God has to be in **total control** over every area of your life – not just some or part of it.

In these two prayers, you will see I have you surrendering your body, your soul, your spirit, and your "entire life" over to God the Father. When you tell God you are willing to surrender your entire life over to Him – He will take you very serious and assume that you literally mean everything and anything in your life – no holding back!

Here are the two specific prayers. Obviously feel free to add any of your own personal words when making this commitment to Him. But the specific wording in these two prayers, if truly done from your heart, will break you into a realm with God that will completely change the course of your entire life.

Making the Initial Full Surrender

"Father God,
In the name of Jesus, I am now willing to place my body, my soul, my spirit, and my entire life into Your hands. I now ask that You place me into Your perfect will for my life. From this moment on, I will choose to stay fully surrendered to You all the days of my life, and will allow You to lead and direct my life in the direction that You will want it to go in.
Thank You Father God.
Thank You Jesus.
Thank You Holy Spirit."

To Stay in the Full Surrender

"Father,
In the name of Jesus, I continue to place my body, my soul, my spirit, and my entire life into Your hands. I am choosing to stay fully surrendered to You all the days of my life, and I ask that You will continue to keep me in Your perfect will for my life.
Thank You Father God.
Thank You Jesus.
Thank You Holy Spirit."

If you are willing to make this full surrender to the Lord, He will then start to take full control of your life and steer it in the direction that He will now want it to go in. You have now just stepped from the dugout out onto the real playing field of life – where God can now use you to complete His divine purpose for your life.

I will now leave you with three very profound verses from Scripture nicely summarizing the above argument as to why each and every Christian needs to commit to making this full surrender with the Lord.

The first one will be on the verse that unless God is the One to build the house of your life, then you will be laboring in vain with the house you are trying to build all on your own efforts and wisdom.

The second verse is from Jesus where He states that unless you build your house on Him, the Rock, then it will eventually fall completely apart as soon as any storm clouds start to come against it.

The third verse sums up this whole argument when God says that He is giving each person a real, big choice to make in this life. They can either choose to receive true life by choosing to follow God and all of His ways for their lives – or they can choose a life of death and cursing by following their own ways, the ways of someone else, or the ways of this world.
The key words in this last verse is that you **"cling to Him,"** that you **"obey His voice,"** and that you **"love the Lord your God."** Clinging to God means that you are walking very close with Him in this full surrender.

He leads, we follow – just like the sheep follow the shepherd. The Bible tells us that Jesus is our Shepherd and as such, it is our job to fully follow Him in this life.

These three verses perfectly capture the big picture as to what is really most important in this life and who we should really be living this life for. Here they are:

127 **Unless the LORD builds the house,
They labor in vain who build it;**
Unless the LORD guards the city,
The watchman stays awake in vain.

Psalm 127:1

[24] "**Therefore whoever hears these sayings of Mine, and does them, I will liken him to a wise man who built his house on the rock:** [25] **and the rain descended, the floods came, and the winds blew and beat on that house; and it did not fall, for it was founded on the rock.**
[26] "But everyone who hears these sayings of Mine, and does not do them, will be like a foolish man who built his house on the sand: [27] and the rain descended, the floods came, and the winds blew and beat on that house; and it fell. And great was its fall."

Matthew 7:24-27

[19] I call heaven and earth as witnesses today against you, *that* I have set before you life and death, blessing and cursing; therefore choose life, that both you and your descendants may live; [20] that you may love the LORD your God, that you may obey His voice, and that you may cling to Him, for He *is* your **life and the length of your days**; and that you may dwell in the land which the LORD swore to your fathers, to Abraham, Isaac, and Jacob, to give them."

Deuteronomy 30:19-20

I feel the evidence is absolutely overwhelming that God the Father wants this full and complete surrender from each and every one of us so that He is fully free to guide our lives in the directions that He will want to take them in.

However, I also feel that the Lord has conveyed to me that this decision is one of the hardest for many of His people to make. There is something inside each one of us that wants to control our own destinies, call all of our own shots, decide who we are going to marry, and decide what goals and aspirations we should be striving for in this life.

This natural desire for independence inside of each one of us is actually good, as it helps to prevent us from falling into human and demonic slavery. Our world is a perfect example of that spirit in operation when we gained our full independence. However, that same spirit has no place in our personal relationship with God.

The Bible specifically says that all men and all women have sinned and fall way short of the glory of God and that without Jesus, we can do absolutely nothing of any consequence. We are imperfect in every way, shape, and form. We are powerless within our own beings to accomplish anything of any real worth with the Lord. Only God is all-powerful and all-knowing, and He is the only One who can anoint us with His divine power, and then guide us every step of the way to accomplish anything meaningful in this life before we die and cross over to be with Him for all eternity. Many Christians feel that if they make this full surrender with the Lord, that they will lose all of their freedom and independence – even if it is God Almighty Himself they are serving. However, the Bible tells us that there is liberty and freedom where the

Spirit of the Lord is at. **In other words, you will have much more freedom, liberty, and independence by serving and following God than you would if you serve yourself or someone else.**

The apostle Paul could not have said it any better when he says that he is a **servant to all – but a slave to none!** Here are two very good verses from the apostle Paul giving us this powerful piece of revelation:

[19] For though **I am free from all** *men*, **I have made myself a servant to all**, that I might win the more;
1 Corinthians 9:19

[23] You were bought at a price; **do not become slaves of men.**
[24] **Brethren, let each one remain with God in that** *state* **in which he was called.**
1 Corinthians 7:23-24

The way Paul has this last verse worded – you are a slave if you are not serving God and operating in the specific call that He has set up for your life.
By being willing to fully surrender your entire life to the Lord – not only will you find what you were created to be and exactly what your true, divine destiny is going to be in this life – but you will also find a new sense of freedom and liberty that you never knew could exist in a world where many people are constantly trying to control one another to one degree or another.

God highly respects your free will and He will work very closely with you as He starts to guide your steps on an everyday basis. You can totally trust Him to perfectly handle you and your life.

The choice is now yours for those of you who have not made this full surrender with the Lord. You must now choose this day whom you will serve.

Chapter 7: Sanctification

Our Father God's ultimate and highest aim for all of us is our sanctification in Him. God wants us to be more like Himself. He wants to transform us into the image of His Son Jesus Christ.

God wants to sanctify us completely in our body, soul, and spirit. Jesus Christ Himself tells us that He wants us to be perfect just like His Father.

The Bible tells us that all men and women have sinned and have fallen way short of the glory of God. Most people think that it is impossible to be Christ like as they think that the bar is set to high to even try and be like Jesus Christ. This is why, many Christians never seek after God to get this sanctification process started in their life and because of this there is very little spiritual growth in their lives. This is also the reason many Christians fall back into their old ways because they think it is too difficult to be Christ like and it is easier to just give up and become part of the world again.

I will show you how easy it is to get sanctified and be more Christ like and after this book you will definitely have a more personal relationship with the Lord Jesus Christ.

We got three specific things as a result of Jesus Christ dying on the cross for our sins. **Redemption, Righteousness, and Sanctification.**
Most Christians only know about – redemption and righteousness – most of them never pick up on the

third thing that is available to us – our **sanctification in the Lord**!

Sanctification is a progressive work done by the Holy Spirit throughout your entire life.

Apostle Paul tells us that we have to "work out" our salvation with fear and trembling. He also says there are "things" we have to work out – and I strongly believe one of those "things" is our sanctification in the Lord.

The process where God set us apart and transform us into becoming more holy instruments of righteousness for His use.

The Hayford's Bible Handbook, defines sanctification as follows:

"The work of God's grace by which the believer is separated from sin and becomes dedicated to God's righteousness. Accomplished by the Word of God and the Holy Spirit, sanctification results in holiness, or purification from the guilt and power of sin. Sanctification is instantaneous before God through Christ and progressive before man through obedience to the Holy Spirit and the Word."

What is sanctification?

Jesus Christ had a lot to say about sanctification in the Book of John, chapter 17. In verse 16 the Lord says, "They are not of the world, even as I am not of the world," and this is before His request: "Sanctify them in the truth: Thy word is truth." Sanctification is a state of separation unto God; all believers enter into this state when they are born of God:

^{30} But of Him you are in Christ Jesus, who became for us wisdom from God—and righteousness and sanctification and redemption—
1 Corinthians 1:30

This is a once-for-ever separation, eternally unto God. It is an intricate part of our salvation, our connection with Christ.

^{10} By that will we have been sanctified through the offering of the body of Jesus Christ once *for all*.
Hebrews 10:10

If you have never really sought after the Lord to release this kind of supernatural work in your life – study these verses very, very carefully. God is giving you an incredible spiritual secret that can dramatically change the quality of your life down here on this earth. You do not have to wait until you get to heaven to have God start this sanctification-transformation process in your life. It can start right now if you are willing to fully surrender your entire life over to the Lord and then ask Him to begin this sanctification process in your life.

Many people have no interest in the spiritual things of God. Most people major goal in this life is to more material things in this life and they do not care who they have to step on or who they hurt in the process.

Many Christians have been labeled as being "not cool" and "goody two shoes" by their friends and family. Many of our teenagers are made fun of in their schools if they do not join the crowds in abusing alcohol, doing drugs, or engaging in premarital sex.

God's ways are not the ways of this world! God clearly tells us that we will become His enemies if we become too friendly with the things and ways of this world. God is calling you to become more holy and more righteous in the Lord. The only thing that really matter is what God thinks, not what the world thinks. We will all be judged by God and not by the world.

So many people entering a life of drugs or alcohol abuse. Many people are committing adultery. Others are chasing after their one and only god "money".

Have you ever thought why so many people engage with alternative forms of spirituality, such as the occult and the many facets of the New Age movement.

They are all looking for that **"high"** that make them **"feel good."**

They want to get a quick fix to get that next high.

All of the free sex, drugs, and alcohol, and all of the money in this world, and all of the material things money can buy us, will never buy us that true state of inner happiness, that true state of well-being that we are all really searching for.

Too many Christians have become more attached to the things of this world rather than to God and the things that He wants us to get involved in. This is way many Christians are unhappy.

Accepting Jesus Christ as your personal Lord and Savior is just the beginning once you have done this God wants to build you up in Him and all of His ways for your life.

The first thing that God will want you to do is to be willing to enter into a full surrender with Him so He can then set you up on the divine path that He will want you to follow in this life. Then God will want you to establish a personal relationship with Him.

Many Christians have already done both of these things, but they still feel there is something missing in their lives.

They are following God's perfect will and plan for their lives. They know how to be led by the Holy Spirit on a daily basis. They have established very good personal relationships with the Lord but there is still something missing in their lives and they cannot pin point it.

I personally believe that the missing ingredient in many believer's life is the sanctification process. Many have not entered into it because they simply do not know about it, or they really do not want to go this far with the Lord.

The sanctification process with the Lord, can be a bit painful at times, since God will be working with you to fully expose and prune out all the negative qualities that He do not want in your personality.

It will be your responsibility to work with the Holy Spirit in order to be able to get God to move you into this deeper realm of making you to become more holy.

God will transmit and impart His love, His peace, and His kindness into your personality.

Once the sanctification process starts, it is then that you will really be able to feel and experience the sense of well-being that God intended all of us to have in Him.

When God Himself, through the Holy Spirit, starts to enter into your mind, soul, and heart will you feel that high that everyone is really looking for these days.

You Are Now Sanctified in Jesus Christ

Jack Hayford on sanctification says that sanctification is **"instantaneous before God through Christ,"** but that it is **"progressive before man through obedience to the Holy Spirit and the Word."**

The below two Scripture verses are telling us that we are now **"sanctified in Jesus Christ,"** and that we now receive sanctification, along with redemption and righteousness, through the blood that Jesus Christ has shed for all of us on the cross. We have to go through a progressive process through the Holy Spirit and the Word in order to become more holy and sanctified in the Lord.

We have already received His sanctification, like we have already received His redemption and righteousness as a result of being saved and born again.

Here are the two verses:

²To the church of God which is at Corinth, **to those who are sanctified in Christ Jesus, called *to be* saints**, with all who in every place call on the name of Jesus Christ our Lord, both theirs and ours:

1 Corinthians 1:2

³⁰ But of Him you are in Christ Jesus, who became for us wisdom from God—and righteousness and sanctification and redemption—
1 Corinthians 1:30

God the Father has given us a full redemption and a full pardon for all of our sins. It is now your turn to start the process of being sanctified through the power of His Holy Spirit to become the saints that He wants you to become in Him. The following three words will mean much more to you over the next couple of days.

Redemption, Righteousness, and Sanctification! Just stop and think for a moment. All of this is coming directly from God Almighty if we are willing to accept His free gift of eternal salvation through His Son Jesus Christ.

The Progressive Process of Sanctification

Now here are the two main verses that will show us that becoming sanctified in the Lord is a progressive process. The two keys words in these verses are **"being sanctified."**

If we were all instantaneously sanctified at the moment of our conversions with Jesus Christ, then the Bible would not read **"being sanctified."** The word **"being"** is telling us that this is a progressive and ongoing process.

[11] For both He who sanctifies and those who are **being sanctified** *are* all of one, for which reason He is not ashamed to call them brethren,
Hebrews 2:11

[14] For by one offering He has perfected forever those who are **being sanctified**.
Hebrews 10:14

God is Calling YOU Sanctification

God is calling everyone to be sanctified in Him. The verses below are very direct and straight-to-the-point. The first verse tells you that God wants to sanctify you **"completely"** in all three parts of our being – body, soul, and spirit!

²³ Now may the God of peace Himself **sanctify you completely; and may your whole spirit, soul, and body be preserved blameless** at the coming of our Lord Jesus Christ.

1 Thessalonians 5:23

¹⁵ but as He who called you *is* holy, you also be holy in all *your* conduct, ¹⁶ because it is written, "Be holy, for I am holy.

1 Peter 1:15-16

³ **For this is the will of God, your sanctification**: that you should abstain from sexual immorality; ⁴ **that each of you should know how to possess his own vessel in sanctification and honor,** ⁵ not in passion of lust, like the Gentiles who do not know God

1 Thessalonians 4:3

⁷ **For God did not call us to uncleanness, but in holiness.**

1 Thessalonians 4:7

7 Therefore, having these promises, beloved, **let us cleanse ourselves from all filthiness of the flesh and spirit, perfecting holiness in the fear of God.**

2 Corinthians 7:1

²⁰ But in a great house there are not only vessels of gold and silver, but also of wood and clay, some for honor and some for dishonor. ²¹ **Therefore if anyone cleanses himself from the latter, he will be a vessel for honor, sanctified and useful for the Master, prepared for every good work.**

2 Timothy 2:20-21

⁴⁸ **Therefore you shall be perfect, just as your Father in heaven is perfect.**

Matthew 5:48

¹⁹ I speak in human *terms* because of the weakness of your flesh. For just as you presented your members *as* slaves of

uncleanness, and of lawlessness *leading* to *more* lawlessness, **so now present your members *as* slaves *of* righteousness for holiness.**
[20] For when you were slaves of sin, you were free in regard to righteousness. [21] What fruit did you have then in the things of which you are now ashamed? For the end of those things *is* death. [22] **But now having been set free from sin, and having become slaves of God, you have your fruit to holiness,** and the end, everlasting life.

Romans 6:19-22

If you are honest with yourself, you can feel and sense how big the gap is between where you are right now with the Lord in your present spiritual level and how far God would really like to take you in this realm. Many Christians never even attempt to give God a chance to start the sanctification process through them.

Sanctification can only be done by the Word and the Holy Spirit

Trying to achieve the state of holiness that God the Father would like to bring you up into is completely impossible if you try to do it through your own flesh and through your own efforts.

Many Christians are trying to achieve this state of holiness without the presence and power of the Holy Spirit. You can easily spot those who are being properly sanctified through the Holy Spirit and those who are not, those are the people who are not genuine. Their holiness is not coming from the heart. You get the sense they are just trying to put on a show. There just seems to be something fake and plastic about them and the way they operate. Even nonbelievers can see right through them.

The person who is properly sanctified by the Holy Spirit, stand out because there is something different about this type of person. This person does not flaunt his or her goodness, or holiness. They are very humble about it. Everything they do comes from the heart and everything appears to be done very naturally. There is no pretentiousness or sense of false piety in their actions or attitudes.

This sense of real holiness they are projecting through their personalities literally has a drawing power to it. You find yourself gravitating to these types of people. You can almost sense or see a radiance or glow about them. The love of God just radiates from their countenance. You are very comfortable in being in their presence and talking with them. You can see that their holiness is genuine and that it really is coming from the heart of God Himself.

Sanctification in the Lord is done by the power of the Holy Spirit operating through the knowledge that the Word (the Bible) will give you. It is the Word and the Holy Spirit working together that will cause this sanctification process to begin and occur in your life.

It is the Holy Spirit who will be the One to cause this transformation to occur in your personality.

The Holy Spirit does not work without the Word. Why? Because the Word of God will give you the knowledge that you will need in order to be able to work with the Holy Spirit in this process. You have

to know exactly what it is that God wants to change about you before the Holy Spirit will move to cause some of these changes to start to take place in your personality.

A good example of some of the specific qualities that God want to impart into your personality is the 9 fruits of the Holy Spirit.

The Bible will tell you exactly what these nine fruits are. Then once you know exactly what they are, then you can start to work with the Holy Spirit to get more of these fruits manifested and imparted into your personality. But if you do not learn exactly what these specific fruits are to begin with by reading about them from the Bible, then the Holy Spirit will have nothing to work with and He cannot do much with you in this realm. More on the 9 Fruits later in this book.

All born again Christians have the Holy Spirit inside them. The Holy Spirit is anxious to with you in every area of your life where you may need His help on, especially in the area of being sanctified in the Lord. However, many Christians have not spent much time in the Word and they are thus lacking the **"working knowledge"** they will need to work with the Holy Spirit in this deeper realm. As a result, there is very little, true spiritual growth over the course of their lives. Sanctification is for the real seekers. The real seekers will be diving into God and His Word to find out exactly what it is God wants to do with them, and then will only be too anxious to work with the Holy Spirit during this process – having no fear of doing it, and being willing to fully submit to the Lord with how He wants to handle all of it.

These verses are giving you the **"key"** that you will need to open up the door of sanctification to come into your life and change it forever.

¹³ But we are bound to give thanks to God always for you, brethren beloved by the Lord, because God from the beginning chose you for salvation through **sanctification by the Spirit and belief in the truth,**
2 Thessalonians 2:13

¹¹ And such were some of you. But you were washed, **but you were sanctified**, but you were justified in the name of the Lord Jesus and **by the Spirit of our God.**
1 Corinthians 6:11

¹⁸ **But we all, with unveiled face, beholding as in a mirror the glory of the Lord, are being transformed into the same image from glory to glory, just as by the Spirit of the Lord.**

² elect according to the foreknowledge of God the Father, **in sanctification of the Spirit**, for obedience and sprinkling of the blood of Jesus Christ:
Grace to you and peace be multiplied.

A Heavenly Inheritance
³ Blessed *be* the God and Father of our Lord Jesus Christ, who according to His abundant mercy has begotten us again to a living hope through the resurrection of Jesus Christ from the dead,
1 Peter 1:2-3

¹³ For if you live according to the flesh you will die; **but if by the Spirit you put to death the deeds of the body**, you will live.
Romans 8:13

²⁵ Husbands, love your wives, just as Christ also loved the church and gave Himself for her, ²⁶ **that He might sanctify and cleanse her with the washing of water by the word,** ²⁷ that He might present her to Himself a glorious church, not having spot or

wrinkle or any such thing, but that she should be holy and without blemish.

Ephesians 5:25-27

The Word of God (the Bible) is like water. The more you read it the more you get sanctified.

²² Since you have purified your souls in obeying the truth through the Spirit in sincere love of the brethren, love one another fervently with a pure heart, ²³ having been born again, not of corruptible seed but incorruptible, through the word of God which lives and abides forever

1 Peter 1:22-23

Notice in the last verse it says that your soul can become purified by **"obeying the truth through the Spirit."** You can only get God's truth in you if you read His Word. Learn the truth by studying the Word of God, and then combine this with walking in the power of the Holy Spirit, and then your soul can become purified.

Jesus Christ can cleanse and sanctify His church, which are the individual body of believers, by the **"washing of water by the word."** In other words, you can be washed clean by His Word (the Bible) if you are willing to soak into the Scripture verses like you would soak in a bath of water to clean off. The Word of God has that kind of power in it!

The truth from God can set you free in many areas of your life – but you first have to learn what those truths are before they can start to work to set you free. And the only way to find the spiritual truths that will change the quality of your life and help set you free is by reading and studying from the Bible. There is no other way!

It is by the Holy Spirit Himself that this sanctification process is done in your life. Put all of these verses together, and God the Father is telling you exactly how this sanctification process can be done in your life and it is by the power of the Holy Spirit operating through the knowledge that the Word will give you.

Entering into the Sanctification Process with the Lord

It may seem like a tall order in the type of world we live in today, but it isn't. I have personally seen God do a sanctifying work in several people I know, and the changes in these people's personality have been dramatic and powerful. They are no longer the people I used to know. They are now true saints in every sense of the word.

The Holy Spirit is powerful and He is the Spirit of God Almighty Himself. Seeing the Holy Spirit sanctifying someone to make them to become more holy and Christ-like in their spirit, souls and body is truly an incredible sight and is even more miraculous than watching someone get healed.

To those of you who would like to tread into this type of deeper waters with the Lord, but are somewhat fearful of what He may do with you – the one thing that I can personally tell you is that you can completely trust God the Father to begin this work in you. He knows you better than you can ever know yourself.

Below is a simple 4 step process that will lead you into the sanctification realm if you decide you want to give God the green light, what I cannot give you is exactly what God will personally do with each and everyone of you once this sanctification process starts up.

Everyone is operating at different levels of spiritual development with the Lord. Some people have more baggage to clean up than others. Some people will be more resistant to the Holy Spirit wanting to remove certain negative qualities than others will. Some will progress at a faster rate of speed than others will because they will be more honest with the Lord and will be more open to receiving revelation on exactly what it is God wants to put in them and exactly what it is He wants to take out of them.

Sanctification is a process. It will not happen overnight. You can trust God to perfectly handle the time frame in which He wants to operate in. He will not overwhelm you. He will give you plenty of reasonable time to work with the Holy Spirit once the Holy Spirit starts to impart revelation and knowledge to you.

Do You Really Want It

The first thing you will need to do is to make a personal decision as to whether or not you really want to enter into this sanctification realm with the Lord. Many Christians really do not want God to do any type of sanctifying work in their lives. The reason for this is that they know He will be coming after some of their vices and character flaws, and they simply are not willing to give up some of these vices, or attempt to try and work with Him to change certain parts of their personalities.

So the first thing you will have to do is to make a personal decision as to whether or not you really want the Lord to begin this type of deeper work in your life. This is not something that you can go halfway with Him on. This is an all-or-nothing decision.
You are either going to go all the way with the Lord once He begins to do it with you or you are not.

Ask God to Begin the Sanctification Process

To get God to start to move you into this sanctification realm will only require one thing – and that one thing is that you go before the Lord in serious and heartfelt prayer, and ask Him to start this sanctification process in your life through the power of the Holy Spirit.
The Bible says to ask – and **then** you will receive. The Bible also says you have not because you ask not. Once you put this request on His altar, keep reminding the Lord to keep this sanctification process going for the rest of your life at least once or twice a year for the rest of your life. By reminding God to keep this sanctification process going on for the rest of your life, you are showing Him that you mean serious business with Him, and that you want the Holy Spirit to keep working with you in this realm as long as you are in this physical body.

Here is a prayer you can use:

"Father,
In the name of Your Son Jesus Christ, I now approach Your throne with a very special request. Your Word

tells me that You want to completely sanctify me through the special workings of the Holy Spirit. Your Word tells me that You want to shape, mold, and transform me into the express image of Your Son Jesus Christ. Father, I now want to work in cooperation and in partnership with both You and the Holy Spirit to begin this deeper sanctifying work in my life.

Father, I now ask that You begin to completely sanctify me in both my body, my soul, and my spirit. I now give You the green light to begin this sanctification process in my life. Father, I now ask that You hold nothing back once You begin this sanctifying work in me and my life. I will now be willing to work with both You and the Holy Spirit in any area of my life and in any area of my personality that You feel needs to be cleaned up, sanctified, and made more holy. Father, I now have full faith and belief that You will honor this request and will begin this sanctification process in my life in the way and manner You deem most appropriate at the level of spiritual development that I am currently operating at with You.
Thank You Father.
Thank You Jesus.
Thank You Holy Spirit." Amen

If you can truly approach God with this prayer, and you are really meaning it from your mind and your heart, then God will hear you loud and clear, and He will then begin to start this sanctification process in your life right where you are at the moment you put this request before Him.

Study the Word for the Knowledge needed

There are two things you must now be willing to do. You will not be passive in all of this, expecting God to do all of the work for you. He will need you to do your part in this.

Firstly you must study the Word (the Bible) on a regular and frequent basis. As some of the above Scripture verses have stated, it is the combination of the Holy Spirit working with the Word and the knowledge that the Word will give you that will cause this sanctification process to move into high gear in your life.

As stated at the beginning of this chapter, you have to have the actual knowledge on exactly what it is God wants to change about you. And the only way you can get this knowledge is by reading and studying from the Bible.

It's the Word and the Spirit working in conjunction with one another that will take you on this road to holiness in the Lord. Your part is to get into the Word. The Holy Spirit cannot do this part for you. Many Christians do not spend much time in the Bible and this is one of the main reasons why there is not much spiritual growth in their lives.

The Holy Spirit will personally guide you in this life as to how often and how frequently you will need to read from the Bible.

Work with the Holy Spirit during this process

The apostle Paul says that God wants to sanctify you completely – body, soul, and spirit. Do not be surprised if one of the things that the Holy Spirit will move in on is any particular vices you may have that could be harming your physical body. Good examples of this would be smoking cigarettes, smoking pot, abusing alcohol, and overeating on the wrong kinds of foods.

Many Christians are addicted to smoking cigarettes. I have seen God move on quite a few of them on this particular vice. Some of them have been successful in kicking the habit, and others have not. The power of the Holy Spirit is there to help break this addiction off you, but you have to really want to have this vice removed before God will move in to break this addiction off you.

Some people really do not want to give this up for the Lord. When that happens, God will respect your free will on the matter and back off. However, I have seen Him come back in waves on that person, and every so often He keeps coming back and knocking on their doors, letting them know once more that He would really like to have this addiction removed from their lifestyle.

I have discovered there is some slack with the Lord on the cigarette thing, but there is much less slack with Him on the pot issue! Every Christian who I have known that has smoked pot, and then really came into a full surrender with the Lord, have all had the pot taken out of their lives very quickly.

Bottom line – God will be letting you know very early on which of these vices He would like to have removed from your personality and lifestyle. His divine power is there to help break these addictions off your back, but you will have to be the one to make this personal decision for yourself as to whether or not you will work in cooperation with the Holy Spirit to take these addictions out of your life for good.

I have seen God break many of these types of addictions off people and they did not have to go through any type of physical withdrawal during the weaning off process. God, through the power of the Holy Spirit operating on the inside of you, has the full power to be able to set you completely free from any vices or addictions you may have. There is nothing that the power of God cannot totally defeat and overcome if you are willing to allow God to work with you in these areas.

Other areas of your life that God may want to move in on are some of your attitudes. If you are holding any un-forgiveness towards others for things they may have done to you in your past – expect God to move in very strongly to try and get you to forgive these people and to let all of the wrongs they may have ever done to you into His hands. Vengeance and payback in this life belong to the Lord, not to you or anyone else! God will be righting all the wrongs ever done to you in this life. Your job is to forgive all of those who have ever hurt or wronged you and get on with the rest of your life.

If you are operating in any type of a judgmental, critical, controlling, or manipulating spirit – expect the Lord to deal very heavily with you on these issues. These kinds of attitudes and behaviors are poisonous and toxic to all of those who come in contact with them. They are all unacceptable in the eyes of God, and the Holy Spirit will be moving very strongly on you with conviction and insight to tackle these kinds of attitudes and behaviors.

Bottom line – God, through the power of the Holy Spirit, will be letting you know very clearly what good, positive, and godly qualities He will want to try and **"put on"** into your personality, and what negative qualities and vices He will want to try and **"put away."** Once all of this knowledge and information has been given to you by the Lord, then it will be up to you as to whether or not you will want to work in cooperation with the Holy Spirit to get all of this accomplished.

If you are willing to work with the Lord in the specific areas that He will target – then the Holy Spirit will start to do the miraculous and supernatural work of removing all of the bad things that He will not want operating in your personality and life, and then impart all of the positive and godly things that He will want have operating in your personality and life. And once this starts to happen, God the Father will then start to transmit and impart part of His divine nature and personality right up into your mind, soul, and spirit.

God's love, joy, peace, patience, boldness, goodness, gentleness, and kindness will all start to move up and mesh into your personality, thereby increasing your ability to be able to walk, live, and operate in these saintly and godly qualities.

When this starts to happen, you will have officially entered into a true, progressive, sanctified state – where the very life of God Himself will now be flowing through you and out of you so that you can reach others with His message of eternal salvation, and His message on how to properly live this life the way He wants His people to live it.

The Bible tells us that God wants us to become fishers of men for Him. You can become a much better fisherman, representative, and ambassador for the Lord if you are willing to allow Him to lead you into this sanctification process. Nothing will draw others to the Lord more than a Spirit-filled, anointed, and truly sanctified saint who has the fruits and qualities of the Holy Spirit operating through their personality.

This sanctification process is available to every single born again believer. However, it is up to each and every Christian to make this personal decision for themselves. This is something that the Lord will not force on anyone due to the individual cooperation that is needed from each person to really get this process started.

Chapter 8: God is the Potter, we are the Clay

One of the most powerful analogies in the Bible regarding our transformation and sanctification in the Lord has to be the analogy of the potter and the clay.

The Bible says that God is the Potter and we are the clay. It is up to God to mold, transform, and sanctify us as we journey through this earthly life.

Whenever God gives us a specific analogy in the Bible, this means that we have to seek into the revelation of that analogy in order to pick up what He is trying to tell us with the analogy. If we do, then we will see exactly what God is trying to tell us in reference to the actual analogy itself. In other words, we have to find exactly how pottery is made if we want to fully understand what God is trying to tell us in this most incredible analogy.

Here is the key verse from the Bible that will give us this specific revelation that God is the Potter and we are His clay:

8 But now, O LORD,
You *are* our Father;
We *are* the clay, and You our potter;
And all we *are* the work of Your hand.

Isaiah 64:8

I have never made pottery myself, so I had no idea how it was actually made. But I always had a feeling that God would somehow bring someone along that would show and demonstrate how this process is actually done so we can see exactly how this analogy fits into what God wants to do with each one of us in our own personal growth in Him.

Pastor Pat Lazovich used to make pottery before God called him into full time ministry work. As a result of his previous experience in actually making pottery, God now has him traveling to different churches, giving real live demonstrations on exactly how pottery is made, and then how this analogy perfectly fits in and lines up with how God wants to mold, shape, and transform all of us in our personal growth in Him. You can watch the video on our ministry website.

His explanation of this analogy is excellent. I cannot recommend this man highly enough with his demonstration on the potter and the clay. If any of you would like to have him come to your church to do this demonstration for you, he is the senior pastor of Calvary Chapel in Sierra Vista, AZ.

In this chapter, I will give you the main steps on exactly how pottery is made, and then the appropriate explanations on how all of this fits into the analogy that God is the Potter and we are His clay.

Grab a hold of this very powerful revelation, because it will both visually and dramatically show you not only how God molds and transforms us in this life, but exactly why He does some of the things He does with us in this molding process, as this process can be quite painful and unpleasant at times.

I will break down the main steps on how pottery is actually made, along with the appropriate explanations as to how all of this perfectly fits into God's actual sanctification with us under the specific captions below.

God Needs the Word in Us Before He Can Start the Sanctification Process

The first thing Pat will show you is the lump of clay that he will actually use to make the piece of pottery he is looking to make. Before Pat can put this piece of clay on an electric wheel to start the actual molding process to make the kind of pottery he wants to make, he first has to add enough **WATER** into it in order to make it pliable and soft enough for him to be able to actually use it. If he does not add enough water into the clay, the clay will remain too hard and rigid for him to be able to actually use.

When the water is added into the clay, it makes the clay soft and pliable. If the clay is not soft and pliable enough, the potter cannot begin to use it to make the pottery he wants to make. The analogy for us to pick up on this first step is that the water used in this process represents the Word of God (the Bible).

Here is a good verse giving us the actual revelation that the word **"water"** in the Bible is symbolic of the Word of God. In other words, the Word of God is like water to our souls. Just like our physical bodies need water in order to be able to live and survive in this world, in the same way our souls need God's Word flowing through us in order to feed us on the inside in our inner man.

> [26] that He might **sanctify and cleanse her with the washing of water by the word,** [27] that He might present her to Himself a glorious church, not having spot or wrinkle or any such thing, but that she should be holy and without blemish.
>
> **Ephesians 5:26-27**

What this is telling us is that God cannot even begin to mold and transform us in this life unless we are first willing do our part. And our part has to be to get into His Word and try to read, understand, and assimilate what is in the Bible as best we can, with the Holy Spirit also helping us to understand what we are actually reading.

The Bible says that we are to grow in the knowledge of God, and one of the main ways that you will grow in the knowledge of God is to read from the one Book that will give you this direct knowledge – the Bible! There is no other way into the knowledge of God other than through the Bible.

If you do not spend enough reasonable time in this life trying to read from the Bible and assimilate the actual knowledge that is in this Book as best you can, then God will have very little to work with in your own personal growth with Him, and you will see very little, if any actual spiritual growth in Him in this life.

The reason why so many of God's saints are not spiritually growing in this life and being properly sanctified in the Holy Spirit is because they are not spending enough time trying to read and understand the Bible as best they can, and then see how the actual knowledge in this Bible can be implemented into their daily lives.

The Holy Spirit needs something to work with in order to get this growth process kicked into full gear – and that something is knowledge – and that knowledge can only be gained by reading the Bible. There is no other way!

Just as the potter cannot use the clay unless there is enough water added into it – in the same way God cannot start the sanctification process in our lives unless we first start to get enough of the Word in us. The Word cannot start to effectively work in you and your life unless you first start to attempt to get it into you in the first place.

So without question, the very first step you have to take, if you really want God to mold and shape you into the kind of person He really wants you to become in Him in this life, is to spend enough reasonable time in the Word (the Bible) – trying to understand, with the help of the Holy Spirit, all of the knowledge that is contained in it, and exactly how all of this knowledge can be incorporated into your personal life and walk with the Lord.

You Have to Be Properly "Centered" in Jesus Christ

After Pat adds enough water into the clay to make it soft and pliable so he can now start to work with it – the next thing he will do is put the piece of clay in the **center** of an electric wheel. This wheel will then start to spin so he can then use his hands to start the molding and shaping process with the clay as it is actually spinning on the wheel.

However, if the piece of clay is not **properly centered** in the middle of the wheel, then he will not be able to work with it, and he will not be able to make the pottery he wants to make.

Pat said having the lump of clay **perfectly centered** in the middle of the electric wheel is the first step in being able to actually make a piece of pottery. If he tries to make a piece of pottery with a lump of clay that is not properly centered in the middle of the wheel, it will eventually tear apart before he can finish the process.

In the same way that the clay has to be properly centered in the middle of the wheel before the potter can even begin to mold and shape it – we have to be properly centered in Jesus Christ before God can start to mold and shape us.

So what does it mean to be properly centered in Jesus? I believe what it means to be properly centered in Jesus is that you have to be under a complete and full surrender of you and your entire life with Him where He is now in full control of your entire life. Jesus has to become both Lord and Savior in your life, not just your Savior. Too many Christians do not have Jesus as the real Lord in their lives.

Bottom line – you have to enter into God's perfect will for your life before He will start to guide both you and your life in the direction that He will want to take it in. God will not fully guide you to your divine destiny in Him, and fully sanctify you to the degree that He would really like in this life unless you first come into this full surrender with Him. It's your all for His all.

Just like the potter cannot mold the piece of clay into the piece of pottery that he is trying to make unless it is **perfectly centered** in the middle of the wheel – in the same way the Lord cannot begin to properly work with us in this life unless we are **perfectly centered** in Him in a full surrender.

Pat actually shows this with a piece of clay. With it not being properly centered in the middle of the wheel, he gets it about halfway to where it needs to go and then all of a sudden it rips and tears apart from the wheel – all because it was not perfectly centered in the middle of the wheel in the first place.

In the same way, if we try to live our lives without Jesus leading and guiding the way, our lives will eventually fall apart and we will never reach and fulfill the divine destiny to which God has called each one of us in this life. This is why Jesus tells us in His Word that without Him we can do absolutely nothing – and that if we try to build our own houses without His direct guidance, that we will end up laboring **"in vain"** if we try to do it all through our own efforts and wisdom.

127 Unless the LORD **builds the house,
They labor in vain who build it;**
Unless the LORD guards the city,
The watchman stays awake in vain.

Psalm 127:1

Sanctification is a Slow, Steady, and Progressive Process

The next thing that Pat points out is how "slow" and "steady" the electric wheel turns as he is using his hands to mold the pot. He explains that to get the lump of clay to the pot he wants to make, that the wheel has to turn at this slow and steady pace. If he speeds up the wheel to any faster degree, the lump of clay will again tear completely apart before he can make it to the finish line.

In the same way, we have to have patience with the Lord on how He wants to work and build our lives up in Him. In our fast-paced, self-centered world, we are used to instant everything. But in God's realm, He usually works things out in a much slower time frame than we are used too. And if we do not learn how to go with His slower flows and time frames, we could end up getting very frustrated and impatient, and then eventually end up losing our peace and joy in Him, not to mention our possible calls in Him.

Just as a teenager will get stretch marks on their skins if they grow too fast during puberty, in the same way we have to let God build us up in Him in this slow and steady manner. If we try to push the envelope too far and too fast with Him, different parts of our lives could totally unravel and fall apart.

Not waiting on God's timing on who you should be marrying in this life could cause you to marry the wrong person in this life. I know what I am talking about, I made that mistake. You can read more about this in my book Witchcraft in the Church.

Not waiting on the next new job you should be taking could cause you to take a major wrong turn in the divine destiny that God already has planned out for your life, and it could then end up costing you years of wasted and unproductive time, if not completely cause you to lose your entire call in Him all together.

Just as a good potter has to take his time when molding and forming out this piece of pottery as it is spinning on the wheel – in the same way God has to mold, shape, and transform all of us in this same, slow, and steady manner. This is why one of the 9 fruits of the Holy Spirit is the fruit of patience. We all need the patience of the Holy Spirit operating in us to help keep us in God's timing with how He wants to work things out in our lives, especially in the fast-paced world in which we all live in.

God's Hand Will Personally Mold, Shape, and Transform You

The next thing you need to grab a hold of in your sanctification in the Lord, is that it is literally the hand of God Himself, operating through the Holy Spirit on the inside of you, that will supernaturally transform and sanctify you. This is a direct, supernatural work done by the Holy Spirit Himself.

Once Pat has the lump of clay properly centered in the middle of the wheel, and enough water has been added into the clay to make it soft and pliable to work with, then Pat starts the actual molding process with the lump of clay.

What he first does as the lump of clay is spinning on the wheel is to take his hand and push it down on the top of the clay to create an opening in it. Once this opening has been made at the top of the clay, Pat's hand then goes down deep inside the middle of the clay as it is forming out, and he then uses his hands to properly shape the piece of clay as it is building up during this spinning process on the wheel.

Pat's hands are thus working on both the inside and outside of the clay to mold, shape, and transform it into the pot he wants to make as it continues to spin on the wheel. His hands are literally making and forming all of this out with this original shapeless lump of clay. Pat says that he cannot make a pot unless his hands go down deep in the middle of that pot as it is forming out.

In the same way, God's own hand literally goes down deep into the middle of our souls and spirits where the inner sanctification work is actually done – to mold and transform us into the saints He wants us to become in Him. This is why we have to give God a full, solid, green light to do this type of inner sanctification work in us, as He needs our full co-operation in order to be able to get that deep on the inside of us.

Since God is doing the actual supernatural work on the inside of us, it can become rather painful and unpleasant at times, since He will be removing all of the bad and negative qualities that He will not want us to have operating in our personalities – and at the same time, instilling and imparting all of the good, positive, and godly qualities that He will want us to have.

Pat also has to apply a good amount of **pressure** with his hands as he is molding and shaping this lump of clay. In the same way, God has to apply some **serious pressure** on all of us from time to time in order to get us to change to become the kind of person He wants us to become in Him.

Removing toxic qualities such as pride, arrogance, bad tempers, complaining, gossiping and lust can all be very painful due to our flesh wanting to keep these negative qualities operating in our personalities. But let God do this inner surgery work in you through the Holy Spirit, and you will eventually be molded and shaped into the godly saint that He is calling you to become in Him – and true joy, happiness, and fulfillment will be all yours in this life.

Let God develop you to your fullest potential in this life

The next thing Pat will show you is that as his hands start to work with both the inside and outside of the clay, the lump of clay now starts to actually grow as it continues to spin on the wheel. It starts to get bigger and taller.
However, he then all of a sudden stops working the clay, with it being about half-way to where it needs to go. He then points out that we all need to let God take us as far as He will want to take us in this life. He said

no one is going to pay for a pot that is only half-done and half-completed.

In the same with the Lord, we should not quit and bail out on Him as we are about half-way up the mountain He wants us to climb in our calls and divine destiny in Him. We always need to continue to press on and let God take us as far as He wants to take us. Too many Christians quit and bail out on the Lord as they are about half-way up the mountain He is asking them to climb for Him. As a result, they never find out how much further they could have gone with God had they just continued to press further on.

Pat says that once you start this process with the Lord, let Him decide how far He wants to take you in this life, and do not be afraid if God really wants to stretch your abilities and horizons in the divine plan that He has already set up for your life.

You only have one chance in the eternal scheme of things to leave your mark in this world in the calling that God has placed on your life. Let God take you as far as He wants to go and you won't ever have to worry about having any second regrets once you leave and depart from this life and enter into heaven for all of eternity. You can leave this life knowing that you have fully accomplished everything that the Lord was wanting you to accomplish for Him if you just stay the course with Him and do not bail out due to fear or laziness.

God knows exactly what He wants to do with your life

The next thing Pat will point out as he is building this piece of clay into the exact pot he wants to make, is that he knows **exactly** what kind of pot he is going to make before he even starts the process. He knows **exactly** how tall and how wide it will end up being, because he already has a **perfect plan** for the pot before he even begins to sit down to start to work with it.

In the same way, God the Father already has our lives **perfectly planned** out for all of us. He knows **exactly** what He wants us to become in our callings in Him, who we should be marrying in this life, how many children He would like us to have, and exactly how to get to all of these specific milestones so we can make it there safely and in one piece.

Just as the piece of clay needs to fully trust the potter to make it into the exact pot he wants to make – in the same way we need to fully trust the Lord to mold, shape, and transform our personalities, along with leading our lives into the specific directions that He will want to take them in.

Since God is all-perfect and all-powerful and we are not – then it only stands to reason that we can **fully trust** God to build the **"house"** of our lives in Him rather than us trying to do it all on our own efforts and wisdom, or the wisdom and efforts of anyone else in our lives.

Do not stretch beyond the boundary lines that God has set up for your life

The next thing Pat will show you is that even though you want to make this pot into what you had originally designed it to be, you need to be very careful that you do not make this pot too tall or too wide and go beyond what your original design and plan for the pot was. If you do, it will tear apart and completely unravel, thereby completely destroying what you originally wanted to do with the pot in the first place. In the same way with the Lord – though we are to press on and go as far as God will want to take us in this life in our specific callings in Him, we also have to realize there is another side to this two-sided coin. We also have to make sure that we do not stretch beyond what God is calling us to do for Him, or stretch into positions that He does not want us going into.

If God is calling you to be an attorney, pastor, or doctor – do not try and stretch into other callings that He does not want you to be going into. If God is calling you to play third base on His team, do not try and stretch into the position of the shortstop or left-fielder.

Stay in the boundary lines that God will be setting up in your life. If you stretch beyond those boundary lines, you will stretch beyond your divine calling and there will thus be no anointing, no protection, and no fruit for you in those other endeavors. God knows exactly how far He wants to take us and we need to respect the boundary lines that He will be setting up for our lives.

Billy Graham was called to be an evangelist and he perfectly stayed in that calling during his entire life. He did not try to be a musician or a pastor. He stayed within the boundary lines that God had initially set up for his life and as a result, he will end up going down as one of the greatest evangelists of all time because of all of the good fruit he has produced for the Lord in that specific calling.

God's eyes and attention are always on you

Another good point that Pat brings up is that his eyes are always on the clay once he starts to work with it. If he takes his eyes and attention off the pot as he is shaping and molding it, he could make a big mistake and damage the pot in the process.

In the same way, once we come into this full surrender with the Lord, God will never take His eyes and attention off you. You will always have His complete and undivided attention, since He is omnipresent and no respecter of persons. God obviously has His eyes on everyone since He is omnipresent, but until you come into that full surrender with Him, He will not start to work and build up your life in the direction that He will want it to go in.

What this means is that you can fully trust God to complete the work that He has begun with you until the day you die and depart from this earth. As a result, you will be able to leave this life with most, if not all of your divine missions fully accomplished for Him as long as you stay the course and do not bail out on Him anywhere along the way.

God will always be doing major pruning in your life

The last thing that Pat will do is to take a knife and start cutting off any excess clay that has accumulated around the pot as he was molding and shaping it on the spinning wheel. What Pat is doing is smoothing out all of the rough edges so the pot turns out complete and beautiful to the natural eye.

In the same way, God will always be pruning out different things and different qualities that He will not be wanting you to have in this life. God may want to prune out some of the bad and negative friends you are hanging out with due to the negative influences they may be having on you and your spiritual development in Him.

He may also want to prune out some bad habits you may still have on you such as smoking cigarettes or the overeating of the wrong kinds of foods – and He will definitely be pruning out some of the bad and negative qualities you may still have operating in your personality such as some of the ones mentioned previously.

Though this cutting and pruning can be very painful at times due to your attachments to some of the above things, just realize that it is always for your own good in the long run, and you will be much better off by going with the Lord on anything that He will want to prune out of your life or out of your personality. Resist God on this pruning and you may never reach to the heights, to the calling, and to the person that He will want you to become in Him in this life.

Let God mold you into the specific person He wants you to become in Him

After Pat completes the process of turning this lump of clay into a beautiful piece of pottery, he then makes the comment to let God mold and shape you into the **specific person** He wants you to become in Him, not what other people want you to become.

You have been created by God to be a **unique person** – unlike any other person that has ever been created and born into this world. Realize that only God can mold and shape you into the **finished person** that He wants you to become in Him.

God, as our Father and Potter, is the only One who has the full knowledge, the full power, and the full means to be able to truly sanctify us to become the beautiful, godly, and righteous saints He is calling all of us to become in Him in this life.

Chapter 9: Seeking After the Lord with All of Your Heart

There are two main themes that you will see repeated over and over in many of our chapters. The first theme is the extreme importance that each and every Christian enters into a full surrender with the Lord so that He can then enter them into His perfect plan and destiny for their lives.

The second main theme that you will see repeated over and over again is the extreme importance that each and every Christian seek to establish a good, close, intimate, personal relationship with the Lord.

When you really stop and think about the big picture and what is really most important in this life, and then study the Bible to see where all of our priorities should be set at in this life – there is one special message and revelation that comes jumping off all the pages of the Bible. This one special message and revelation is that God the Father, His Son Jesus Christ, and His Holy Spirit are looking to establish and make a direct, one-on-one, intimate, personal relationship with each person He has created.

God knew beforehand that Adam and Eve were going to blow it in the Garden of Eden. God knew beforehand that every man and woman that would be born after them would all turn out to be unholy sinners in His sight, and that none of us would ever be good enough or righteous enough to be able to enter into His kingdom on any our own good works.

At this point, God could have easily given up on the entire human race after the fall of Adam and Eve, but for some strange reason, He chose not to do so. Why?

When you really stop to think about what unholy sinners we all really are, and how fallen and corrupt our human nature really is, you have to wonder – what does God see in any of us that makes us so redeemable in His sight?

Why would God the Father go to such extreme and painful lengths to bring us all back to Himself by sending down His one and only Son Jesus Christ to our cursed earth to go through the worst and most horrible form of physical death that anyone could have possibly undergone at the time He came down to our world – crucifixion by nails?

For God the Father to go to such an extreme and painful length to get all of us back to Himself shows us only one possible thing – and that one thing is how much our God really, truly, and unconditionally loves each man and each woman He has ever created.

There is no way that God the Father is going to send down and sacrifice His one and only Son on a cross if He did not have some kind of special, maximum intense, passionate, jealous, all-consuming type of **fire love** for each person He has ever created.

The fact that God and Jesus would ever allow this kind of scenario to unfold just to be able to save us and bring us back to Themselves is truly a maximum kind of intense and unconditional love that our human minds have a hard time in really being able to fully grasp. This kind of total, complete, unconditional, and perfect love is beyond our ability to fully understand or comprehend, especially in the type of world we live in today.

So why does the Lord have this kind of an intense and passionate love for each one of us since we have all been proven to be such unworthy and unholy sinners in His sight? What exactly does God see in all of us that make us so redeemable in His sight? God is obviously seeing something in all of us that is making us salvageable in His sight; otherwise He would have never wasted His time sending His Son Jesus down to our earth to save us.

After studying the Bible from start to finish, I believe there is one main reason why the Lord has gone to such extreme and painful lengths to bring all of us back to Himself – and that one main reason is for intimate fellowship.

I believe the main reason that God created the first man and the first woman was for intimate fellowship. And God was not only wanting intimate fellowship with Adam and Eve, but He was also going to want it with every man and woman that would follow after them.

Though Adam and Eve blew it for every man and woman that would be born after them, God still has not changed His mind from what his original intentions were going to be. God still has this incredible perfect and unconditional love for each one of us, and He has now made a way for all of us to be able to receive that divine love – and that way is through His Son Jesus and the Blood that Jesus has personally shed for each one of us on the cross.

The Blood that Jesus has personally shed for each and everyone of us on the cross now gives us full entrance back into the kingdom of God the Father. Our spiritual relationship with God the Father, which was completely torn and severed with the first sin of Adam and Eve, has now been fully restored through the Blood of Jesus Christ.

We have now all been made spiritually whole and complete again if we are willing to accept Jesus Christ as our personal Lord and Savior. We have now come full circle again! We have now got back what Adam and Eve lost in their first original paradise. Our spiritual relationship has now been fully restored back with God the Father.

Now that we have come full circle again with God the Father, there is now one more thing that each Christian must decide on in this life.

The veil has now been torn apart between God and us. There are now no more walls, barriers, hindrances, and roadblocks between us and God. There is now nothing but clear and smooth sailing ahead of us as far as our own personal relationship with God is concerned. The Bible tells us that we are now all free to approach the throne of God anytime we want for prayer and intimate communication with complete confidence and boldness.

God is now waiting with wide and open arms for all of us to approach Him. And what exactly is God waiting for? Intimate fellowship, intimate prayer and communication, intimate dialogue and conversations about anything and everything, and intimate sharing of our most personal, private, and secret thoughts.

Bottom line – God is looking for seekers! God is looking for those who will not be afraid to try and establish a one-on-one, personal, on-fire, passionate, intense, and willing to tell-all and share-all love relationship with Him.

God is looking for a maximum intense kind of personal relationship with no holds barred. He is looking for on-fire and passionate people who will try and tear into Him, who will try and take a hold of Him, and who will try to understand Him and all of His ways.

The Scripture verses I will list in this chapter are the bridge, the key, and the secret to being able to find and make direct contact with the Lord in this lifetime. As result of having the Holy Spirit now residing on the inside of us, we now have a direct link and a direct connection back to both God and Jesus in heaven. We can now all pray, talk, and communicate direct to God and Jesus through the Holy Spirit.

Now that the channels have been completely opened back up between God and us, each Christian must now make a personal choice in this life as to whether or not they want to make an attempt get to know this awesome and loving God of ours by establishing this kind of deep, close, intimate, personal relationship with Him.

For those of you who would really like to enter into and start to establish this kind of a deeper personal relationship with the Lord, the Scripture verses I will list below will give you the key and secret to being able to really do this in this life. You do not have to wait until you get to heaven to be able to make direct contact with God. You can learn how to establish a good, powerful, personal relationship with the Lord right where you are standing at right now.

The key and secret to being able to establish this kind of deeper, personal, intimate relationship with the Lord in this life is dependent upon one, simple, little thing – and this one, simple, little thing is that you have to be willing to seek after it!

The verses below are really spelling and shouting out this secret. Study the specific wording in these verses very carefully. As you will see when you study the wording in these specific verses, God is telling us that we have to be the ones to first initiate making some kind of direct contact with Him!

Seek, and **then** you will find God. Draw near to God, and **then** He will draw near to you. Ask, and **then** you will receive. Knock, and **then** the doors will open up for you.

In each one of the verses making these profound statements, we have to be the ones to first start out by doing the actual seeking, asking, knocking, and drawing near to God. If we do, these verses are then telling us that God will allow us to **"find Him."** We will be able to make direct contact with both God and Jesus through the Holy Spirit if we show God that we mean serious business with Him by putting in a certain amount of intensity in our seeking of Him.

If there is one personal secret that I have learned in my own personal walk with the Lord in order to try and get Him to become much more active in my daily life – is that I have to be a seeker after Him and all of His ways. If you are not willing to put in a certain amount of quality time to seek after the Lord – and then to try and develop an active, dynamic, personal relationship with Him, then you will have very little, if any true spiritual and supernatural activity coming from Him.

The verses below are all showing us that we have to be the ones to try and get the ball rolling with God on this seeking. I believe God is letting us know with the specific wording of these verses are that there is a spiritual law that is in operation in His kingdom – and that spiritual law is the seeking law. Seek after God, and then you will find Him. And the more that you seek after God, the more you will find of Him and the deeper and stronger your personal relationship will become with Him.

I believe there is a direct correlation between the quality and intensity of your seeking with the Lord and how much He will interact back with you. The deeper, stronger, and more intense you seek after God – the deeper, stronger, and more intense God will come and seek after you!

Not only is God telling us in these verses to seek and attempt to draw near to Him, but He is also telling us to seek after Him with **"all of our heart"** and with **"all of our soul."** Seeking after God with **"all"** of our heart and "**all**" of our soul is showing us that God wants us to come after Him with maximum intensity, not with a half-hearted or lukewarm attempt.

This would be no different in how we see professional and amateur athletes compete with one another in the sports games they play. A true professional athlete will give it his best and give it his all every single time he goes out to compete in his particular sport. In the same way, God wants all of us to show Him the same amount of intensity in our own personal relationship with Him and in our own personal seeking of Him and all of His ways.

I know many Christians, when they first read these types of verses, get scared and a bit overwhelmed at the specific wording being used by the Lord. These verses need no fancy interpretation. They mean exactly what they are saying.

God is telling all of us that He wants us to be seeking after Him, drawing near to Him, trying to take a hold of Him, and trying to understand Him and all of His ways. And not only does God want us to initiate and make an attempt to do this type of seeking after Him, but He wants this seeking to be done with maximum effort and maximum intensity.

When many Christians first realize how much intensity God is really looking for in this type of seeking, they realize they are not operating anywhere near this level of intensity with Him, and they then back off never giving God any kind of real chance to help work this kind of intensity in their own personal relationships with Him.

Rome was not built overnight, and neither will your own personal relationship with the Lord. **All God is looking for is that you give Him the best effort you can at your current level of spiritual development with Him.** If you do, then God will more than meet you halfway in this realm.

When two people first meet and start dating, they usually do not fall madly and passionately in love with one another. It usually takes a certain amount of time for this kind of true, passionate, and intense type of love to form out and build up. It's the exact same with God the Father. God does not expect this kind of passionate intensity to be built up overnight. For many, this will be a slow and gradual process, with the Holy Spirit being the One to slowly guide you further and deeper into this realm with God.

Again, seeking after the Lord to try and establish a good, deep, intimate, personal relationship with Him is all part of the sanctification process that God would like to do with each and everyone of us.
Before I give you the verses on this topic, and then end the chapter with some of the different ways that you can seek after the Lord in this lifetime, I first want to make one more statement so you can fully grasp the importance and the incredible profound reality that we are dealing with – in that the one and only God of this entire universe is looking to make and establish a direct, one-on-one, personal relationship with each person He has ever created.

We are dealing with only one God – but one God in three separate and complete Persons – God the

Father, His Son Jesus Christ, and the Holy Spirit. All Three of Them want more than anything else in this world to be able to make direct contact with you so They can then start to establish and create this unique, special, one-of-a-kind, personal relationship direct with only you.

God the Father has an equal and unconditional love for each person He has ever created. The Bible tells us that God shows no personal favoritism to any man or woman He has ever created. What this means is that we are all equal in the eyes of God. We are all on an equal footing with the Lord. He loves you just as much as He loves anyone else in this life.

What this means is that you can establish and develop just as much of a special, deep, personal relationship with God as anyone else can. God will give you just as much time, attention, effort, and intensity as He would with anyone else.

Just stop and think for a moment what kind of reality we are dealing with – that the one and only God of this entire universe can become your best Friend and your one and only true Father! I repeat – your best Friend! A true best Friend who will never harm you, hurt you, mistreat you, lie to you, leave you, or forsake you!

So many people in this life have been abused, hurt, wounded, mistreated, and discarded by their parents, by their spouses, and by some of their so called good friends. As a result, they have a hard time in being able to trust anyone, including God Himself.

The Bible tells us that we have to learn how to fully trust in the Lord. God is the only One who is perfect in His very nature and personality, and He thus is the only One that we can perfectly trust in this life. All other men and women in this life are fallen and imperfect creatures. This is why each and every Christian has to learn how to place all of their faith and trust in the Lord – not in the world, and not in all of the other people in this world.

God has already shown us how much He really does love all of us by being willing to send down and sacrifice His one and only Son. All God is asking from each one of us is that we be willing to fully trust Him, and then be willing to enter into this special, intimate, personal relationship with Him.

For those of you who are really looking for true love – true love can only be found in a perfect Being – and God is the only perfect Being in the entire scheme of things.
Though we are to do the best we can in establishing good, healthy, personal relationships with all of our family and friends – realize that only God is totally perfect in His very nature and personality – and only God can give you a perfect, true, and unconditional love that no one else will be able to give you in this life.

If you place all of your love and trust in the other people in this life rather than direct to God Himself, then sooner or later you will find yourself hurt, wounded, and bitterly disappointed. Imperfect people are not capable of giving you any type of perfect and unconditional love – no matter how hard they try, and no matter how hard they will try and tell you otherwise.

So many people are chasing after other people and other material things in this life in an effort to try and find perfect happiness, peace, and fulfillment. And then sooner or later it happens. All of their marriages, all of their good friends, all of their earthly wealth and possessions, and all of their personal accomplishments leave them feeling dead, empty, and lifeless on the inside. All of the good friends they may have made, and all of the earthly material wealth they may have acquired and accumulated in this life fail to fill the void and emptiness that is on the inside of each and everyone of us.

God has purposely created all of us with a void and a vacuum on the inside of each of us – and the only thing that can fill that void and emptiness is the Lord Himself. There is nothing else in this world that can fill that little hole that is in all of our souls. This hole can only be completely filled by God the Father, His Son Jesus Christ, and the Holy Spirit.

Some people manage to find this revelation and truth in their lives, but sadly, most people do not. As Christians, we all have something that no one else has in this life – we have the real God in God the Father, we have the one and only real Savior of this world in Jesus Christ, and we have the one and only Holy Spirit who will come and live on the inside of us once we have accepted Jesus as our personal Lord and Savior. As the Bible has already told us, we literally have the kingdom of God residing on the inside of us once we have become saved and born again.

We literally have the one and only true fountain of perfect peace and happiness – and that is the Lord Himself! And it is all there for the taking for those who are willing to dive into Him and start to seek and drink from Him. Jesus has already told us that He Himself is the fountain of living waters and that we will never hunger or thirst again if we would only be willing to drink directly from Him. **The water is Jesus – and the drinking is our seeking to establish a close, intimate, personal relationship with Him.**

God is waiting for each and every person He has created to come to Him to try and establish this kind of close, intimate, personal relationship with Him. And this can be done if you will just seek after Him with all of your heart, with all of your mind, and with all of your soul.

Now here are some of the main verses from the Bible giving us this profound secret and revelation direct from the Lord Himself. I will break these Scripture verses down under 5 separate captions so you can see exactly what the Lord is trying to convey to all of us in these very powerful verses.

God Is Looking For Seekers

These first two verses will perfectly set the stage for all of us in reference to learning how to develop a good personal relationship with the Lord.

This first verse will tell us that God the Father is actually looking down on this earth from His heaven for those who will seek after Him and who will try and understand Him.

The second verse perfectly completes this first verse when it tells us that God is looking for those who will try and take a hold of Him.

Put these two verses together side by side, and God the Father is telling all of us, loud and clear, that He is looking for passionate and intense seekers who will try and take a hold of Him, who will try and figure Him out, and who will try to understand Him and all of His ways. Here are two very profound verses giving us this incredible piece of revelation:

² **The LORD looks down from heaven upon the children of men,
To see if there are any who understand, who seek God.**
Psalm 14:2

⁷ **And *there is* no one who calls on Your name,
Who stirs himself up to take hold of You**;
For You have hidden Your face from us,
And have consumed us because of our iniquities.
Isaiah 64:7

To think that this one and only all-powerful God is actually looking down on this earth from His heavenly throne to try and find people who are willing to seek after Him. This verse is shouting from the roof tops two very powerful words – **open invitation!**
God the Father is giving every single one of us an open invitation to come in and make some kind of attempt to seek after Him. And what will happen next if we make some kind of attempt to seek after Him? This will now lead us into the next set of verses.

Seeking After the Lord

These next set of verses will tell us that not only does God the Father want us to seek after Him, but they will tell us that if we make some kind of attempt to seek after Him, that we will actually **"find Him."** In other words, we will end up making some kind of direct contact with God.

Think of the ramifications of what these next set of verses are trying to tell us – that if we make some kind of attempt to seek after God, that we will be able to find Him, that we will be able to make some kind of direct contact with Him where He can then start to communicate back to us.

Study these next set of verses very, very carefully. Meditate on what the Lord is trying to tell us. These verses in particular are giving all of us of a major and profound secret in that this incredible and awesome God of ours can actually be **"found"** to some degree in this life if we are willing to make enough of an effort on our end to seek directly after Him.

⁸ **Draw near to God and He will draw near to you.** Cleanse *your* hands, *you* sinners; and purify *your* hearts, *you* double-minded.
                                                    James 4:8

⁴ For thus says the LORD to the house of Israel:
"Seek Me and live;
⁶ **Seek the LORD and live,**
Lest He break out like fire *in* the house of Joseph,
And devour *it,*
With no one to quench *it* in Bethel—
                                                    Amos 5:4,6

[11] Seek the Lord and His strength;
Seek His face evermore!

               1 Chronicles 16:11

[13] And you will seek Me and find *Me,* when you search for Me with all your heart.

               Jeremiah 29:13

[29] But from there you will **seek the Lord your God, and you will find** *Him* **if you seek Him with all your heart and with all your soul.**

               Deuteronomy 4:29

119 Blessed *are* the undefiled in the way,
Who walk in the law of the Lord!
[2] Blessed *are* those who keep His testimonies,
Who seek Him with the whole heart!

               Psalm 119:1

¹² Sow for yourselves righteousness;
Reap in mercy;
Break up your fallow ground,
For *it is* time to seek the LORD,
Till He comes and rains righteousness on you.

            Hosea 10:12

⁹ With my soul I have desired You in the night,
Yes, by my spirit within me **I will seek You early;**
For when Your judgments *are* in the earth,
The inhabitants of the world will learn righteousness.

            Isaiah 26:9

¹² **Then they entered into a covenant to seek the LORD God of their fathers with all their heart and with all their soul**

           2 Chronicles 15:12

⁹ "As for you, my son Solomon, know the God of your father, and serve Him with a loyal heart and with a willing mind; for the LORD searches all hearts and understands all the intent of the thoughts. **If you seek Him, He will be found by you; but if you forsake Him, He will cast you off forever.**

           1 Chronicles 28:9

63 O God, You *are* my God;
Early will I seek You;
My soul thirsts for You;
My flesh longs for You
In a dry and thirsty land
Where there is no water.

            Psalm 63:1

42 As the deer pants for the water brooks,
So pants my soul for You, O God.
² **My soul thirsts for God**, for the living God.
When shall I come and appear before God?

Psalm 42:1-2

⁶ But without faith *it is* impossible to please *Him,* for he who comes to God must believe that He is, and *that* He is a rewarder of **those who diligently seek Him.**

Hebrews 11:6

When you read each one of these verses one right after the other – the message is coming through loud and clear. God is looking for intense seekers who are willing to seek after Him with all of their heart and with all of their soul. He will not settle for anything less. These verses are not only telling us that God wants all of us to seek after Him – but He is also telling us that we will be able to find Him to some degree and to some extent if we keep pressing in to make this kind of direct connection with Him. Our seeking will not be in vain. The last verse tells us that the Lord will reward those who are willing to **"diligently seek"** after Him.

God Created Us for Intimate Fellowship

As I said the beginning of this chapter, I believe the main reason God created the human race was for intimate fellowship – and that is intimate fellowship direct with Him, His Son Jesus Christ, and His Holy Spirit.

The different Bible Dictionaries and Commentaries describe the word **"fellowship"** as the following:

- Sharing together
- Communion with God
- Sharing things in common with others
- Companionship, friendly association, mutual sharing

- The bond of common purpose and devotion that binds Christians together and to Christ

Not only does God want us to learn how to fellowship with other people in this life, but He also wants us to learn how to fellowship direct with Him, His Son, and His Holy Spirit. Here are two very powerful verses giving us this revelation that we can have fellowship direct with all three Persons of the triune Godhead.

3 that which we have seen and heard we declare to you, **that you also may have fellowship with us; and truly our fellowship** *is* **with the Father and with His Son Jesus Christ.**
1 John 1:3

2 Therefore if *there is* any consolation in Christ, if any comfort of love, if any **fellowship of the Spirit**, if any affection and mercy
Philippians 2:1

The first verse tells us that we can fellowship direct with both God and Jesus. The second verse tells us that we can have fellowship direct with the Holy Spirit Himself. Put both of these verses together side by side, and God is telling all of us loud and clear, that He wants us to have intimate fellowship with both Him, His Son, and His Holy Spirit.

Talk to God Like You Would Talk to a Best Friend

Probably one of the greatest stories in the Bible about someone who was not afraid to approach God and attempt to commune and talk to Him like you would a best friend has to be the story of Moses.

Without question, this man's story and adventure in God will go down as one of the greatest God-stories of all time. This one man, in a 40 year period, was able to talk direct to God, see God personally manifest His presence from His back side, receive all of the 10 commandments, and help prepare a younger generation to go in and possess the Promised Land.

As a result of his incredible, face-to-face encounters with the Lord, God ended up giving this man two of the highest compliments any human could ever hope to receive from the Lord in this lifetime. Here are the two verses giving Moses these two incredible compliments from the Lord:

[10] But since then there has not arisen in Israel a prophet like Moses, whom the LORD knew face to face

Deuteronomy 34:10

[11] **So the LORD spoke to Moses face to face, as a man speaks to his friend.** And he would return to the camp, but his servant Joshua the son of Nun, a young man, did not depart from the tabernacle.

Exodus 33:11

The first verse says that Moses **"knew"** God face to face. The word **"knew"** is implying that Moses had established a very good personal relationship with the Lord. The second set of words, where it says that Moses knew the Lord **"face to face,"** is also implying that he made a good type of personal connection with the Lord in an effort to try and get to know Him better. Notice that Moses was seeking after the **"face"** of God, not after His hand. Too many Christians only seek after the hand of God, which represents what He might be able to give them or help bring their way. Seeking after the **"face"** of God means that you are seeking directly after God in an effort to try and get to know Him better as a Person. You are seeking after God to get to know His personality.

The Bible tells us that no one can see the face of God and live. God told Moses, when He was getting ready to manifest His presence before him, that He would not be able to show him His actual face, but only His backside. So when the Bible uses the words that Moses knew God **"face to face,"** it is showing us that Moses ended up coming to know God in a very personal and intimate way. It is not referring to Moses being able to actually see the face of God.

This now leads us to the revelation that is in the second verse. This second verse then goes one step further and tells us that Moses spoke to God face to face **"as a man speaks to his friend."** This is where I am picking up the revelation that we are to learn how to talk to God as we would with a best friend.

When God the Father Himself is spelling out these specific words in that we are to commune and talk with Him as we would with a good friend, then you know we are dealing with a major and profound revelation from the Lord. This is why I have been using the best friend analogy to help try and explain what kind of personal relationship God is really looking to establish with each one of us.

Jesus Himself further expounds on this friend analogy with what He has to say in the following verse:

¹⁴ **You are My friends if you do whatever I command you.** ¹⁵ No longer do I call you servants, for a servant does not know what his master is doing; **but I have called you friends,** for all things that I heard from My Father I have made known to you.

John 15:14-15

Jesus is calling us His friends. God the Father is telling us that Moses learned to how to speak and talk to Him like you would a good friend. Put all three of these verses together, and God and Jesus are telling us that They want a best-friend type of personal relationship with each one of us. If God has to be number one in your life, then it is only logical to conclude that God wants to become your best Friend, over and above any other best friends that you may have in this life.

These two verses on Moses' personal relationship with the Lord may only be two, short, one-line sentences in the Bible, but they are both giving us an incredibly profound secret in the Lord – and that secret is that we learn how to develop a best-friend type of personal relationship with the Lord. God does not want to settle for anything less.

What Moses managed to accomplish with the Lord should serve as a powerful example for all of us on how we are to interact with God and what we should really be seeking and striving after in this life.

Without question, our number one goal and priority in this life should be to establish a good, close, intimate, personal relationship with the Lord. I believe that trying to establish this kind of good, close, personal relationship with the Lord is even more important than completing whatever His perfect plan and destiny is going to be for our lives.

You could end up doing great and mighty works for the Lord in this lifetime, but if all those works are not being done operating in a good, close, personal relationship with Him, then you could end up feeling sad, lonely, and despondent.

All of the good works that you can do for the Lord in this lifetime will not fill that hole and void that is on the inside of your soul. The only thing that can fill that hole and void is the Lord Himself, not the actual works that you are doing for Him. And the only way that you can get the Lord to fill that hole and void is to enter into a good, personal relationship with Him.

God is Looking for Passionate and Intense People

Not only are the above verses telling us that God is actually looking for seekers, but He is also looking for people who will seek after Him with a certain amount of intensity in their seeking of Him.

These next three verses will put the icing on this entire cake. The first verse will tell us that Jesus Himself will spew us out of His mouth if He finds that we have become too lukewarm in our own personal relationship with Him and in the works that we will do for Him in this life. This verse is so extreme, that Jesus is telling us that He would rather find us to be too cold than too lukewarm. At least if you are too cold, you are operating at the other extreme end of the scale.
I believe the reason Jesus is telling us that we have to learn how to seek after Him with a high level of

intensity is because nothing will kill a personal relationship faster than if one or both of the parties start to go dead and lukewarm in the way they interact with one another.

Many spouses end up wandering into the arms of another lover behind their spouses back as a result of the deadness and lukewarmness that has infected their marriage relationship. Just as this same kind of lukewarmness can kill a good marriage relationship, it can also hurt or possibly kill our own personal relationship with God Himself.

God has made all of us after His own image and likeness. As a result, God has created and wired all of us for maximum intensity. Just as our God is a God of maximum intensity, this same God has created and wired all of us for this same kind of maximum intensity. This is why God will not settle for any type of lukewarmness in our own personal relationship with Him.

This is why so many people are such avid sports fans. Sporting games give all of us a chance to release maximum intensity for the teams and players that we are shouting for.

When you really study this part of God's personality – we are seeing a God who is not dull, boring, or lukewarm. We are looking at a God who is extremely passionate and intense.
In the same way, God wants all of us to learn how to live this life at a higher level of passion and intensity. He wants all of us to learn how to live more of this life at a full throttle, at a full pedal to the medal type

mentality in how we serve Him, in how we interact with Him, and how we work for Him in this life.

There is nothing more contagious, more infectious, and more energetic than to be around a true Spirit-filled Christian who is fully alive in the Lord, and who is fully serving and working for the Lord with maximum passion and intensity.

Now here are three very special verses from the Lord showing us what He is really looking for in how we interact and work for Him in this life.

¹⁵ "I know your works, that you are neither cold nor hot. I could wish you were cold or hot. ¹⁶ So then, because you are lukewarm, and neither cold nor hot, I will vomit you out of My mouth.
Revelation 3:15-16

⁸ 'These people draw near to Me with their mouth,
And honor Me with *their* lips,
But their heart is far from Me.
⁹ And in vain they worship Me,
Teaching *as* doctrines the commandments of men.
Matthew 15:8-9

¹³ "For My people have committed two evils:
They have forsaken Me, the fountain of living waters,
And hewn themselves cisterns—broken cisterns that can hold no water.
¹⁹ Your own wickedness will correct you,
And your backslidings will rebuke you.
Know therefore and see that *it is* an evil and bitter *thing*
That you have forsaken the LORD your God,
And the fear of Me *is* not in you,"
Says the Lord GOD of hosts.
Jeremiah 2:13,19

Not only is the Lord looking for on-fire, passionate, and intense people, but this passionate intensity has to be coming from our heart. Notice in the second verse that Jesus is ripping on those who are just paying Him lip service. These types of people may talk a good game, but they are not really talking about God and serving Him from their heart with any kind of real passionate intensity. It's all words and show, with no real substance behind their words, actions, and behaviors.

The last verse perfectly sums up what God the Father thinks about people who will eventually end up forsaking Him and leaving Him. He is telling anyone who is willing to forget, forsake, and leave Him – that they are committing an evil and bitter act against Him.

Bottom line – God the Father has made all of us for Himself. God has made all of us with a hole, a void, a vacuum, and an emptiness inside our souls that can only be filled up by His presence.
We can thus either learn how to start seeking after God so we can enter into this powerful, personal, and intense relationship with Him – or we can turn our back on God, completely forsake Him, and trade Him in for all of the carnal and fleshly pleasures of this world.

I am afraid with all the luxuries and material wealth this world has to offer, many Christians have forsaken and abandoned their God and have now traded Him in for a life of total carnal pursuit.

The last verse stated above is a real bone-chilling verse when it says that is an evil and bitter thing to have forsaken the Lord for all the material wealth of this world that has nothing but leaks and holes in it and will never hold any real water. All of the earthly wealth you may be able to collect and accumulate in this life will never be able to hold any real water because it will eventually rot and perish away.
In other words, all of the earthly wealth and possessions that this world has to offer has leaks in them, and they will all sooner or later completely perish and be taken away from you on your deathbed.

And the only thing that will be left standing, when everything is all finally said and done, is you standing totally alone before the Judgment Seat of Christ, with Jesus judging you on how well you have served Him and followed Him in this life. None of your earthly wealth and possessions will be going over with you when you finally die and cross over to meet Jesus head on for this personal judgment.

God has so plainly and clearly laid out how He wants all of us to live this life and exactly what it is that we all should be seeking after – but yet so many Christians keep missing the mark and fail to get their priorities straight in how they should be living this life, and exactly what it is they should be seeking after in this life with the Lord.

Our two main goals in this life should be to first seek to enter into a full surrender with the Lord so that He is fully free to guide us into His perfect plan and destiny for our lives. The second thing that each fully surrendered Christian should be willing to do is to seek after God with all of their heart and with all of their soul so they can start to establish and enter into this maximum intense kind of personal relationship with Him.

5 Ways To Seek After the Lord

Now that we know the Lord definitely wants all of us to seek after Him – exactly how do we go about really seeking after Him?
I will give you 5 basic ways in which you can seek after the Lord in this life so you can improve the quality and depth of your personal relationship with Him.

Your Prayer Life With the Lord
Without question, the number one way that you should seek after the Lord is in your own personal private prayer life with Him. Your personal prayer life with the Lord has two sides to it.

On the one side is where you are praying to God for something very specific, whether it be directly for you or for someone else you may be praying for.

The second part to your prayer life, and this is the one that I really want to concentrate on for this chapter, is where you walk and talk with God much like what you would do with a best friend. This is not where you are asking God for anything in particular. You are just walking and talking with God just like you would do with a best friend.

If there is one major, whopper secret that will open up the door to God's heart, it has to be the secret of learning how to talk and communicate with Him much in the same way as you would do with a best friend. For those of you who have a best friend or who used to have one, you will know exactly what I am about to talk about.
A true best-friendship is without question, the most unique and special of all the personal relationships that you can have with anyone else.

Granted, there is nothing like the bond and love that exists between parents and their children. But as great and powerful as that bond is, a true best-friend relationship can actually go farther and deeper than what can transpire between some parents and their children. It would really be nice if all of the relationships between parents and their children could turn into and develop into true best friendships, but for many in this life, this never really happens.

This type of best-friendship should really be occurring between parents and their children, and between spouses in their marriages due to the large amount of close interaction that occurs in a family unit. But for many different reasons, this type of best-friendship really never develops in the way that it should in many households across this world, and you thus have many parents and children living and breathing right next to one another with no real passionate love and intimacy ever being established and forged with one another. As a result, many people are forced to try and find a true best friend outside the family unit.

There is obviously nothing wrong in making best friends with other people outside the family unit, but every family, if they are walking right with the Lord, should also be making and developing many of these best friend relationships right there in the middle of their own household – husbands with wives, parents with their children, and children with the other siblings in the household. There is so much quality time that everyone is spending with one another in a family unit, that this kind of quality time should be leading to more people in a household becoming best friends with one another.

But as we all know, for many different reasons, this does not occur with everyone in the family unit. As a result, many people are forced to try and find a true best friend outside the family unit. I cannot even begin to count the number of married men and women I have personally met who no longer feel their spouse is their true best friend. And they are now stuck feeling totally isolated and alone right in the middle of their actual marriage.

As I said in the beginning of this chapter, the real reality is that imperfect people are incapable of giving perfect love to one another, so most people have to be very careful when they start to seek and search for a true best friend. But when you do find one, you have found a true treasure in this life.

The one thing that is so unique and special about a true best friendship is the incredible comfortableness you will feel in the relationship. All guards and shields will start to come down. You can totally trust this person. You can totally be yourself around this person. As a result of being so comfortable with this person, you feel totally free to express your most intimate and secret thoughts with one another. There is literally nothing that you cannot talk about or freely discuss. You can tell your best friend things that you could never tell your spouse or your own children. You feel like you and this best friend are one in spirit and one in mind. You start to get to the point where you can sometimes read each other's minds and thoughts. You can sometimes feel their pain to the same degree they are feeling it.

For those of you who have this type of best-friendship with someone, you know exactly what I am talking about. This type of special, unique, close, personal relationship is exactly what God is looking for from each one of us.

The Bible tells us to seek after the **"face"** of God, not after His hand, which represents what He might be able to give to you. Seeking after the face of God means that we are to seek directly God's heart and personality. We are to seek directly after His personality so we can start to get to know Him in a much better and deeper way.

Bottom line – we should seek after God in the exact same way we would seek into a true best friend. All of the above verses are telling us that we will be able to **"find"** this awesome God of ours if we are willing to expend some quality time and energy to seek directly after Him. And once we find Him, then the doors will be opened up between Him and us!

God will now be willing to open up His heart, His mind, His ways, some of His thoughts, and some of His actual emotions direct to us. In other words, God is looking to share a part of His personality with us if we would only be willing to do the same with Him – just like what we would be willing to do with a true best friend. Except with God, we are dealing with a Being who is totally and completely perfect in His personality.

We are thus looking and gazing on a perfect Being who has the ability to transmit and release perfect, true, unconditional love in a way that no other human will ever be able to do in this life.

If there is one major, whopper, profound, can't shout-it-out-loud enough thing that God is looking for from each one of us – it has to be this revelation that we try and seek to establish this kind of best-friend relationship with Him.

Talk to God just like you would talk to your best friend. Share your most intimate, private, and personal thoughts and feelings with Him that you would never consider sharing with anyone else.

Be willing to completely open yourself up to the Lord, with no holds barred. Be willing to lay yourself totally bare. Be available to God 24/7, not for just 2 hours a week in a Sunday church service. Be willing to talk and communicate with God anywhere and at anytime. Just like you have total freedom to call your best friend up anytime you want, do the exact same thing with God. The Bible tells us that God never sleeps or slumbers. He is always on duty, day or night, rain or shine, storm cloud or no storm cloud. He is always there for you, 24/7, 365 days every year.

God already knows all the thoughts of your mind and heart, so there is nothing you can hide from Him anyway. And not only does He know every single thought and word that is floating around in your mind and heart to begin with – but He knows what you are going to say and think before you even begin to say it or think it, since He has perfect knowledge on all future events, including what will be coming out of your mind or your mouth.

If you are willing to open yourself up to the Lord with this kind of open and honest intimacy with Him, then you will have just touched the heart of God – and He will now more than blow you away with what He will do with you and how He will handle your life from here on in.

I believe this best-friend type of personal relationship that God is looking to establish with each one of us is the main reason that He has created the human race. God is so jealous and so possessive of the human race that He has created, that He has purposely made all of us to only be able to live in this life and the next life to come only if we are willing to bond and graft directly into Him through the Blood that His Son Jesus has already shed for us on the cross.

In other words, we either learn how to bond and graft into our Lord with the kind of close, intimate, personal relationship that He is really looking for – or we will eventually die and be cast off from Him forever.

Jesus Himself is telling us that He will spew us out of His mouth if we ever get to the point of taking Him too much for granted or start to get too lukewarm in our own personal relationship with Him. The last verse perfectly spells it out for all of us in that if we ever forsake or turn away from our Lord, then we will have committed an evil and bitter act in His sight.

Reading and Studying From the Bible

The next big way that you should attempt to seek after God is by reading and studying from the Bible. The Bible is God's only true Word to us in this life.

God has given us everything that we will ever need to be able understand Him, His Son, His Holy Spirit, and all of His ways in just this one Book. Just as God made it as easy as possibly He could for Adam and Eve by telling them to stay off one simple tree – in the same way God has made it as easy as He possibly could by putting all of the information, knowledge, and revelation that we will ever need to find and understand Him in one special Holy Book. And yet most Christians will go their entire lives having never read this one special Book in its complete entirety. As a result, they never really get to learn much about God, His ways, and how He likes to work and operate.

I believe the Bible is serving as a real litmus test between God and us in this life. If you are a true, saved, born again, on-fire Christian, then God is going to sit back and see how much of a desire you really have to try and get to know Him. There are two main ways that He is going to do this.

The first main way that God is going to test you on this is to see how far and to what extent you will attempt to make some kind of personal contact with Him in order to try and establish a good personal relationship with Him. The second main way that God is going to test you is by watching to see if you will make some kind of attempt to learn more about Him by reading and studying from the Bible.

If you are really in love with God, and are really wanting to increase the depth and quality of your own personal relationship with Him, then you will have a very strong natural desire and hunger to want to get into His Word so you can then start to feed off all the knowledge and revelation that is contained in the Bible.

There is simply no other book on this earth that we can feed off that will give us the amount of direct revelation and knowledge about God and who He really is as the Bible can. And again, God has made it as simple and easy as He possibly could by putting everything that we would ever need all in this one Book.

This is why I say the Bible is the real litmus test between God and us – as it will be what will separate the true, passionate, on-fire seeker from the lukewarm, lazy, and worldly Christian who could really care less about God and any of His ways on how we are to live in this life.

With the Blood that His Son Jesus has already shed for all of us on the cross, God the Father has now opened up the gates to His heaven and the gates direct to Himself.

All we have to be willing to do is to believe and accept Jesus Christ as our personal Lord and Savior – be willing to seek after God by making some kind of an attempt to enter into a good personal relationship with Him – and then seek to learn more about Him and all of His ways by reading and studying from His Word. If we do, then we will spiritually grow and mature in this life beyond anything that we ever thought was possible.

Reading and Studying From Other Christian Books
In addition to the wealth of knowledge and revelation that is contained in the Bible, there is also an enormous amount of information and knowledge in other good anointed Christian books.

God the Father has anointed many teachers in this day and age to be able to teach from His Word. Many of these teachers have written some very good books covering a wide range of issues and topics that will also help you grow in the knowledge and ways of the Lord.

For the real seeker in the Lord, there is a whole treasure chest of goodies at your local Christian bookstore. You can find good, anointed, Christian books covering just about any topic or issue you may be interested in.

If you can combine the study of Scripture with the reading of other good anointed books, you will spiritually grow at a rate that will truly astound you. Going into this kind of heavy seeking mode trying to acquire as much knowledge as you can about the Lord will really move the Holy Spirit to want to work on your behalf.

If you are willing to spend some good quality time trying to increase your knowledge base on the Lord and all of His ways, then the Holy Spirit will really start to move to help you out in understanding and assimilating what you are reading so that true spiritual growth can occur in this life. This is a direct supernatural work that the Holy Spirit can do for every single believer who is willing to put forth the time and effort to try and learn more about our Lord.

Fellowship With Other Believers
Another powerful way that you can seek after the Lord is by being willing to fellowship with other like-minded believers. When you are attempting to fellowship with other believers, you are willing to share your walk, your testimonies, and your knowledge base with them – and they in turn will do likewise with you.

As a result of sharing your stories, your testimonies, and your knowledge base with one another, you will get to learn more about the Lord from these other believers. God will be doing different things with some of them than maybe what He has done with you. As a result, you can each learn from one another in the personal experiences that you have had in the Lord.

I cannot tell you how much more my knowledge base has increased in the Lord over the years as a result of learning from some of my other close born again friends and what God is doing in their lives. And I am still continuing to learn from each and everyone of them as they continue to share their walk and journey in the Lord with me.

By being willing to learn from other believers, you will be showing the Lord your strong desire to want to learn more about Him and all of His ways, and that you are leaving no stone unturned in your seeking and pursuit of Him. God loves to be the center of attention, and He loves it when His people sit around and talk about Him and share their knowledge base with one another. When you do this with other believers, you are seeking directly after the Lord.

Watch For the Lord to Move in Your Everyday Life
This next area is one area that many Christians are missing out on. Once you enter into a full surrender with the Lord where He is now fully free to guide you into His perfect plan and destiny for your life, and then you combine that with seeking directly after Him in order to establish a good, strong, personal relationship with Him – you will have opened up a major supernatural door with the Lord, and He will now start

to move in many different areas of your life to help you maximize your walk and call with Him.

And this is where it really gets fun, interesting, and exciting. Once you put the pedal-to-the-medal with the Lord in your seeking of Him, then He is now going to move very strongly on your behalf, and He will now start to show Himself to you in a wide variety of miraculous ways.

What this means is that you now have to keep your radars up each and every day, as you never know when, where, or how God will move next. Your job will be to try and pick it up when God does move in some kind of supernatural way to help you out.

God can move in your life in a wide variety of ways and in a wide variety of matters. God can move to help give you favor with your bosses and supervisors at your places of employment. He can supernaturally open up doors to the next new job that He may want to promote you into.

He can help you with the everyday activities of your job. He can help you with the raising and parenting of your children and all of the everyday activity that goes on in the family. He can help you solve problems, handle different types of emergencies, and help warn and protect you of oncoming dangers.

There are literally an infinite number of things or situations that God can get actively involved in within your own normal everyday life. God is much more active in people's daily lives than most people actually realize or see.

If you are willing to go into this kind of intense seeking mode with the Lord where you have your radars up each and everyday looking for God to move in your life in some way or some fashion – then the Holy Spirit will help open up your eyes and help increase your ability to be able to spot it, recognize it, and actually see it when it does occur so you can fully appreciate it and be very thankful for it when it does happen.

The Bible calls the Holy Spirit the Helper, and there is no area of your life that is too small or too trivial that He will not be willing to give you a helping hand on when His help is really needed.

Chapter 10: Living a Good and Righteous Life before the Lord

The Bible tells us in 2 Timothy 3:1 that as we start approaching the end times, that the love of many will grow cold and that lawlessness and immorality will start to abound. It also says in this verse that men will become lovers of self and money, along with becoming unholy, blasphemers, unloving, unthankful, and disobedient to parents, unforgiving, slanderers, without self-control, traitors, headstrong and lovers of pleasure rather than lovers of God.

3 But know this, that in the last days perilous times will come: ² For men will be lovers of themselves, lovers of money, boasters, proud, blasphemers, disobedient to parents, unthankful, unholy, ³ unloving, unforgiving, slanderers, without self-control, brutal, despisers of good, ⁴ traitors, headstrong, haughty, lovers of pleasure rather than lovers of God, ⁵ having a form of godliness but denying its power. And from such people turn away!

2 Timothy 3:1

As bad as the moral state of man is right now, believe it or not, it is going to get a lot worse in the coming years according to the above verse.

When it comes to the real big picture with our Lord, the age old question is simply why – why did Satan and one third of the angels have to choose with their own free wills to go against God and His holy and righteous ways? Why couldn't they just do the right thing and stay loyal to the Lord and choose to live good and righteous lives before Him?

And then when God decides to create a second race of beings, the human race, again, why couldn't Adam and Eve have chosen with their own free wills to obey one simple little command from the Lord to stay off one forbidden tree?

And then when they couldn't pass their one simple little test, and then the rest of the human race is created and born into a now fallen and cursed world, we now once again still have the same old problem.

Again, why does a certain percentage of the human race still have to choose with their own free wills to go against God and all of His holy and righteous ways just like one third of the angels managed to do?

As you will see in the verses I will list below, God has written His basic laws into the heart of every created being. We all know basic right from basic wrong, and yet so many of us still choose to this day with our own free wills to do the wrong thing at certain times, with some of the more evil people in this life doing some really bad and evil things that a normal person would never consider doing like robbing, raping, killing, kidnapping and torturing.

There is not a day that goes by that we do not see some kind of extreme evil being committed on some kind of a regular basis across the entire world. With all the advancements in technology, and with the world now becoming a much more smaller and closer space due to how inter-connected we all now are, many still have not learned from the history lessons of our past, and we still have many people who are out there acting out on their evil and fleshly impulses with no regard as to who they hurt, kill, or destroy. Some people are as primal now as they were 5000 years ago.

Many people who have had some type of evil crime committed against either them or one of their close loved ones have always asked themselves **why** when it happens to one of them? How can some people commit such horrible and evil acts on another fellow human being? Why can't we just all live in peace and harmony with one another?

And not only can man not get along with his fellow man, but we also have nations always wanting to stir up trouble with other nations, as the Bible tells us that as we approach the end times, that there will be wars and rumors of wars, and that nations will be going against other nations and that kingdoms will be going against other kingdoms.

When you step back and look at the real big picture, it is just heart-breaking to see all of this kind of carnage play itself out every single day across much of the world. And again, why can't most of the human race just get it right with the Lord and learn how to follow His holy and righteous ways so we can all learn how to live in peace and harmony with one another?

God has given all of us a free will, and we all have the ability to choose between the good and righteous side of this life or the evil and dark side of this life. Even though we still have demons who are still roaming in the air trying to get us to do their evil bidding, God will still hold all of us personally accountable for any kind of bad and evil acts we will end up committing in this life.

Though Satan was the one who tempted Eve to disobey one simple little command, God still held both Adam and Eve totally responsible for what they did in the Garden of Eden, even though it was Satan who was the one who put the pressure on them to try and get them to do it. For most of us, the excuse that "the devil made me do it" will not be washing with the Lord once we die and cross over and meet Him head on for all of our own personal judgments.

Demons cannot make you do anything against your own free will, as God will not let them violate that space that you have within your own being. All demons can try and do is persuade you and tempt you to do evil things. But the choice will always remain up to each one of us as to whether or not we will fall for their evil suggestions. Just because a demon plants a thought and a desire in your head to go out and kill someone does not mean you have to actually try and do it.

Unless you are mentally ill to any serious degree, God will watch your response to these demons just like He did with Adam and Eve in the Garden of Eden – and He will then hold you personally accountable if you decide to act out on any of their evil suggestions. If you decide to act out on any evil thoughts or desires that are playing in your mind, your day of judgment will eventually come before the Lord, and you will then have to pay the full price for your sins if you do not get saved and get those sins fully forgiven by the blood of Jesus before you die and cross over.

Even the apostle Paul, who I believe was the greatest of all of the New Testament apostles, had a problem in controlling his flesh and dark side. Here is the verse straight from this man's mouth on he, himself having some problems controlling some of his own thoughts and actions. This statement is a classic statement on the sin nature that we all have in us.

[15] For what I am doing, I do not understand. For what I will to do, that I do not practice; but what I hate, that I do.
Romans 7:15

In other words, Paul is finding out like the rest of us that we all end up doing things in this life that we know we should not be doing. We can all witness to this classic statement, as we all have problems from time to time in doing things that we know that are not right in the eyes of God.

As we have said before, no man, no woman, and no angel is ever going to become the 4th person of the Divine Godhead (Trinity). Only God, Jesus, and the Holy Spirit are completely and totally perfect in Their divine personalities. They are completely and totally perfect all the way down the line in every single one of Their personality qualities.

However, this now leaves God with a bit of a dilemma. This means that every single being that He will ever create is not going to be perfect like He is and they will now be capable of malfunctioning to the dark side.

With one third of the angels malfunctioning to the dark side, and a good percentage of the human race now doing the exact same thing, there is simply no other conclusion that we can come to. We are simply all fallen and sinful creatures and only the blood of Jesus Christ can make us righteous and clean enough before God the Father to get us into heaven, as the Bible tells us that all men and women have sinned and fallen way short of the glory of God.

As you will see in one of the verses I will list below, we are actually born into this world through our mother's womb in sin and iniquity. In other words, we are all born doomed and damned right off the bat unless we receive and accept the free redemptive pardon that Jesus Christ is offering to each one of us through His sacrificial death on the cross.

Again, here are 7 very good verses showing us that we have all been born into this world as sinners in the eyes of God – but if we accept what Jesus Christ has done for all of us on the cross, then His very own righteousness can then be imputed upon all of us where God the Father will then take us back and grant us entrance into heaven once we die and cross over.

2 Corinthians 5:21 below perfectly spell this out for us. The rest of the verses will then show us how we have all been born into this world as sinners, and that there is absolutely no one in this world who is truly righteous and holy before the eyes of God the Father.

[21] For He made Him who knew no sin *to be* sin for us, that we might become the righteousness of God in Him.

2 Corinthians 5:21

⁵ **Behold, I was brought forth in iniquity,**
And in sin my mother conceived me.

Psalm 51:5

¹⁰ As it is written:
"There is none righteous, no, not one

Romans 3:10

²³ **for all have sinned and fall short of the glory of God**

Romans 3:23

²¹ For since by man *came* death, by Man also *came* the resurrection of the dead. ²² For as in Adam all die, even so in Christ all shall be made alive.

1 Corinthians 15:21-22

¹² Therefore, just as through one man sin entered the world, and death through sin, and thus death spread to all men, because all sinned—

Romans 5:12

⁶ **But we are all like an unclean** *thing,*
And all our righteousnesses *are* **like filthy rags;**
We all fade as a leaf,
And our iniquities, like the wind,
Have taken us away.

Isaiah 64:6

Once you really think about and meditate on these specific verses, it just blows the human mind to think that God the Father would allow the very own righteousness of His Son Jesus to be imputed upon us so we can all be made righteous enough before Him to be able to cross over into heaven when we die and cross over – especially when we ourselves have done absolutely nothing to be able to earn or achieve any of this on our own. This is all simply a free and holy gift that is being given to us by the Lord.

The last verse above says that even if we did try to be as good and as perfect as we possibly could before the Lord, that all of our good works would be nothing but as filthy rags before Him because we simply do not have the ability within our own natural makeups to attain His state of perfection and holiness.

If we are really honest with ourselves, we can all see how we are really sinners before a holy and righteous God, and that no matter how hard we try, there is simply no way we can ever achieve any state of true perfect holiness that would be pleasing enough to God. And again, the apostle Paul in the above verse perfectly sums up that reality even for himself.

However, as Christians, we now have something that the unbeliever does not have on himself. Not only are we born again with the Holy Spirit, who is now residing in our human spirits, but we are now also clothed with the very righteousness of Jesus Christ Himself, which will now be good enough to grant us entrance into heaven once we die and cross over.

However, there is now one more thing each Christian must get a real grip on after they have fully realized this astounding fact and revelation.

Even though we are now all fully clothed with the righteousness of Jesus Christ Himself, and we have now been given a free ticket to heaven once we die and cross over, this does not mean that we can try and abuse or take advantage of this grace and righteousness that we now have upon us from the Lord. We still have to make every concerted effort on our end to try and live a good and righteous life before the Lord.

This new found righteousness that we now have in Jesus Christ does not give us the liberty, the right, or the excuse to be able to keep on sinning. We should all still be doing our best to try and live a good and righteous life before the Lord and staying out of any unacceptable sins.

And when we do find ourselves falling short or having a hard time in staying out of certain sinful activities, we now have the Holy Spirit Himself, who can now give us His divine power to be able to put of any heavier sins that we may have fallen into.

Bottom line – once we have become saved and born again through the shed blood of Jesus Christ, we should all do our best to allow God to start the sanctification process within us. And once God the Father starts this sanctification process within each one of us, we should then do our best to live this life the way that He will want us to live it, not the way we or the world will want us to live it.

The Bible very clearly lays out all of the ways and commandments of our Lord, and exactly what He wants all of us to do, and exactly what He wants all of us to stay away from in this life. We also have the Holy Spirit on the inside of each one of us whose job is to not only **guide us** and **teach us** in this life, but to also **convict us** when we do start to stray and get off into any sinful activities that the Lord will not want us engaging in.

Again, no one person will ever become the 4th person of the Holy Godhead (Trinity). We will never become perfectly holy like God is, but we should still make every effort on our end to try and live good and righteous life before the Lord so that we can become well pleasing to Him, and so that He will then approve of the way that we have lived our lives down here and conducted ourselves among our fellow man.

Before I get into the actual Scripture verses on how God wants all of us to have a good and righteous walk with Him, here are two good definitions on what the word righteousness means from some of the different Bible Dictionaries and Commentaries:

- **Without guilt before God, acting in accord with God's laws**
- **Inherent or imputed guiltlessness before God**

Now I will give you some very good verses from Scripture on the importance that we all try to do the best we can to try and live a good and righteous life before the Lord once we have become saved and born again through the shed blood of Jesus Christ.

The Scripture Verses

I will break these Scripture verses down under 4 separate captions so you can fully grasp what the Lord is trying to tell us on this topic. All of these verses mean exactly what they are saying and they do not need any kind of fancy interpretation.

Jesus Did Not Come to Destroy the Law – But to Fulfill It

This first verse I will now list will completely set the stage as far as the law is concerned and what God is expecting from all of us. Though the Bible says that we are no longer under the law, but under grace – this does not mean that we are to fully do away with all of God's moral laws, which are His direct commandments to us on how we are to live in this life.

Granted, there are some laws back in the Old Testament that would not apply in the kind of environment we are now living in. But many of what I call the basic moral laws is still in full play today such as all of the 10 commandments, God's laws on not engaging with anything having to do with the occult, along with staying out of such sins as homosexuality and fornication.

In the Old Testament, they did not have the Holy Spirit living on the inside of them. They thus did not have His power available to them in which to help them overcome some of the sins they were engaging in. Now all New Testament believers have the Holy Spirit on the inside of them and they thus now have His divine power available to them in which to help them overcome the temptation to sin, or if by chance they have fallen into any type of bad sin, the power of the Holy Spirit to actually pull them out of it and set them free.

Here is this first very powerful verse direct from Jesus Christ Himself:

[17] "Do not think that I came to destroy the Law or the Prophets. I did not come to destroy but to fulfill. [18] For assuredly, I say to you, till heaven and earth pass away, one jot or one tittle will by no means pass from the law till all is fulfilled. [19] Whoever therefore breaks one of the least of these commandments, and teaches men so, shall be called least in the kingdom of heaven; but whoever does and teaches *them,* he shall be called great in the kingdom of heaven. [20] For I say to you, that unless your righteousness exceeds *the righteousness* of the scribes and Pharisees, you will by no means enter the kingdom of heaven.
Matthew 5:17-20

Notice that this is Jesus talking in the New Testament, not God the Father talking in the Old Testament. Jesus is flat out telling us that He still wants all of us to still abide by His Father's basic laws and commandments and that He will expect all of us to do so until "all is fulfilled" – which is when we will get the New Heaven and the New Earth after Jesus' millennial rule has ended.

As you will see in the verses that I will list below, all of these basic moral laws and commandments from God the Father are all being given to us for our own good and for our own protection, as the Bible tells us that the wages of sin will be death.

As such, we should all do our best to try and abide by them and keep them as best we can, and when we do run into any problems with any specific sin areas, we have the Holy Spirit Himself to help us get victory over any specific sins that are starting to drag us down.

God Now Has His Basic Laws Written Into Man's Hearts

Not only did God the Father lay out the basic laws and commandments that He wants all of us to live by, but He has even gone one step further. He now has His basic laws actually written into the hearts of men, along with causing their conscience to actually bear witness to all of it.

In other words, we all have God's basic laws written into our hearts and we all know basic right from basic wrong when we are old enough to fully understand what it is all about. This is why the unsaved sinner will have no excuse on his day of judgment with the Lord. He will know, without any shadow of a doubt, that all of his sins were wrong and that they were going against the will and ways of God. As a result, he will not be able to plead any type of ignorance on his day of judgment with the Lord.

Here are 6 very serious verses about God's laws and why we are to take all of them very, very seriously in this life. The first verse is the one that will tell you that God the Father has His basic laws written into the hearts of men.

[15] **who show the work of the law written in their hearts, their conscience also bearing witness**, and between themselves *their* thoughts accusing or else excusing *them*
Romans 2:15

[7] What shall we say then? *Is* the law sin? Certainly not! On the contrary, I would not have known sin except through the law. For I

would not have known covetousness unless the law had said, "You shall not covet."

Romans 7:7

¹⁷ Therefore, to him who knows to do good and does not do *it*, to him it is sin.

James 4:17

²² If I had not come and spoken to them, they would have no sin, but now they have no excuse for their sin.

John 15:22

¹⁹ I call heaven and earth as witnesses today against you, *that* I have set before you life and death, blessing and cursing; therefore choose life, that both you and your descendants may live;

Deuteronomy 30:19

¹³ "Enter by the narrow gate; for wide *is* the gate and broad *is* the way that leads to destruction, and there are many who go in by it. ¹⁴ Because narrow *is* the gate and difficult *is* the way which leads to life, and there are few who find it.

Matthew 7:13-14

First notice that God has to give us His laws. If He does not tell us what He will be expecting from us, then we will not know for certain what real sin is. But once we do have these laws from God, then we will know for certain what sin is and then He will expect all of us to stay away from it and abide by His commandments. That is why no one will have any type of excuse on their day of judgment with the Lord, as we will all know for certain what is wrong and sinful before the eyes of God.

Deuteronomy 30:19 is another in-your-face type of verse. In this verse God is telling all of us how it is going to be in this life whether we like it or not.

Bottom line – God is setting before each one of us a choice to make in this life. Either we choose to follow God and His ways and commandments for our lives, or we choose to disobey Him, go our own way, and then end up reaping eventual death when it is all said and done. In other words, it is either God's way or the highway for each one of our lives. There is no middle or neutral grounds with the way this specific verse is being worded by the Lord.

Matthew 7:13-14 then put the icing on this entire cake. This verse seems to be talking about our salvation in the Lord. If it is, then the majority of people who have lived on this earth are not going to be making it into heaven.

We obviously will not know for sure what percentage of the human race is going to end up making it into heaven until we get there, but with the words in this verse stating that **"there are few who find it,"** this leads me to believe that the majority of the human race is not going to end up making it into heaven when it is all said and done.

This verse in particular has been one of the most bothersome and troubling in all of Scripture for me, as I cannot see how to interpret this verse any other way other than God is referring to our salvation in Him and what is awaiting all of us at the end of our lives. God is flat out telling us that many people will be choosing the wide and broad way in this life, which is obviously a life of sin and going against the will and ways of God. The straight and narrow road represents the road that God wants all of us to travel on, which is the road of His perfect will and ways for our lives.

As we look out upon this world and all of the people we can see, we can easily see who is trying to travel on the straight and narrow road that God wants all of us to travel on, and those who are out there traveling on their own wide and broad roads.

The people who are traveling on their own wide and broad roads are out there doing anything and everything they want in the flesh, and they do not care who they end up hurting or running over in the process. But sooner or later all of their wide and broad roads will eventually end, and then they will have to face God Almighty Himself for their own final judgments and final fate.

Again, Matthew 7:13-14 could not be more scary, more alarming, and more in your face with how God wants us to live in this life. That is why I had the title of this chapter to read, "Living a Good and Righteous Life Before the Lord," so you will know exactly how God wants all of us to live in this life and what He will be expecting from all of us as we journey through this life.

God Still Wants All of Us to Practice Righteousness

As you will see in 1 John 3:10, the first verse I list below, God still wants all of us to continue to practice righteousness in this life, even though we now have the righteousness of His Son Jesus already imputed on us. And again, this verse is coming from the New Testament, showing once again that we still have to do the best we can in obeying all of God's basic laws and commandments, which will include some of the basic laws and commandments that were back in the Old Testament.

The rest of the verses below will really drive home the point on how important it is that we all seek to walk in the ways of our Lord, and that trying to live a good, holy, and righteous life before the Lord will help bring us true **"life"** in this life.

Here are some very good verses on how powerful of a thing it can be for all of us if we try to live a good and righteous life before the Lord. Being good, holy, and righteous for the Lord may not be cool with the rest of the world, but it is definitely cool with the Lord – and that is what we will eventually be rewarded on once we enter into heaven and God then hands out His rewards based upon the good works we have done for Him down here, along with how we have lived our lives for Him.

[10] In this the children of God and the children of the devil are manifest: Whoever does not practice righteousness is not of God, nor *is* he who does not love his brother.
                                                    1 John 3:10

[28] In the way of righteousness *is* life,
And in *its* pathway *there is* no death.
                                                    Proverbs 12:28

[18] The wicked *man* does deceptive work,
But he who sows righteousness *will have* a sure reward.

¹⁹ As righteousness *leads* to life,
So he who pursues evil *pursues it* to his own death.

           Proverbs 11:18-19

56 Thus says the Lord:
"Keep justice, and do righteousness,
For My salvation *is* about to come,
And My righteousness to be revealed.
² Blessed *is* the man *who* does this,
And the son of man *who* lays hold on it;
Who keeps from defiling the Sabbath,
And keeps his hand from doing any evil."

           Isaiah 56:1-2

⁹ The way of the wicked *is* an abomination to the Lord,
But He loves him who follows righteousness.

           Proverbs 15:9

¹⁶ The labor of the righteous *leads* to life,
The wages of the wicked to sin.
¹⁷ He who keeps instruction *is in* the way of life,
But he who refuses correction goes astray.

           Proverbs 10:16-17

³ To do righteousness and justice
Is more acceptable to the Lord than sacrifice.

           Proverbs 21:3

⁷ The righteous *man* walks in his integrity;
His children *are* blessed after him.

           Proverbs 20:7

⁷ When a man's ways please the Lord,
He makes even his enemies to be at peace with him.

⁸ Better *is* a little with righteousness,
Than vast revenues without justice.

Proverbs 16:7-8

³³ Do not be deceived: "Evil company corrupts good habits."
³⁴ Awake to righteousness, and do not sin; for some do not have the knowledge of God. I speak *this* to your shame.

1 Corinthians 15:33-34

¹⁷ **All unrighteousness is sin**, and there is sin not *leading* to death.

1 John 5:17

¹⁶ "Wash yourselves, make yourselves clean;
Put away the evil of your doings from before My eyes.
Cease to do evil,
¹⁷ Learn to do good;
Seek justice,
Rebuke the oppressor;
Defend the fatherless,
Plead for the widow.

Isaiah 1:16-17

¹⁴ Do not enter the path of the wicked,
And do not walk in the way of evil.
¹⁵ Avoid it, do not travel on it;
Turn away from it and pass on.
¹⁶ For they do not sleep unless they have done evil;
And their sleep is taken away unless they make *someone* fall.
¹⁷ For they eat the bread of wickedness,
And drink the wine of violence.
¹⁸ But the path of the just *is* like the shining sun,
That shines ever brighter unto the perfect day.

¹⁹ The way of the wicked *is* like darkness;
They do not know what makes them stumble.

Proverbs 4:14-19

¹² *It is* an abomination for kings to commit wickedness,
For a throne is established by righteousness.

Proverbs 16:12

²⁸ Mercy and truth preserve the king,
And by lovingkindness he upholds his throne.

Proverbs 20:28

Notice how many times the Bible says that righteousness will lead to **"life"** and that any kind of unrighteousness is actually considered sin in the eyes of God. This means that real righteousness is all black and white. There is only God and the devil, heaven or hell, and good and evil when you really sum everything up.

It now becomes up to each person as to which side of the fence they are going to walk on in this life. Again, Joshua could not have said it any better when he said that you must choose this day who you will serve. You will either decide to serve and follow God and follow His ways and live, or you will choose to follow yourself, other people, or the devil and eventually die. There are no middle or neutral grounds as far as God is concerned. God has made it as easy as He possibly could. But we only have one lifetime, and a very short lifetime at best, to make that one final and fateful decision which will then determine what the rest of our eternal life will be like once we die and cross over to the other side, which will either be heaven for the saved or hell for the unsaved.

All of these verses are short, quick-to-the-point, and very easy to understand. God simply wants all of us to walk in His righteous ways and again, when we start to run into trouble with certain types of sins, we have both Him and His Holy Spirit to help pull us out of any sins that He will not want us to be getting caught up in.

Keeping the Commandments of the Lord
Part of having a true righteous walk with the Lord is to make sure that we simply obey all of His basic laws and commandments as best we can. These next set of verses will really drive this point home.

Many in the world today want to scoff and make fun of the ways, laws, and commandments of our Lord. They want to be able to live in their flesh, doing anything they can that will feed their flesh. They do not want to be told that adultery, fornication, homosexuality, abortion, and other alternative forms of spirituality are not acceptable to the one and only living God.

As a result, they will either make up their own little gods to worship, or they will try and say that they are a god and an island all unto themselves and that they do not need to answer to any type of Higher Power. This is all done so they can rationalize and explain away all of their sinful behaviors before the Lord.

Again, our Lord could not make things any simpler and any easier than with the way that He has everything set up. All we have to do is accept the fact and reality that we are all fallen sinners and that we all need the shed blood of Jesus Christ to be able to receive eternal salvation from God the Father. From there, we are to walk out the rest of our earthly life serving God in the divine destiny that He already has set up for our lives, along with trying to live a good and righteous life before Him.

But so many people still to this day cannot see this simple and obvious truth, or if they can, they are still refusing to be told that they have to serve anyone, even if it is God Almighty Himself. Just as pride and major stupidity took out one third of the angelic race, I am afraid that same kind of pride and stupidity is going to be taking out a much larger percentage of the human race when it is all finally said and done.

Again, these next set of verses are really going to drive home the point that we fully appreciate the basic laws and commandments that God has set out for all of us.

These laws and commandments from the Lord will be telling us what is right and what is wrong in this life. They will act as a **compass** and a **guide** for us so we will know how to live and act in this life for the Lord. These laws and commandments are again, all being given to us for our own good and for our own protection, for without them, we would just keep falling into one pit after another.

[16] Now behold, one came and said to Him, "Good Teacher, what good thing shall I do that I may have eternal life?"
[17] So He said to him, "Why do you call Me good? No one *is* good but One, *that is,* God. But if you want to enter into life, keep the commandments."

Matthew 19:16-17

¹⁰ If you keep My commandments, you will abide in My love, just as I have kept My Father's commandments and abide in His love.

John 15:10

⁶ This is love, that we walk according to His commandments. This is the commandment, that as you have heard from the beginning, you should walk in it.

2 John 1:6

² By this we know that we love the children of God, when we love God and keep His commandments. ³ For this is the love of God, that we keep His commandments. And His commandments are not burdensome.

1 John 5:2-3

³ Now by this we know that we know Him, if we keep His commandments.

1 John 2:3

²³ For the commandment *is* a lamp,
And the law a light;
Reproofs of instruction *are* the way of life

Proverbs 6:23

¹⁶ He who keeps the commandment keeps his soul,
But he who is careless of his ways will die.

Proverbs 19:16

The highway of the upright *is* to depart from evil;
He who keeps his way preserves his sou

Proverbs 16:17

3 My son, do not forget my law,
But let your heart keep my commands;

² For length of days and long life
And peace they will add to you.

Proverbs 3:1-2

²⁸ Observe and obey all these words which I command you, that it may go well with you and your children after you forever, when you do *what is* good and right in the sight of the LORD your God.

Deuteronomy 12:28

7 My son, keep my words,
And treasure my commands within you.
² Keep my commands and live,
And my law as the apple of your eye.
³ Bind them on your fingers;
Write them on the tablet of your heart.

Proverbs 7:1-3

¹⁸ Oh, that you had heeded My commandments!
Then your peace would have been like a river,
And your righteousness like the waves of the sea.

Isaiah 48:18

⁹² Unless Your law *had been* my delight,
I would then have perished in my affliction.

Psalm 119:92

¹³ "Oh, that My people would listen to Me,
That Israel would walk in My ways!
¹⁴ I would soon subdue their enemies,
And turn My hand against their adversaries.

Psalm 81:13-14

⁸ This Book of the Law shall not depart from your mouth, but you shall meditate in it day and night, that you may observe to do

according to all that is written in it. For then you will make your way prosperous, and then you will have good success.
Joshua 1:8

[71] *It is* good for me that I have been afflicted,
That I may learn Your statutes.
[72] The law of Your mouth *is* better to me
Than thousands of *coins of* gold and silver.
Psalm 119:71-72

[18] Open my eyes, that I may see
Wondrous things from Your law.
[19] I *am* a stranger in the earth;
Do not hide Your commandments from me.
[20] My soul breaks with longing
For Your judgments at all times.
Psalm 119:18-20

[165] Great peace have those who love Your law,
And nothing causes them to stumble.
Psalm 119:165

[10] With my whole heart I have sought You;
Oh, let me not wander from Your commandments!
[11] Your word I have hidden in my heart,
That I might not sin against You.
[12] Blessed *are* You, O LORD!
Teach me Your statutes.
[13] With my lips I have declared
All the judgments of Your mouth.
[14] I have rejoiced in the way of Your testimonies,
As *much as* in all riches.
[15] I will meditate on Your precepts,
And contemplate Your ways.

¹⁶ I will delight myself in Your statutes;
I will not forget Your word.

Psalm 119:10-16

³² I will run the course of Your commandments,
For You shall enlarge my heart.
³³ Teach me, O LORD, the way of Your statutes,
And I shall keep it *to* the end.
³⁴ Give me understanding, and I shall keep Your law;
Indeed, I shall observe it with *my* whole heart.
³⁵ Make me walk in the path of Your commandments,
For I delight in it.

Psalm 119:32-35

⁷ The law of the LORD *is* perfect, converting the soul;
The testimony of the LORD *is* sure, making wise the simple;
⁸ The statutes of the LORD *are* right, rejoicing the heart;
The commandment of the LORD *is* pure, enlightening the eyes;
⁹ The fear of the LORD *is* clean, enduring forever;
The judgments of the LORD *are* true *and* righteous altogether.
¹⁰ More to be desired *are they* than gold,
Yea, than much fine gold;
Sweeter also than honey and the honeycomb.
¹¹ Moreover by them Your servant is warned,
And in keeping them *there is* great reward

Psalm 19:7-11

1 Blessed *is* the man
Who walks not in the counsel of the ungodly,
Nor stands in the path of sinners,
Nor sits in the seat of the scornful;
² But his delight *is* in the law of the LORD,
And in His law he meditates day and night.
³ He shall be like a tree
Planted by the rivers of water,

That brings forth its fruit in its season,
Whose leaf also shall not wither;
And whatever he does shall prosper.

Psalm 1:1-3

When you read each one of these verses one right after the other, it is a real mouthful. God is simply trying to drive home the fact that we seek to obey all of His ways and all of His commandments. If we do, then note some of the incredible blessings that we can receive from the Lord:

- We will receive life
- We will keep and preserve our soul
- We can have a long life here on this earth
- Great peace will be given to us and it will be like a river
- It will go well with our children
- It will keep us from perishing
- God will subdue our enemies
- Our way will be made prosperous and we will have good success
- Our heart will be rejoiced
- Our eyes will be enlightened
- The law will warn us and keep us out of harm's way

Again, all of God's ways and commandments are all being given to us for our own good and for our own protection. These commandments are not meant to stunt our spiritual growth or steal our joy in the Lord. They are all meant to increase our spiritual growth and increase our peace and joy in the Lord.

As earthly parents, one of the first things we will do with all of our children as they are starting to grow is to tell them what they can and cannot do in this life. We know that if we do not give them fair warning ahead of time as to what they should be staying away from in this life, that we risk them getting seriously hurt, if not possibly killed. We thus give them the basic commandments they are to abide by in this life so we can keep them safe and out of harm's way.

It is the exact same way with God the Father. Except with God the Father, He has full knowledge on exactly what we should all be staying away from in this life since He has absolute perfect knowledge on all things. As such, we should all listen very carefully to what God is trying to tell us in these basic commandments, as they are all being given to us for our own good and protection. God is not trying to hurt us or harm us with all of these basic commandments, He is trying to help us and protect us.

If you really want to see how important it is that we seek to obey all of God's laws and commandments, just take your time and meditate on some of the above verses. King David especially was able to see how important it was that he try and learn the **ways of God** so that he could continue to spiritually grow in Him. That is why some of the above verses are telling us that we will find true life in this life if we can learn how to live righteous lives before the Lord.

As I said at the beginning of this chapter, it is just heart-breaking to see so many people in this life choose with their own free wills to walk on the dark side of this life instead of the good and righteous side of this life.

Since God has given each man and each woman a full free will to make their own choices in this life, He really has no other alternative but to sit back and watch this horror show unfold with the people who will end up rejecting Him, His ways, and His message of eternal salvation through His Son Jesus.

To think that a good percentage of the human race is going to end up in the most horrible place imaginable when they die and cross over, when they could have easily chosen the Lord and His message of eternal salvation for them, is enough to break your heart into a million pieces. I do not believe there is a day or an hour that goes go by where God and Jesus are not crying and weeping for the souls who are descending down into hell with no chance of ever being able to make it back out again.

God initially created all of these lost souls for Himself, and He now has to watch all of them choose with their own free wills to reject Him and His Son Jesus during the course of their earthly lives. And then when they do die and cross over, He has no other alternative but to let them descend down into the pit of hell itself, as they now have to be held fully accountable for all of the horrible choices they have made in this life.

As born again Christians, we do not have to worry about this kind of horrible and final fate. We will all be given full entrance into heaven the minute we die and cross over. But until that final and glorious event actually occurs with each one of us, we should all be doing our best to try and live a good and righteous life before the Lord so that He will be well pleased with us when we do meet Him for our own personal judgments at the Judgment Seat.

Chapter 11: Worshiping the Lord

Another area where the Holy Spirit will move in on in your sanctification process will be in the area of being able to properly worship the Lord. This will be the area where you can really learn how to worship and praise the Lord in the Spirit. This is a supernatural ability that will be given to you by the Holy Spirit Himself if you are open to receiving this from Him.

Since there are so many different denominations and branches in the Body of Christ today, there obviously are going to be differing levels of the way people will worship the Lord. Some of the more conservative types of denominations will have a much less intense way in which they will worship and sing to the Lord in their services as compared to what you will see in some of the non-denominational, charismatic type services.

I have had numerous Catholics tell me that when they decided to switch from the Catholic setting they were raised up in to a more non-denominational, charismatic type of church, their spiritual senses came in for a major shock the first time they walked into a charismatic service.

The first thing they notice is how much more intense the charismatics will worship, praise, and sing to the Lord in the first part of their services. Sometimes you will see a real live band up on an actual stage with musicians playing guitars, keyboards, and drums, along with one or more singers. You will see people with their hands raised up in the air worshiping, singing, and praising the Lord. You will see some people with tears rolling down their eyes. Other people will be jumping up and down and clapping their hands. And others will literally be running around the church or dancing in the middle of the aisles.

If you have not been raised up with this kind of intensity in the denomination that you have been brought up in, you will feel like you have just walked into the middle of a hurricane or tornado due to the high level of passion and intensity these people are worshiping and praising the Lord.

For those of you who have been raised up in the more conservative branches in the Body, and are not used to seeing this kind of intensity in the way these people are worshiping and praising the Lord, I will use this chapter to give you 21 very good verses from the Bible showing you that this type of intensity is definitely biblical, and that these people have not lost their minds or gone too flaky in their walks with the Lord.

What these people are doing are worshiping and praising the Lord in the Spirit, singing in the Spirit, dancing in the Spirit, and running in the Spirit. This is something that is coming directly from the Holy Spirit and this is all being done **"in the Holy Spirit."** This is literally a supernatural ability that can be imparted to each and every believer by the Holy Spirit Himself if they are open to receiving it.

This first verse I will now list will tell us exactly how true worship is made to the Lord.

²³ **But the hour is coming, and now is, when the true worshipers will worship the Father in spirit and truth;** for the Father is seeking such to worship Him

John 4:23

Notice that John 4:23 is telling us that we have to learn how to worship God from our human spirits. The letter **"s"** in the word **"spirit"** is with a small **"s."** This means it is talking about our human spirits. The apostle Paul tells us that we have three parts to our being – body, soul, and spirit.

You are a spirit, you have a soul and you live in a body.

I believe the Lord is trying to tell us two things with the specific wording of this verse. First, we have to learn how to worship the Lord from our spirit, which means that we have to learn how to worship Him from our heart.

The second thing is that we must learn how to worship the Lord in the Holy Spirit. The Holy Spirit lives and dwells in our human spirits. The Holy Spirit enters into our human spirits the moment we accept Jesus as our Lord and Savior and have become saved and born again.

If we are to worship the Lord from our human spirits, and the Holy Spirit is already living in our human spirits, then I believe it is only logical to conclude that the Lord wants us to learn how to worship and praise Him in the Holy Spirit.

I do not want to come down on some of the other more subdued and less intense ways some people will worship the Lord in some of these other less intense branches, but there is definitely a difference between one person who can worship and praise the Lord in the Spirit and another who is just worshiping the Lord out of his flesh and out of his head.

Again, the ability to be able to truly worship the Lord with this kind of intensity, passion, and love can be imparted to you by the Holy Spirit if you will not be afraid to open yourself up to receive it from Him.

To really be able to receive this kind of ability from the Holy Spirit, the first thing you are going to need is the appropriate verses from Scripture to show you that this kind of intense worship is definitely biblical.

Before I list the actual Scripture verses on this topic, I am going to highlight and bullet point several key phrases that you will see listed in these verses. Here are 8 powerful key phrases that will first of all tell us that God the Father wants us to worship, exalt, and magnify Him and His Holy Name.

- Worship the Father in spirit and truth
- Worship the Lord in the beauty of holiness
- Worship at His footstool
- Let us worship and bow down
- All the earth shall worship You
- Give unto the Lord the glory due to His name
- Exalt the Lord our God
- Magnify His name

Here are 5 very good phrases on us being able to give thanks to the Lord:

- Give thanks to the Lord for His goodness
- Give thanks to the Lord, for He is God
- Magnify Him with thanksgiving
- Enter His gates with thanksgiving
- Come before His presence with thanksgiving

Part of what will be included in being able to worship the Lord will also be praising Him. Here are 7 key phrases all pointing out that praising the Lord should be something that we all learn how to do on a regular basis:

- I will bless the Lord at all times
- His praise shall continually be in my mouth
- Let the high praises of God be in their mouth
- Great is the Lord and greatly to be praised
- Praise God in His sanctuary
- Praise Him for His mighty acts
- Praise Him according to His excellent greatness

These next 11 phrases will all point out that it is also biblical that we sing to the Lord, and that God will have no problems with you if you want to sing with some level of intensity in your singing to Him.

- Sing to the Lord
- Sing praises to God
- I will sing praises
- Sing praises with understanding
- Sing out the honor of His name
- Praise the name of God with a song
- I will sing of Your power

- Let them sing aloud in their beds
- Praise Him with stringed instruments and flutes
- Praise Him with loud cymbals
- I will play music before the Lord

These next 3 verses will show you that it is also biblical if you want to dance before the Lord when you are worshiping, praising, and singing before Him:

- Praise Him with the timbrel and dance
- Let them praise His name with dance
- Then David danced before the Lord with all his might

I know some people may think this kind of higher intensity in the way some people like to worship, praise, sing, or dance to the Lord may be a bit on the extreme side – but strongly consider this analogy.

Next time you are watching a sporting event on TV such as a college or professional football, basketball, or baseball game, watch what happens when the cameras start to pan out into the crowd when one team gets ready to score a touchdown, hit that winning shot from the basketball court, or drive in that winning run in the bottom of the ninth inning in a baseball game.

When the cameras start to pan out into the crowd in these kinds of climatic moments, you will literally see just about everyone standing up, clapping their hands, and yelling, screaming, and shouting at the tops of their lungs – all because their team is about to win the game, or make an important touchdown, goal, or hit in order to help them win the game. And all of this kind of

maximum intensity is being shown and expressed over just a simple sports game.

If we can have these kinds of maximum intense emotions, thoughts, words, and feelings over who is going to win a simple sports game, then how much more should we have this kind of maximum intensity in the way that we worship, praise, and give thanks to our one and only Lord and Savior?

For those of you who may be new to all of this as a result of just getting saved, or as a result of having decided to switch from one denomination to another, just realize this higher level of worship that you will see manifested in these types of services is not something that the Lord will expect you to be able to do overnight.

Don't ever feel inferior and not good enough before the Lord because you cannot worship, praise, or sing to Him like some of the other people are able to do in their services. You might be uncomfortable and uneasy with all of it because it is such a big and drastic change from what you had been raised up in. The first thing you really have to grab a hold of when learning how to enter into true worship with the Lord is that this is a very individual and personal matter between you and God. Do not ever compare yourself with anyone else in how they worship and praise the Lord.

We are all operating at different levels of spiritual development with the Lord. Some people are much more outgoing, bold, and brazen in their walks and in their personalities with the Lord. They are not self-conscious, and they have no problems in being able to let go with some level of intensity in the way they worship the Lord in a public setting.

However, there are others who are much more self-conscious, shy, and timid in their walks and in their personalities with the Lord. They do not have the boldness or courage to be able to sing out loud or raise up their hands when worshiping the Lord in a public type of setting like this.

If you fall into this category, do not beat yourself up with condemnation or think of yourself as not being good enough before the Lord. If you will notice in the wording in the first verse that I have listed at the top of this chapter – that we have to learn how to worship God the Father in spirit and in **"truth."**

The words in **"truth"** could be referring to the fact that we learn how to be true to ourselves and learn how to worship the Lord from a true and pure heart – not from a heart of trying to be like everyone else when it is not coming natural to us at the level of spiritual development that we may be currently operating at with Him.

Some people will progress at a faster rate in certain areas of their walk with the Lord than others will. Some people will be able to easily and quickly jump right in to being able to worship and praise the Lord with the more intense kind of singing and worship that you will see in some of these types of services.
If you are having a hard time in being able to release to the Lord with this kind of intensity in the way you want to worship and praise Him, especially in a public

type of setting, then my advice to you would be not to worry about it, and let the Lord gradually bring you up into these higher levels of worship and praise at the pace that He will want to do it in.

Be guided by the Holy Spirit on this. The Holy Spirit will gradually work His boldness, courage, passion, and intensity into you where you will then be able to do this without feeling overly self-conscious or intimidated. Let Him work all of this into you at the pace that He will want to work with.

What you will find in this specific area is that the closer you get to the Lord in your own personal relationship with Him, the less self-conscious you will become in how you interact with Him and how you share Him and His ways with other people. The closer you get to the Lord, the better you will get to know Him. And the better you get to know Him, the more you will want to express your feelings, thoughts, and emotions to Him. And once this starts to happen, you will then start to have a natural and holy desire to want to worship and praise this awesome God of ours. Once you start to really learn more about the Lord as a result of your own personal adventures and walk with Him, the more He will start to blow you away with His goodness, with His awesomeness, with His love, and with how much He really does care for you and how far He will always go to take proper care of you.

Once you break into the real realm and reality of what our Lord is really like and all about – your mind, your heart, and your spirit will want to bow down and worship Him, and Him alone. You will simply want to give and express, to the best of your abilities, all the praise and worship that will only be due to Him.

You will come to realize that every fiber of your being and every ounce of your existence is solely and totally dependent upon Him – and that there is nothing on this earth that can even begin to compare to Him and the depth and awesomeness of His personality.

Once your mind comes into direct contact with who God really is and what He is really all about, then it will become much easier for you to be able to worship Him in the way these Scripture verses are telling you to do.

But again, let the Holy Spirit slowly raise you up to this level if you are not there yet. If you have committed to making a full surrender with the Lord where He is now in complete control of your life, and you have now given Him a full and solid green light to enter you into His sanctification process for your life, then this ability to be able to properly worship and praise Him will be given to you by the Holy Spirit over a certain period of time.

The Scripture Verses
So that you can get the full power effect of these verses, I am going to go ahead and run all of these verses together one right after the other.
Once you read all of these verses one right after the other, then you will be able to understand and witness to some of the more intense levels of worship and praise that you will see in some of the non-denominational, charismatic type of churches.

[23] But the hour is coming, and now is, when the true worshipers will worship the Father in spirit and truth; for the Father is

seeking such to worship Him. [24] God *is* Spirit, and those who worship Him must worship in spirit and truth."

John 4:23-24

[11] "You are worthy, O Lord,
To receive glory and honor and power;
For You created all things,
And by Your will they exist and were created."

Revelation 4:11

[2] Give unto the LORD the glory due to His name;
Worship the LORD in the beauty of holiness.

Psalm 29:2

99 The LORD reigns;
Let the peoples tremble!
He dwells *between* the cherubim;
Let the earth be moved!
[2] The LORD *is* great in Zion,
And He *is* high above all the peoples.
[3] **Let them praise Your great and awesome name—**
He *is* holy.
[4] The King's strength also loves justice;
You have established equity;
You have executed justice and righteousness in Jacob.
[5] **Exalt the LORD our God,**
And worship at His footstool—
He *is* holy.

Psalm 99:1-5

[14] He brought them out of darkness and the shadow of death,
And broke their chains in pieces.
[15] **Oh, that *men* would give thanks to the LORD *for* His goodness,**
And *for* His wonderful works to the children of men!

¹⁶ For He has broken the gates of bronze,
And cut the bars of iron in two.

Psalm 107:14-16

²⁸ You *are* my God, and I will praise You;
You *are* my God, I will exalt You.

Psalm 118:28

34 I will bless the LORD at all times;
His praise *shall* continually *be* in my mouth.
² My soul shall make its boast in the LORD;
The humble shall hear *of it* and be glad.
³ Oh, magnify the LORD with me,
And let us exalt His name together.

Psalm 34:1-3

³ Great *is* the LORD, and greatly to be praised;
And His greatness *is* unsearchable.
⁴ One generation shall praise Your works to another,
And shall declare Your mighty acts.

Psalm 145:3-4

³⁰ I will praise the name of God with a song,
And will magnify Him with thanksgiving.

Psalm 69:30

³³ I will sing to the LORD as long as I live;
I will sing praise to my God while I have my being.

Psalm 104:33

150 Praise the LORD!
Praise God in His sanctuary;
Praise Him in His mighty firmament!
² Praise Him for His mighty acts;
Praise Him according to His excellent greatness!

³ Praise Him with the sound of the trumpet;
Praise Him with the lute and harp!
⁴ Praise Him with the timbrel and dance;
Praise Him with stringed instruments and flutes!
⁵ Praise Him with loud cymbals;
Praise Him with clashing cymbals!
⁶ Let everything that has breath praise the LORD.
Praise the LORD!

Psalm 150:1-6

98 **Oh, sing to the LORD a new song!**
For He has done marvelous things;
His right hand and His holy arm have gained Him the victory.

Psalm 98:1

¹⁶ **But I will sing of Your power;**
Yes, I will sing aloud of Your mercy in the morning;
For You have been my defense
And refuge in the day of my trouble.
¹⁷ To You, O my Strength, I will sing praises;
For God *is* my defense,
My God of mercy.

Psalm 59:16-17

47 Oh, clap your hands, all you peoples!
Shout to God with the voice of triumph!
² For the LORD Most High *is* awesome;
He is a great King over all the earth.
³ He will subdue the peoples under us,
And the nations under our feet.
⁴ He will choose our inheritance for us,
The excellence of Jacob whom He loves. ⁴Selah

---

⁴ The word "selah" is found in two books of the Bible, but is most prevalent in the Psalms, where it appears 71 times. It also appears three times in the third chapter of the minor prophet Habakkuk.

⁵ God has gone up with a shout,
The LORD with the sound of a trumpet.

There is a great deal of confusion about the meaning of "selah," primarily because the Hebrew root word from which it is translated is uncertain. Well-meaning Bible scholars disagree on the meaning and on the root word, but since God has ordained that it be included in His Word, we should make an effort to find out, as best we can, the meaning.

One possible Hebrew word that is translated "selah" is *calah* which means "to hang" or "to measure or weigh in the balances." Referring to wisdom, Job says, "The topaz of Ethiopia shall not equal it, neither shall it be valued with pure gold" (Job 28:19). The word translated "valued" in this verse is the Hebrew calah. Here Job is saying that wisdom is beyond comparing against even jewels, and when weighed in the balance against wisdom, the finest jewels cannot equal its value.

"Selah" is also thought to be rendered from two Hebrew words: s_lah, "to praise"; and s_lal, "to lift up." Another commentator believes it comes from salah, "to pause." From these words comes the belief that "selah" is a musical direction to the singers and/or instrumentalists who performed the Psalms, which was the hymnbook of the Israelites. If this is true, then each time "selah" appears in a psalm, the musicians paused, either to take a breath, or to sing a cappella or let the instruments play alone. Perhaps they were pausing to praise Him about whom the song was speaking, perhaps even lifting their hands in worship. This would encompass all these meanings—praise, lift up, and pause. When we consider the three verses in Habakkuk, we also see how "selah" could mean "to pause and praise." Even though Habakkuk was not written to be sung, Habakkuk's prayer in chapter 3 inspires the reader to pause and praise God for His mercy, power, sustaining grace and sufficiency.

Perhaps the best way to think of "selah" is a combination of all these meanings. The Amplified Bible adds "pause and calmly think about that" to each verse where "selah" appears. When we see the word in a psalm or in Habakkuk 3, we should pause to carefully weigh the meaning of what we have just read or heard, lifting up our hearts in praise to God for His great truths. "All the earth bows down to you; they sing praise to you, they sing praise to your name." Selah! (Psalm 66:4).

Read more: From: gotquestions.org

⁶ Sing praises to God, sing praises!
Sing praises to our King, sing praises!
                                                    Psalm 47:1-6

105 Oh, give thanks to the LORD**!**
Call upon His name;
Make known His deeds among the peoples!
² Sing to Him, sing psalms to Him;
Talk of all His wondrous works!
³ Glory in His holy name;
Let the hearts of those rejoice who seek the LORD!
⁴ Seek the LORD and His strength;
Seek His face evermore!
⁵ Remember His marvelous works which He has done,
His wonders, and the judgments of His mouth
                                         Psalm 105:1-5

100 Make a joyful shout to the LORD**, all you lands!**
² Serve the LORD **with gladness;**
Come before His presence with singing.
³ Know that the LORD, He *is* God;
It is He *who* has made us, and not we ourselves;
We are His people and the sheep of His pasture.
⁴ Enter into His gates with thanksgiving,
***And* into His courts with praise.**
Be thankful to Him, *and* bless His name.
⁵ For the LORD *is* good;
His mercy *is* everlasting,
And His truth *endures* to all generations.
                                         Psalm 100:1-5

95 Oh come, let us sing to the LORD**!**
Let us shout joyfully to the Rock of our salvation.
² Let us come before His presence with thanksgiving;
Let us shout joyfully to Him with psalms.
³ For the LORD *is* **the great God,**

And the great King above all gods.
⁴ In His hand *are* the deep places of the earth;
The heights of the hills *are* His also.
⁵ The sea *is* His, for He made it;
And His hands formed the dry *land.*
⁶ Oh come, let us worship and bow down;
Let us kneel before the LORD our Maker.

               Psalm 95:1-6

66 **Make a joyful shout to God, all the earth!**
² **Sing out the honor of His name;**
Make His praise glorious.
³ **Say to God,**
"How awesome are Your works!
Through the greatness of Your power
Your enemies shall submit themselves to You.
⁴ **All the earth shall worship You**
And sing praises to You;
They shall sing praises *to* **Your name."** Selah

               Psalm 66:1-4

96 Oh, sing to the LORD a new song!
Sing to the LORD, all the earth.
² Sing to the LORD, bless His name;
Proclaim the good news of His salvation from day to day.
³ Declare His glory among the nations,
His wonders among all peoples.
⁴ For the LORD *is* great and greatly to be praised;
He *is* to be feared above all gods.
⁵ For all the gods of the peoples *are* idols,
But the LORD made the heavens.
⁶ Honor and majesty *are* before Him;
Strength and beauty *are* in His sanctuary.

⁷ Give to the LORD, O families of the peoples,
Give to the LORD glory and strength.

Psalm 96:1-7

**³ Let them praise His name with the dance;
Let them sing praises to Him with the timbrel and harp.**
⁴ For the LORD takes pleasure in His people;
He will beautify the humble with salvation.
⁵ Let the saints be joyful in glory;
Let them sing aloud on their beds.
⁶ *Let* **the high praises of God** *be* **in their mouth,**
And a two-edged sword in their hand,

Psalm 149:3

¹⁴ Then David danced before the LORD with all *his* might; and David *was* wearing a linen ephod.

2 Samuel 6:14

²¹ So David said to Michal, "*It was* before the LORD, who chose me instead of your father and all his house, to appoint me ruler over the people of the LORD, over Israel. Therefore I will play *music* before the LORD.

2 Samuel 6:21

When you study all the above verses, and then match it up with the way some people will worship, praise, sing, or dance to the Lord in some of these more intense types of worship services, you will see that everything they are doing is not only biblical, but right on target with the way the Lord would like all of us to be able to truly worship Him.

The very last verse from King David, 2 Samuel 6:21 really sums all of it up when it says that he danced before the Lord with all of his might and that he was not worrying about being dignified.

So the next time you see people running in the Spirit, dancing in the Spirit, or singing intensely in the Spirit, remember what the greatest king that Israel has ever had has just stated – that he was not afraid to dance and worship before the Lord with all of his might!

This is also one of the reasons why God said David is a man after His own heart.

Chapter 12: MINDSET - BE Transformed by the Renewing of Your Mind

The Bible tells us that one of the highest, ultimate goals that God has in store for each one of us is our transformation in Him – and this transformation is accomplished by the renewing of our mind. The Bible tells us that God wants to sanctify us and transform us into the express image of His Son Jesus Christ. He wants to make us into a better and more holy people, both on the inside and the outside.

Here is the specific verse from Scripture that will tell us that this kind of transformation is actually done by the renewing of our minds in the Lord:

[2] And do not be conformed to this world, but be transformed by the renewing of your mind, that you may prove what *is* that good and acceptable and perfect will of God.
Romans 12:2

I believe this transformation process has 3 major steps to it. They are as follows:

Knowledge From The Word
The first thing each Christian must know is exactly what it is that God wants to change about us. If you do not know exactly what it is God wants to do with you in this sanctification-transformation process, then you will have a very hard time in being able to fully cooperate with Him once He does try to start the renewal and transformation process on the inside of you.

There are a million and one self-help books on the market, but there is only one Book that will tell you exactly what it is God wants to do with you on the inside to change you for the better – and that Book is the Holy Bible. There are no other books out there that will tell you the specific and exact points that God is looking to target to make this transformation occur in the way that He would really like.

The Bible tells us that this sanctification-transformation process is actually done by the Holy Spirit. **However, the Holy Spirit will not start this transformation process in you until He has something to work with – and that something is knowledge – and that knowledge can only be obtained from the Bible.**

God expects you to play a direct part in this transformation process if He is going to start to work it in you. In the three steps that will get this transformation process going for you – you will be responsible for doing the first two steps. If you are willing to put some quality time and effort in doing these first two steps, then God will do His part, and He will then actually do **all of step 3** for you in order to make this kind of transformation really possible to achieve in this lifetime.

The first step will be to study the Bible for the specific points that God will be looking to target to change you into the kind of person He really wants you to become in Him. Since many of these verses pertaining to all of this are scattered throughout the entire Bible, I am going to list, in subsequent chapters, some of the most powerful verses in all of Scripture – showing you exactly what godly and saintly qualities God will want to work and impart into the very core of your personality.

King David tells us in the Old Testament that we are to meditate on the Word of God. To meditate means to think about, to chew on, to try and figure out what God is trying to tell us in His Word – and then to try and see how these divine truths can be applied in our daily life, and how we can get some of these positive qualities worked and imparted into our personalities.

This entire book is focused on the full Surrender and the Sanctification process; With this and by studying the Bible you have right at your fingertips exactly what it is that God wants to start working on in your personality. And once you have the basic knowledge of what these positive and godly qualities are going to be that God will be looking to impart into you – then you will be ready for step two.

The reason I have the word **"mindset"** listed in the title of this chapter is because you have to know exactly what it is that you have to **"set your mind on"** before God can really kick this transformation process into full gear – hence the word **"mindset."**

You have to learn how to develop **"right thinking"** in the Lord, but you cannot develop right thinking in the Lord unless you first know exactly what it is that you should be thinking right about. The Scripture verses that is listed in this book will show you all the things that God will want you to think right about in order to help you with this renewing of your mind.

Put On Positive Qualities – Put Away Negative Qualities

You will find two key words that will be repeated several times in many of the Scripture verses that will follow. These two key words are **"putting on"** and **"putting away."**

The Bible tells us that we are the ones who are to try and **"put on"** the good and godly qualities that God will want us to have operating in our personalities, and to **"put away"** all of the bad and negative qualities that He will not want us to have operating in our personalities.

This step right here is where many Christians are missing the boat. They have been walking with the Lord for years and they wonder why there have not been many changes in the very cores of their personalities. Where are the love, joy, peace, sound mind, and self-control that the Bible promises me once I fully commit my life to the Lord? Why is it that I still have a problem in controlling my temper, my cussing, and my critical and judgmental spirit?

Once you know the Bible tells you to have self-control over your bad temper and over your condescending and critical attitudes – then it will be your job at this point to **make some kind of concerted effort to actually "put away" these kinds of negative and destructive qualities from your personality.**

Example – say you have a problem with a bad temper. The least little thing will set you off. The first step, as described above, is to find the specific verses from the

Bible on this topic so you can see exactly what God's Word has to say about having bad and quick tempers.

Once you know what God's opinion really is on the matter through His Word – then you will have the appropriate knowledge to work with in order to try and tackle this problem.
Once you see in God's Word that He does not want His people having bad and quick tempers – then you will now be ready for step 2. Now here is where your part will really come into play.

Now that you know God wants your bad temper removed from your personality – He will now expect you to try and put away this bad and negative quality when it does want to erupt. You will now have to start to engage with your quick and bad temper every single time you find yourself in a situation that will start to trigger its release. You will now have to make some kind of attempt on your end to **"put away"** your bad temper and **"put on"** the quality of self-control.

Say someone has just cut you off in traffic. Your normal response may be to start cussing at this person and try to flip him off if you can get close enough to him to do it. Your bad temper has now been fully triggered like it does every time someone cuts you off in traffic.

At this point, you have to make the best effort you can to try and control the release of your bad temper. You may have to literally bite your tongue to keep all the cuss words from flying out of your mouth. When your bad temper releases on you, it is like a fire that explodes out of your belly. Once this fire starts to explode, you have to make a very strong and concerted effort to neutralize it before the fire hits your mouth and causes you to start cussing.

You will have to try and put on the godly quality of self-control in order to try and douse the fire – like pouring cold water on a hot fire. You will have to tell yourself, and give yourself a pep talk that you will directly engage with your bad temper every single time you find yourself in a situation that will trigger its release.

At first, you may not have much success, because the release of your bad temper has become such an automatic bad habit. It has become an automatic response to certain situations. But if you keep at it, over the course of time you will start to get more self-control over it, and you will then be able to dramatically reduce the number of times that you will actually go off.

The reason your bad temper triggers so easily is because you are weak in the quality of self-control.

Self-control is one of the qualities that God wants to impart and work into your personality. You will see this positive quality mentioned numerous times in the verses to follow.

By attempting to put on this very positive quality into your personality, you will have the live ammunition you will need to not only be able to overcome a bad and nasty temper, but other bad and negative qualities such as too much of a critical and judgmental spirit, an unforgiving spirit, and too much pride, arrogance, and haughtiness. The quality of self-control can really help you **"put away"** many of these bad and toxic qualities that the Lord really does not want operating in your personality.

The same approach goes for trying to incorporate positive qualities into your personality. The Bible tells us that God wants us to be loving, kind, generous, and gentle people.

Some people do not have many of these positive qualities operating in them due to all of the bad things that may have happened to them in this life. What God wants you to do anyway is to try and **"put on"** some of these positive and godly qualities. Try to the best of your abilities to become more loving, more patient, more kind – even if you do not feel like it. If you will make some kind of decent and concerted effort to do this on your end, then God will start to do His part – which will now lead us into step 3.

Each one of us only has a certain amount of mental and emotional strength in our own personal makeups. We can only go so far with step 2. We can only get ourselves to a certain point in being able to become more loving, more kind, and more patient. Our best is obviously not going to be good enough to get this transformation process properly completed to the degree that the Lord would really like in this lifetime.

God wants to make us more loving, patient, kind, and peaceful than we could ever get ourselves to be by using our own natural strength. So how can the Lord do this?

If we have spent good, quality time studying the Bible in reference to the changes God wants to make into our personalities – and we have tried to the best of our abilities to put on the good, godly, and saintly qualities that He would really like to have operating in our personalities – then how can God get us up to the level that He is really looking for as you will see in the Scripture verses to follow?

Since our best is obviously not going to be good enough – how can God complete this transformation process to the degree that would really please Him in this lifetime? This will now lead us into step 3.

By the Power of the The Holy Spirit
As you will see in some of the verses to follow, this transformation process is completed **"by the power of the Holy Spirit."** The Holy Spirit lives on the inside of each born again believer and it is His job to mold, shape, and transform us into the kind of holy and righteous people that God the Father would really like all of us to become in Him.

Many born again Christians already know this. They then wonder why there has not been much change in their personalities after they have been saved. Where is the Holy Spirit? How come He is not removing some of my negative qualities? How come I am still crabby, miserable, and depressed all of the time?

The reason there has been little, if any true changes in a believer's personality after they initially get saved, is because they have not spent enough time doing their part in steps 1 and 2. They have not spent enough quality time in the Word of God to learn exactly what it is that God wants to change about them – and then they have not made any real concerted effort on their end to try and change themselves for the better, to try and put on the godly and saintly qualities that God the Father wants them to have operating in their personalities.

If each born again Christian would do their part as described in the above first two steps – then God the Father would only be too anxious to complete this transformation process for you through the power of His Holy Spirit.

What will happen in this third step is that God the Father will then start to impart His peace, His love, His joy, His kindness, His patience, and His perseverance into your personality through the Holy Spirit. And these will be His divine qualities and attributes being imparted into you – not yours!

You only have a certain amount of love within your own natural personality to give and to express to others. However, once God starts to release His love into your personality – then you will be able to love others in the way that the Lord would really like. Then you can really start loving your children, your spouse, and your friends to the degree that you would really like. It is at this stage that you then can love your enemy.

Once God's divine qualities and attributes start to enter into your personality – then many of the negative qualities that you have in you will start to **wash away.** Once you have God's love, joy, and peace starting to flow through your personality – then you will no longer feel crabby, depressed, and miserable like you did before.

God's love, joy, and peace will now be replacing those negative emotions. You cannot feel depressed and unhappy if the love and joy of God is operating in your personality through the Holy Spirit. This is not to say we will never get crabby, irritable, or down at times.

We all live in a fallen and cursed world and we are living in bodies that are slowly dying and corrupting.

But when God really kicks this transformation process into full gear for you, the down days will not last as long as they used to. You will not have as many of them and when you do, they will not last as long as they use to. With God's peace now flowing through you, you will find yourself not getting as upset as often as you did in the past. You may still lose it from time to time, but not to the same degree and frequency that you use to.

One of the greatest accomplishments anyone can achieve in this life is to find true inner peace, happiness, and contentment in this life.

True happiness can only be found on the inside of your being in your connection and personal relationship with the Lord. All of the material wealth and goods that are out there for the taking will not give you this kind of true inner peace, happiness, and fulfillment.

All you have to do is look around you and see all of the unhappy, depressed, and miserable people that are out there – especially those who are rich and supposedly have it "all." Ever wonder why so many of the Hollywood movie stars are doing drugs and seeing therapists? They are finding out that all of their material wealth, fame, and notoriety are not giving them the true inner peace, happiness, and fulfillment they thought that this kind of life would bring them.

As born again, Spirit-filled Christians, we all know that this true inner peace and happiness can only be found on the inside of our beings through establishing a close, intimate, personal relationship with the Lord. There is no other way! Nothing else in this life will give us this kind of true inner peace and happiness.

However, many Christians are not finding this true inner peace and happiness. The Bible talks about it, the preachers talk about it on Sunday, but many are still not finding it. Why? Once you get saved, that is just the beginning.

After you get saved, God expects you to grow, develop, and mature in your walk with Him. Many born again Christians are missing out on this sanctification-transformation process that is available to them through the power of the Holy Spirit. This sanctification process is what will really lead you into true inner peace, happiness, and fulfillment that everyone is looking for these days.

However, God is not going to give you a free lunch on this process. You will have to be willing to do your part before God will be willing to do His part.

The Bible tells us that with the measure we use, will be the measure measured back to us. In other words, if we want God's best, then we have to give Him our best. When it comes to this sanctification-transformation process – we have to give God our best by reading and studying the Word for the changes that He will want to make with us – and then make our own attempt to put on the good and godly qualities that He will want us to have – and then to put away all of the bad and negative qualities that He will not want us to have.

If we give the Lord our best in doing both of the above, then God will give us His best – and God's best will be when He starts to transmit and impart His saintly and godly qualities right up into the middle of our personalities though the Holy Spirit. Think about this incredible possibility – that God Himself can literally impart and transmit part of His divine nature into our personalities through the Holy Spirit if we are willing to work with Him during this transformation-sanctification process.

One last point before I give you all of the power verses showing you the godly and saintly qualities that God will want to try and work into us. Once you read all of the qualities that God would really like to have instilled in us, some of you may get a bit dismayed and distraught after you read what is in these Scripture verses. You may feel overwhelmed, realizing that you may be a long way off in being able to have some of these positive godly qualities worked and imparted into your personality.

Some Christians read these verses and feel so overwhelmed – they do not even feel it is worth trying for because these ideals just seem to be too high to strive for. The one thing we all have to realize is that every single one of us is flawed to some degree. We all have our character flaws and rough edges. No exceptions. We all have issues that need to be dealt with, and we all need God's transformation-sanctification process to occur in our lives so the Lord can transform us into the holy righteous saints He really wants all of us to become in Him.

This sanctification process is not done overnight. This is a process that will occur over the rest of your earthly life. If you are willing to work with the Lord in this process, God will then gradually and progressively transform and sanctify you to make you into the kind of person that He really wants you to become in Him.

Your reward for allowing God to do this type of inner sanctifying work in your life will be a joy, a peace, a love, and a zest for life that you never knew was really possible to obtain in this life. You will find true inner peace, happiness, and fulfillment. You will find what everyone else is looking for these days and cannot find, and many people will be drawn to you as a result.

Many non-believers have stated that what drew them to certain born again Christians that ended up getting them saved was the peace, joy, and love that seemed to be operating through their personalities. They said they were drawn to those personality qualities like a magnet.

Not only will you be more happy and fulfilled by allowing God to do this with you, but you will also be a joy for others, and they will be drawn to the light of God that will be shining through you.

As a result, many people, including other Christians will start asking you what it is that you have operating in you. Why are you always so happy and upbeat?

How can you have so much peace and contentment in your life in this crazy and tumultuous world we now live in?

As a result of this kind of inner spiritual transformation, you will be able to lead many more non-believers into eternal salvation through Jesus, and disciple many other believers into a deeper walk with the Lord.

This sanctification process is available to all believers. God wants to do this with every single one of us. The problem is that many of God's people are not willing to do their part in it. As a result, the Body of Christ has many flaky hypocritical representatives for God who are doing more harm than good.

They are turning people away from the Lord because they are not truly manifesting God's nature and personality though their own personalities – and this is all due because God could not properly get the sanctification process started in their lives due to ignorance and lack of knowledge on their part on how to actually enter into it, or possibly due to open rebellion and stubbornness on their part.

They may not be open to admitting to God what some of their problems and character flaws really are. They may be full of too much pride and arrogance to admit they have any character flaws that really need to be dealt with, and God thus will not be able to properly reach them to start this sanctification process within them. As a result, they will end up presenting a haughty, prideful, arrogant, and know-it-all witness that will do nothing but turn people off and away from the Lord.

If you decide you really want God to start this sanctification process within you all you have to do is go to God in prayer and tell Him that He has a full and solid green light from you to start this process.
Tell God that you really want this transformation-sanctification process to start to occur in your life – and that you will be open to allowing it to occur over the rest of your life down here on this earth.

Your job will be:

- To get into the Word and study the verses that will give you the knowledge on what positive qualities God will want to impart into you and what negative qualities that He will want to take out of you.
- Make the best attempts you can to "**put on**" the good, positive, and godly qualities that God will want you to have operating in your personality – and then "**put away**" all of the bad, negative, and destructive qualities that He will not want you to have operating in your personality.
- And then be open and sensitive to any communication that you may receive from God

on any specific areas He may want to work with you on. God will let you know exactly what these specific areas are going to be and exactly how He will want to deal with each one of them.

When this starts to occur, it may be a bit painful at times. It's hard for many of us to admit to anyone, including ourselves or to God, that we may have problems in certain areas of our personality. But let God do His inner surgery on you through the Holy Spirit and you will be much better off for it in the long run.

Remember, the Holy Spirit needs something to work with – and that something is knowledge – and the Scripture verses I will be giving you in each Chapter in this book is a good start to this knowledge. These verses are the major door openers that will get God to start the sanctification process within you and change your life for the better.

Chapter 13: You Are What You Think

Each and every chapter in this book set the stage to show you that it is the will of God for your life that you let Him enter you into a sanctification process in order that He may fully consecrate you to Himself and start to mold, shape, and transform you into the express image of His Son Jesus Christ.

One of the first things you will find the Lord will want to do with you is to try and put right thinking into your mind and thought process. Joyce Meyer has a very catchy phrase when describing this. She has said that too many people have **"stinkin thinkin."**

What you choose to think about and dwell on in this life will make or break you as to what type of person you will end up becoming in this life.

Leave it to God the Father to perfectly capture, in one simple one-line sentence from the Bible, the secret to being able to have good mental health in this life.

When I first saw this verse back in the Old Testament, it literally blew off the page at me. As soon as I saw it, I saw incredible amounts of revelation behind it.

Many Christians have never heard of this verse since it is back in the Old Testament in the Book of Proverbs. This powerful verse should be memorized by all Christians, as it is giving us a major spiritual secret in being able to acquire good mental health in the Lord.

⁷ For **as he thinks in his heart, so** *is* **he.**
"Eat and drink!" he says to you,
But his heart is not with you.

Proverbs 23:7

The key word in this verse is the word **"thinks."** The word **"thinks"** is telling you that God is targeting your thought process – what you think about on a daily basis.

Interpretation – you are what you think! You can become what you think!

This principle is easily seen in our world today. You can really tell who is properly operating on this principle in the way the Lord has intended for all of us to operate with it and who is not.

The people who always seem to be more happy, upbeat, and fulfilled with their lives are the people who have a good sound mind and who are always thinking about and dwelling on the more positive things in this life. They choose, with their own free wills, to dwell on the more positive side of this life as versus always thinking and dwelling on the darker and negative side of this life.

The people who are not happy and fulfilled, and who are always pessimistic and depressed all the time, and have negative attitudes towards anybody and anything, are all choosing to think and dwell on the negative side of this life.
Granted, this cursed and fallen world in which we all live in has a mixture of both life and death in it. Jesus

Himself said that we would all have to go through various types of trials and tribulations in this life from time to time.

However, there is a flip side to this coin. On the one side of the coin is the darker side of this life, but on the other side of this coin is the good, positive, and brighter side of this life. It is not all death, doom, and destruction. Even in the worst case scenarios and situations, there is always a hope and a light at the end of that storm cloud tunnel. As Christians, we all have God Almighty Himself on our side to help us take on any storm clouds that may come our way in this life.

The difference between these two types of people is in their **thought life**. The people who are always happy, upbeat, and positive have chosen to look on the brighter side of things, even in some of the worst case scenarios imaginable.

The negative type of people have chosen to think and dwell on all of the bad things that can happen or go wrong in this life. No matter what good may come their way, they will always think that something better could have come their way. As a result of all of this negative and morbid type of thinking in their thought process, nothing ever makes them happy or content because nothing is ever good enough for them.

The Bible is very clearly telling us in the above verse that we can all choose what to think about and dwell on. We do not have to become slaves to negative and pessimistic type thinking. In other

words, we can choose to think about what we want to think about!

Our thinking and thought process does not control us – we control it! Negative type thinking can be broken. For many, it has become an actual mental stronghold because they have been mired down into this type of negative thinking for such a long period of time.

However, as you will see in some of the Scripture verses I will list below, the Bible tells us that we can actually take **"captive"** what we think about. The verse that will give us this revelation says we have to bring every thought into captivity to the obedience of Jesus.

What this means is that we are directly responsible for choosing what we think about and dwell on – and then make sure that our thinking always lines up with the Word of God and how He wants us to think about things.

The power lies with us. We cannot blame anyone else, including God Himself, if we have chosen with our own free wills to constantly dwell on the negative and darker side of this life.

Bottom line – we all have to learn how to develop right thinking in our thought process. Our part is to do the best we can to try and think and dwell on the things that God wants us to be concentrating and focusing on. However, as we all know, most of us only have a certain amount of mental and psychological strength in this area. Some will naturally go farther in this realm than others will.

This is where the Holy Spirit will really be coming in big time to help you get your thinking process straightened out and grounded in the Lord in the way that He will want it to be. This is all part of the sanctification process that God wants to start with each one of us.

Once again, remember this process will not be accomplished overnight. If you have been operating in a negative type of mindset for a long period time, God will start to gradually and progressively move you out of it into a better, clearer, and healthier type of thinking.

Your job will be to work very closely with the Holy Spirit once He starts this sanctification process within you. You will see Him start to target specific areas in your thinking where you are really off base. Once this revelation has been given to you by the Holy Spirit, then it will be up to you as to whether or not you will choose to work with Him to get this particular area cleaned up to the degree that the Lord would really like.

If He tells you that you are too judgmental and too critical of others – then your part will be to do the best you can to try and cast down these types of negative and destructive thoughts and replace them with more positive and godly types of thoughts.

For many, this will be a very painful process because you will be forced to admit that you have some character flaws and imperfections that will need to be dealt with in your mind, soul, and personality.

The Holy Spirit is the Master Surgeon – and He will be attempting to do inner spiritual surgery on you to take out what He does not want to be operating in your mind and thought process, and put in what He does want to be operating in it.

Your job will be to choose, with your own free will, to work and co-operate with the Holy Spirit once He makes it very clear to you what specific changes He will want to make with you. He will not force these changes on you. He will let you know very clearly exactly what it is He wants to put in your system and exactly what it is He wants to take out.

If you choose to move and cooperate with the Holy Spirit on what specific changes He will want to make with you – then God the Father will allow the supernatural power of His Holy Spirit to truly begin to transform and sanctify you in the way and manner that will most pleasing to Him.

And one of the main areas the Lord is definitely going to want to target is your private thinking and thought life – what you choose to think about on a daily basis. In other words, God wants to clean up and straighten out your thought life.

With all of the different types of material and sexual lusts that are operating in our world today that are competing for our time and attention, for many, this will initially be a very big battle.

But if you are really wanting the Lord to help clean you up in some of these areas, especially in your private thought life, the Lord will only be too anxious to help get you over some of these mental hurdles through the incredible supernatural power of His Holy Spirit.

This kind of inner transformation and sanctification can be accomplished in this life if you are willing to do your part by fully cooperating with the Lord once He starts it up with you.

Now I will give you some very good verses from the Bible all showing you that God the Father really does want to come after your thought life and attempt to put right and positive type thinking into your mind.

You Are What You Think

⁷ For as he thinks in his heart, so *is* he.
"Eat and drink!" he says to you,
But his heart is not with you.

Proverbs 23:7

This verse very clearly sets the stage that God the Father really wants to come after our thought life and get it properly cleaned up.

You Are Transformed By the Renewing of Your Mind

These next two verses will again show you that God really wants to come after your mind. And part of your mind is your thought process – what you choose to think about and dwell on. Both of these verses are using the words **"renewing"** and **"renewed"** in reference to your mind.

In other words, part of the transformation-sanctification process with the Lord involves getting your mind properly renewed through His Word and by His Spirit.

12 I beseech you therefore, brethren, by the mercies of God, that you present your bodies a living sacrifice, holy, acceptable to God, *which is* your reasonable service. ² **And do not be conformed to this world, but be transformed by the renewing of your mind**, that you may prove what *is* that good and acceptable and perfect will of God.

Romans 12:1

²² that you put off, concerning your former conduct, the old man which grows corrupt according to the deceitful lusts, ²³ **and be renewed in the spirit of your mind**, ²⁴ and that you put on the new man which was created according to God, **in true righteousness and holiness.**

Ephesians 4: 22-24

¹⁶ Therefore we do not lose heart. **Even though our outward man is perishing, yet the inward man is being renewed day by day.** ¹⁷ For our light affliction, which is but for a moment, is working for us a far more exceeding *and* eternal weight of glory, ¹⁸ while we do not look at the things which are seen, but at the things which are not seen. For the things which are seen *are* temporary, but the things which *are* not seen are eternal.

2 Corinthians 4:16

Notice Paul says in 2 Corinthians 4:16 that our inner man is being renewed day by day. He is using the same word **"renewed"** as the above two verses are using when they are talking about our minds being renewed. This means that God wants both our minds and our inner man to be renewed on a daily and progressive basis.

When God says that our inner spiritual transformation is done by getting our minds properly renewed in Him – He is giving all of us an incredible, powerful, spiritual secret. Again, this is all part of the sanctification process that the Lord wants to start with each and everyone of us.

We Now Have the Mind of Christ
1 Corinthians 2:16 is making one of the most profound statements in all of Scripture. This verse says that we now have the **"mind of Christ."** Think of the implications, ramifications, and power of this statement.

> [16] For "who has known the mind of the LORD that he may instruct Him?" But we have the mind of Christ.
> **1 Corinthians 2:16**

As a result of having the Holy Spirit residing on the inside of us – we now have direct access to both God and Jesus who live in heaven. As a result of having this direct access to Jesus through the Holy Spirit – we now have His mind, or to put it another way, we can now have His mind operating through us.

Jesus, through the Holy Spirit, can now start to impart His thoughts and His ways of thinking direct into our minds. This transmission of His thoughts direct to us through the Holy Spirit is so clear, so perfect, and so powerful – that the Bible can now say that we have the "mind of Christ."

So not only do we have the power of the Holy Spirit operating on the inside of us to help get our thought life cleaned up – but we now have the power of Jesus Christ Himself available to us since He will now allow us to have direct access into His own mind so that we can truly learn how we should act and think in this life.

1 Corinthians 11:1 says that we are to now "imitate Christ." In other words, we are to act the way Jesus wants us to act.

> 11 Imitate me, just as I also *imitate* Christ.
> **1 Corinthians 11:1**

Put these two verses together side by side like two pieces of a jigsaw puzzle – and Jesus is telling us loud and clear that He wants all of us to think like He thinks and act like He acts. He now becomes our perfect role model in which to pattern our inner life and our outer life after.

Again, being able to be tapped into the mind of Jesus Christ so that His thoughts and ways can be transmitted to us is all a part of the sanctification process that God can start with each and everyone one of us.

God Has Given Us a Sound Mind
2 Timothy 1:7 is another major power verse, especially in the times we now live in. If you will notice, many non-believers, and even some carnal Christians, are not operating with very sound minds. All you have to do is spend five minutes with some people and you will be able to quickly tell who is operating with a sound mind and who is not.

⁷ For God has not given us a spirit of fear, but of power and of love and of a sound mind.

2 Timothy 1:7

The sexual and material lusts of this life have been so overwhelming for some of these people, that the only thing they have their minds constantly set on is trying to get as much sex, money, and power as they possibly can. As a result of these types of material and lustful pursuits, their thinking has become totally distorted, warped, debased, and downright unstable.

Many marriages and good friendships have been broken up as a result of these people's minds becoming very unsound as a result of the corruption and deterioration that will occur in a person's mind if they chase after these types of material and lustful pursuits for too long of a period of time.

I have personally seen some men and women in a 20 year period go from being very clear and sound thinking to men and women who have become totally unstable and unsound in all of their ways. As a result of this deterioration in their minds, many of them have lost their marriages, and their good relationships they had with their children and some of their good close friends. Some of them had literally deteriorated down to the point where they had actually ended up committing suicide.

One of the most incredible blessings that we can be given as a born again Christian, especially in the type of world we live in today, is the blessing of being able to have a good, clear, sound mind in the Lord! For those who are walking very close with the Lord and have your act together with Him, the Holy Spirit will really move to impart this sound mind to you.

In this verse, God is telling us that not only can we get a sound mind from Him, but we can also get a mind that has a spirit of power and love in it. This verse actually starts out by telling us that we have not been given a spirit of fear, but a spirit that is of power, love, and sound mind.

Think about these 3 specific words – **power, love, and sound mind!** God is really trying to drive home a major point in the way that He has worded this specific verse.

No matter how severe of a storm cloud you may be forced to deal with – realize that you now have the mind of Jesus Christ and the power of the Holy Spirit operating through you to help keep your thinking "sound" and "powerful." This kind of mindset from the Lord is already in you. You just have to learn how to connect up to it, believe it, ground on it, and act on it.

Your Thoughts Will Be Established by the Lord
Since God is all-knowing and all-powerful, then this means He is the only One who has direct access into your thought life. Demons and other people cannot read your mind or your thoughts. This is your private area only. However, since God can perfectly read into your thought life – this leaves you with not being able to hide anything from Him.

Many people are very good at hiding everything from those around them, but you can never fool God or hide anything from Him, as He is always one step ahead of you – even in your own personal and private thought life and what you choose to think about and dwell on.

[26] The thoughts of the wicked *are* an abomination to the LORD,
But the words of the pure *are* pleasant.
                                                            Proverbs 15:26

This verse also tells us that the **"thoughts of the wicked are an abomination to the Lord."** This verse is telling us that God can literally read our thoughts since this verse is using the word **"thoughts."** I believe the word **"thoughts"** is referring to the thoughts in our minds, which are our unspoken words.

Also notice the Lord is using a very intense word when describing the thoughts of people who are considered really wicked and evil – and that word is **"abomination."**

God does see and watch our thought life. This is why each born again Christian should do the best they can to try and clean it up.

Proverbs 16:3 gives us another very nice promise. It says that if we are willing to commit our works to the Lord – then our **"thoughts will be established."**

[3] Commit your works to the LORD,
And your thoughts will be established.
                                                              Proverbs 16:3

If we are committing our works to the Lord, then we are operating in a full surrender with Him. And if we are operating in a full surrender with Him, then the

Holy Spirit can really start to work with us in helping us to establish and solidify our thought life.

Bring Every Thought into Captivity to the Obedience of Jesus

2 Corinthians 10:3 is telling us to bring every thought into captivity to the obedience of Jesus. What this means is that we are directly responsible for what we choose to think about and dwell on.

> [3] For though we walk in the flesh, we do not war according to the flesh. [4] For the weapons of our warfare *are* not carnal but mighty in God for pulling down strongholds, [5] casting down arguments and every high thing that exalts itself against the knowledge of God, bringing every thought into captivity to the obedience of Christ, [6] and being ready to punish all disobedience when your obedience is fulfilled.
>
> **2 Corinthians 10:3**

A girl who I used to work with got herself into major trouble with the Lord when she went one time to see a hypnotist to try and quit smoking. When she came out after just this one session, she literally lost 50% of her ability to remember and retain things. Both her short and long term memory abilities were severely affected. When she first came to work for me and told me what had happened, I told her under no circumstances are we to ever blank our minds out to let a hypnotist gain control of what kinds of suggestions or thoughts he wants to plant into our minds – even if these are positive types of suggestions.

I then gave her this Scripture verse that says that we are the ones to bring every thought into **"captivity"** to

Jesus – not anyone else – including any hypnotist who wants to plant his suggestions into your mind.

She violated a major spiritual law that is in operation in reference to our thought life and the privacy that we have with the Lord on this issue. As a result of violating this major spiritual law, she drew a demon on her and this demon was then allowed to cause this short and long term memory loss in her.
Once I found out how all of this occurred, I was then able to give her the correct advice on how to get the demon out and have her long and short term memory ability fully restored back to her.

Bottom line – we decide what we want to think about in the privacy of our own thinking. We can either choose to think about good and godly things – or we can choose to think about bad and evil things. The choice is ours.

God makes it very clear in His Word as to what kinds of thoughts He would like us to be dwelling on. But not even God Himself will force His will on us in this realm of our being. We have to be the ones to make that choice.

When God uses the word **"captivity"** in the following verse, I believe He is trying to tell us that we have to make some kind of concerted effort on our end to try and control our thought life and not let it get out of control – especially in the area of bad and fleshly type thoughts. We are to grab a hold of our thoughts and make sure that our thinking and our thoughts always line up with the way that He would like us to be thinking about things.

With all of the material and sexual lusts of our world hitting us full force through the media and everything else we encounter on a daily basis, this is a real tall order for many of us to keep proper control of all the bad thoughts that can cross our minds.

But again, this is where the Holy Spirit can really help you out if you are willing to allow Him to enter you into this sanctification process with the Lord. Your job will be to do the best job you can in controlling your thought life. But where you will fail, and where you will have certain issues that will be harder to conquer using your own will power, is where the Holy Spirit will come in and supernaturally give you His help and strength in order to help get you over some of these harder hurdles.

Chapter 14: Death and Life Are in the Power of the Tongue

As part of your sanctification process with the Lord, expect God the Father to come after three main areas in your walk with Him.

The first area will be with your **"thought life"** – which is the area of your unspoken words.

The second area God will be targeting will be your **"word life"** – which has to do with the words that are being released out of your mouth to other people.

The third area God will be coming after will be your **"action life"** – which will be how you act and behave towards others. Your actions and behaviors toward others have to always line with up with your sanctified thinking and your sanctified speech. The Bible says we have to be **"doers"** of the Word, not just hearers.

This chapter will be dealing with the second area, which will be your **"word life"** towards others. You can have a certain amount of your thinking and thought life cleaned up to some degree in the Lord with the sanctifying help of the Holy Spirit, but if you cannot make the next step and transmit the right kinds of words to others in your own personal dealings with them, then all of the sanctification that you went through to get your thinking and thought life cleaned up will have all been for nothing.

In this chapter, I am going to give you several powerful verses from the Bible on this topic. When you string all of these verses together like I will do in this chapter, you will really be able to see exactly what God wants to do with you in this area. These verses are once again giving all of us some major profound revelation from the Lord in just this one area alone.

Your "**word life**" with others will make or break you in your own personal relationships with other people in this life. If you do not learn how to speak to other people in a positive and godly manner, then sooner or later no one will want to have anything to do with you, and you will eventually find yourself being totally isolated and alone.
I simply cannot stress enough the power that is on these particular verses – and that each and every Christian do the best they can to clean up their speech and the way they express themselves to other people in this life.

The very first verse I will list below will give us perfect revelation from the Lord on this issue. This one verse is so powerful from the Lord that I have decided to name the title of this chapter just after this one verse. This one verse is telling us that **"death and life are in the power of the tongue."** Just stop and think for a minute what the Lord is trying to convey to us with these specific words. There are two things to pick up from this verse.

The first thing that God is trying to tell all of us is that we have a certain amount of "power" in our tongues. Our tongue is referring to the verbal words that we speak out of our mouths to other people.
When God is using the word "power," He is telling us that every single one of us has a certain amount of

power residing in our mouth and in our tongues with the words that we can release to other people.

And with this kind of power residing in our ability to release spoken words to other people – God then tells us what can happen with this kind of power. This power can either be used to bring life or death to the person that we are speaking to. Think of the responsibility and ramifications of this revelation – that our spoken words to other people can either bring them life or bring them death!

You can either choose to learn how to speak and release positive words of love, encouragement, and edification to other people in your own personal dealings with them, or you can choose to release negative words of condemnation, criticism, coldness, and harshness. The choice is yours!

God the Father makes it very clear with the way that He has worded all of these Scripture verses which way He wants all of us to take with the power that we already have residing in our tongues.

Every single one of us can stop and think how good we have felt when someone has released and spoken words of love, encouragement, and edification to us. Words can cut right through you like a knife, and when those words are positive and constructive, they can have an incredible way of building up your own sense of self-esteem, self-worth, and self-confidence.

One of the verses I will list below says that good words can literally be health to our bones. In other words, good and positive types of words can give you better physical health as a result of the boost your immune system will receive.

However, just the reverse is also possible. If all a child ever hears from his parents as they are growing up are stern and abusive words of condemnation, criticism, and negativity – then that child's self-esteem and self-worth can be severely affected if it is not properly counter-balanced by other people in his life who will speak out the right kinds of words of love and encouragement to him.

If a child does not get properly watered with words of love and encouragement from his own flesh-and-blood parents during his early growing years in the family, then sooner or later he will end up believing in all of the lies of his parents as a result of their constant bombardments – and he will then end up growing up thinking that he will never be good enough to amount to anything worthwhile.

There are many grown adults who never end up accomplishing everything that God would've had in store for them in this life as result of not being able to pull out of all the negativity and pessimism that their parents had heaped on them during their earlier growing years in the family. And all of their possible growth in the Lord in this lifetime ends up getting stunted as a result of the **"death"** that was brought upon them by the negative and abusive words spoken to them by their own natural parents.
This is why the Lord is telling us in this verse that some kind of death can literally be brought about as a result of speaking out the wrong kinds of words to

someone – especially words spoken between parents and their own children.

This same type of "death" can also occur in marriages between husbands and their wives. Many married women have had all of their healthy sense of self-respect, self-worth, and self-confidence beat right out of them as a result of all the verbal abuse they have had to put up with from their verbally abusive husbands.

As Christians, we should all work very closely with the Holy Spirit in allowing Him to help us clean up our word life and how we verbally express ourselves to other people in this life.
If we can learn how to get this part of our life properly cleaned up and sanctified under His direction and guidance, then not only we will become more pleasing to the Lord, but we will also dramatically increase the quality of our own personal relationships that we can have with other people in this life.

For the Holy Spirit to really be able to start to work with you in this area, you will need the knowledge that the following Scripture verses will give you. I will once again break these verses down under their appropriate captions so you can fully grasp the revelation the Lord is trying to convey to you.

The Scripture Verses

If you can grasp what the Lord is trying to tell you with the knowledge and revelation that is in these verses, and then start to work with the Holy Spirit in trying to learn how to change, control, and curb some of your bad speech habits – you can change the way you talk and express yourself to other people, with all of it being for the better.

I have personally seen the Lord take several people who used to cuss like sailors, and who were very demeaning and abusive in the way they would talk to other people, and completely change and transform them into sanctified saints who no longer cuss, and who now treat their spouses, their children, and their good personal friends in the godly way and manner that He would like all of us to do.

Death and Life Are in the Power of the Tongue
The very first verse I will list below is the one that will tell us that death and life are in the power of the tongue. The rest of the verses will further extend off this revelation with some very interesting wording being used by the Lord to try and drive home the point of how powerful our words really are – and how they can either be used to bring life, love, edification, and encouragement into a person's life – or bring death, destruction, negativity, and torment.

I will list each one of the verses one right after the other, and then point out and highlight some of the key phrases that are in some of these verses so you can really see the powerful revelation that is in these verses.

[21] Death and life *are* in the power of the tongue,
And those who love it will eat its fruit.

Proverbs 18:21

[18] There is one who speaks like the piercings of a sword,
But the tongue of the wise *promotes* health.
Proverbs 12:18

[13] Keep your tongue from evil,
And your lips from speaking deceit.
Psalm 34:13

[20] A man's stomach shall be satisfied from the fruit of his mouth;
From the produce of his lips he shall be filled.
Proverbs 18:20

[4] "The Lord G<small>OD</small> has given Me
The tongue of the learned,
That I should know how to speak
A word in season to *him who is* weary.
He awakens Me morning by morning,
He awakens My ear
To hear as the learned.
Isaiah 50:4

[5] Walk in wisdom toward those *who are* outside, redeeming the time. [6] *Let* your speech always *be* with grace, seasoned with salt, that you may know how you ought to answer each one.
Colossians 4:5-6

[11] The mouth of the righteous *is* a well of life,
But violence covers the mouth of the wicked.
Proverbs 10:11

[4] The words of a man's mouth *are* deep waters;
The wellspring of wisdom *is* a flowing brook.
Proverbs 18:4

⁴ A wholesome tongue *is* a tree of life,
But perverseness in it breaks the spirit.

Proverbs 15:4

²⁴ Pleasant words *are like* a honeycomb,
Sweetness to the soul and health to the bones.

Proverbs 16:24

²⁵ Anxiety in the heart of man causes depression,
But a good word makes it glad.

Proverbs 12:25

15 A soft answer turns away wrath,
But a harsh word stirs up anger.
² The tongue of the wise uses knowledge rightly,
But the mouth of fools pours forth foolishness.

Proverbs 15:1-2

³ He who guards his mouth preserves his life,
But he who opens wide his lips shall have destruction.

Proverbs 13:3

²³ Whoever guards his mouth and tongue
Keeps his soul from troubles.

Proverbs 21:23

²⁸ The heart of the righteous studies how to answer,
But the mouth of the wicked pours forth evil.

Proverbs 15:28

³ Set a guard, O Lord, over my mouth;
Keep watch over the door of my lips.

Psalm 141:3

If you will notice, some of these verses have two sides to them. On the one side are the positive benefits and blessings one can receive as the result of learning how to speak properly to others. On the other side are the negative things that can occur as a result of not properly expressing yourself to others – either in the specific words that you choose to say to a person, or in the way or manner in which you say these words to a person.

So you can fully grasp both sides of this coin, I will first bullet point all of the positive things that are in the above verses, and then I will bullet point all of the negative things. Here is the positive side of the coin:

- The tongue of the wise promotes health
- The truthful lip shall be established forever
- A man's stomach shall be satisfied from the fruit of his mouth
- Let your speech always be with grace and seasoned with salt
- The mouth of the righteous is a well of life
- The wellspring of wisdom is a flowing brook
- A wholesome tongue is a tree of life
- Pleasant words are sweetness to the soul and health to the bones
- A good word can make someone's heart glad
- A soft answer turns away wrath
- The tongue of the wise uses knowledge rightly
- He who guards his mouth preserves his life
- He who guards his mouth and tongue keeps his soul from trouble

When you read all of these key phrases one right after the other, you can really start to see how powerful of a thing it really is if you can learn how to properly express yourself to other people in this life. Notice in 3 of the middle bullet points, that someone who can speak to others in a righteous and godly manner will be like a well of life, a flowing brook, and a tree of life to that person.

Pleasant words, good and uplifting type words, and a wholesome tongue can also help serve to lift a person's spirit up, help make their hearts glad and happy, be able to turn away possible wrath and anger, and also help to guard and preserve your own personal life. One wrong word to the wrong person at the wrong time could lead you to having an early departure from this life.

If more people would learn how to walk and abide in the revelation and knowledge that is in these verses, and learn how to express themselves in a more positive and godly manner to others – we would have less tensions and conflicts in our marriages, in our families, in our personal friendships, and in the workplace.

Now here is the negative side of this same coin:

- Keep your tongue from evil and speaking guile
- Violence will cover the mouth of the wicked
- A perverse tongue will break the spirit
- A harsh word stirs up anger
- He who opens wide his lips shall have destruction
- The mouth of the wicked pours forth evil

Jesus has already told us that those who will live by the sword will also die by the sword. The second bullet point above tells us that violence can chase after and literally come upon someone if their speech to others is wicked and evil.

These key phrases are telling us that those with big mouths and those who like to speak harsh words to others can bring sudden destruction down on them and possibly those who may be close to them. Flip off and cuss out the wrong guy on the highway, and he may be the last person you will ever see alive again. Put both sides of this coin right next to one another, and you can see very clearly how the Lord wants us to express ourselves to other people in this life.

Rebuking the Wicked
Though the Lord wants us to be able to talk to others in a civil, loving, and uplifting way and manner – this does not mean we have to become submissive doormats and be too afraid to engage with the wicked and evil people in this life if we have to.

Jesus Himself did not mince any words when attacking some of the high ranking Jewish leaders of His day. He also did not hold back when throwing out the money changers who were trying to do business in His house of worship.

The next set of verses are very interesting, especially in the day and age we now live in where everyone is trying to be politically correct and are too afraid to verbally engage with someone for fear of offending them.

Here are 5 very good verses telling us not to be afraid to engage when we have to, and be willing to take a stand and tell the truth even if it means initially hurting or offending someone.

[25] But those who rebuke *the wicked* will have delight,
And a good blessing will come upon them.
Proverbs 24:25

[5] Open rebuke *is* better
Than love carefully concealed.
[6] Faithful *are* the wounds of a friend,
But the kisses of an enemy *are* deceitful.
Proverbs 27:5

[23] He who rebukes a man will find more favor afterward
Than he who flatters with the tongue.
Proverbs 28:23

[30] Blows that hurt cleanse away evil,
As *do* stripes the inner depths of the heart
Proverbs 20:30

[25] Therefore, putting away lying, "*Let* each one *of you* speak truth with his neighbor," for we are members of one another. [26] "Be angry, and do not sin": do not let the sun go down on your wrath, [27] nor give place to the devil. [28] Let him who stole steal no longer, but rather let him labor, working with *his* hands what is good, that he may have something to give him who has need. [29] Let no corrupt word proceed out of your mouth, but what is good for necessary edification, that it may impart grace to the hearers.
Ephesians 4:25-29

Many pastors across the world are afraid to call out the sin of abortion and same sex relationships for the abomination that it really is for fear of offending those who may be pro-choice in their congregations. As all of the above verses are trying to tell you, anyone who is too afraid to call out these types of obvious sins are failing to make an attempt to clean away an evil sin and abomination.

Notice that several of these verses are telling you that if you would be willing to take a strong stand and express the Lord's opinion on these kinds of hot issues and topics, that you initially may hurt and offend a few people, but afterwards you will end up finding much more favor with others, will help impart grace and knowledge to these people, and then possibly end up receiving a good blessing from the Lord for being willing to do this.

This same principle also applies between parents and their children. Stop any bad and inappropriate behavior as soon as you start to see it surface and manifest and you just may save your son or daughter years of possible trouble down the road.

Do Not Bear False Witness Against Your Neighbor
In the very litigious claims conscious society we now live in, many people are filing unscrupulous lawsuits. And in some of these lawsuits, the plaintiffs are bearing some type of false witness against either an employer, a co-worker, a company or corporation, or a total stranger. In other words, they are flat out lying against a defendant, all in an effort to try and make some type of financial gain either against an individual or a particular company.

As you will see in the verses I will list below, when God the Father has it set up as one of His 10 commandments that you should not be bearing any type of false witness against your neighbor, and then tops it off by saying that this type of lying will be considered an abomination in His sight – any Christian will get himself into major trouble with the Lord if they try and do this to either unjustly hurt the person they have targeted as a matter of trying to get some type of personal revenge against them, or if they are doing it to try and make some kind of financial gain.

You will have the vengeance and wrath of God Almighty Himself come down on you and your life if you ever try to hurt anyone else with any type of false accusation or false charge. Let these verses be a major warning to any Christian who is thinking about doing this for either personal revenge or any type of monetary gain.

[28] Do not be a witness against your neighbor without cause,
For would you deceive with your lips?
[29] Do not say, "I will do to him just as he has done to me;
I will render to the man according to his work."
Proverbs 24:28-29

[5] A false witness will not go unpunished,
And *he who* speaks lies will not escape.
Proverbs 19:5

[11] Do not speak evil of one another, brethren. He who speaks evil of a brother and judges his brother, speaks evil of the law and

judges the law. But if you judge the law, you are not a doer of the law but a judge.
James 4:11

²² Lying lips *are* an abomination to the LORD,
But those who deal truthfully *are* His delight.
Proverbs 12:22

⁶ Getting treasures by a lying tongue
Is the fleeting fantasy of those who seek death.
Proverbs 21:6

Notice the second verse says that anyone who bears false witness will not go unpunished. The first verse tells us that we cannot even try to bear false witness against someone even as a matter of personal revenge. The Bible tells us that any type of vengeance or payback in this life always belongs to the Lord. It does not belong to you, or to any of your friends who would like to try and get even for you.

The last verse perfectly describes what people are doing when filing unjust lawsuits based upon trumped-up, false allegations. Trying to obtain treasures and financial wealth by way of a lying tongue is a fleeting fantasy, and eventually judgment will be rendered against them at the hands of God Himself.

As a Christian, do not ever tempt your hand or your fate with the Lord by crossing over into this kind of forbidden territory with Him.

Shun Profane and Vain Babblings
In addition to never, ever, considering bearing any type of false witness against anyone, these next set of

verses will tell us to learn how to shun profane and vain babblings.

The word **"babblings"** means **"foolishness and meaningless type of talk."** In other words, try to keep unnecessary and foolish type of gossiping and talk to a bare minimum. I know in the work place where many people are huddled very close together, this is a real hard one to try and keep on top of. But as you will see in several of the verses listed below, if the one you are gossiping and talking about eventually finds out that you have been doing this behind their back, you will lose a good friend if that person was your friend to begin with, or you will end up making an enemy if that person was not a close friend.

One verse below says that **"a brother offended is harder to win than a strong city."** Two other verses say that **"a whisperer"** and one who **"repeats a matter"** will **"separate the best of friends."**

Many people have lost some of their best friends as a result of getting caught talking behind their backs and spreading personal information about them. Once that personal trust has been violated to any significant degree in a good friendship, it will be very hard to get them to ever be able to trust you again.

These next 6 verses are a true word to the wise.

¹⁶ But shun profane *and* idle babblings, for they will increase to more ungodliness. ¹⁷ And their message will spread like cancer. Hymenaeus and Philetus are of this sort,

2 Timothy 2:16

²³ In all labor there is profit,
But idle chatter *leads* only to poverty.

Proverbs 14:23

¹³ A talebearer reveals secrets,
But he who is of a faithful spirit conceals a matter.

Proverbs 11:13

¹⁹ A brother offended *is harder to win* than a strong city,
And contentions *are* like the bars of a castle.

Proverbs 18:19

²⁸ A perverse man sows strife,
And a whisperer separates the best of friends.

Proverbs 16:28

⁹ He who covers a transgression seeks love,
But he who repeats a matter separates friends.

Proverbs 17:9

Per the chapter that we have titled "Choose Your Friends Carefully," if you have been given several good God-friends by the Lord, really value and cherish these kinds of personal relationships and do not ever be tempted to betray their trust by engaging in unnecessary babblings and gossiping behind their back. True good God-friends are hard to find in this life.

I also believe that cussing, cursing, and swearing can also be included in what the Bible calls **"profane babblings."** There are many Christians who still like to cuss out of their flesh, even as they continue to grow in the Lord.

Let there be no filthiness nor foolish talk nor crude joking, which are out of place, but instead let there be thanksgiving.
Ephesians 5:4 (ESV)

But now you yourselves are to put off all these: anger, wrath, malice, blasphemy, **filthy language** out of your mouth.
Colossians 3:8

However, sooner or later what you will find out as you start to draw closer to the Lord in your own personal relationship with Him, is that your desire to want to keep on cussing will start to wane. Not only will you be receiving the conviction of the Holy Spirit Himself when you do start to cuss, but you will also find your own natural desire to want to keep on cussing will start to get fewer and further apart until you complete stop.

The reason for this is because you will find yourself wanting to become more pleasing to the Lord in your actions, thoughts, and spoken words. Your desire to want to please God will increase and once it does, you will start to lose all desire to want to cuss anymore because you will sense how displeasing it is to Him and that He really does find it offensive.

If you really stop and examine all of the cuss and curse words we use, most of them are either attacks directly against God, Jesus, and the Holy Spirit, or they have to do with some type of nasty bodily function. Many people cuss out of habit and they never really stop and think of the actual words they are using when they are cussing.

Just remember, God the Father is watching your every movement, your every thought, and your every action. He sees and hears every thought and every word that comes out of your mouth. If we really love our one and only Savior, then we will lose all desire to want to cuss, curse, or swear in His sight. It's not only offensive to Him, but it's also offensive to anyone else who may be around you when you start spouting off.

God Will Judge You By Your Words

[36] But I say to you that for **every idle word** men may speak, they will give account of it in the day of judgment. [37] For by your words you will be justified, and by your words you will be condemned."

Matthew 12:36-37

The above Scripture verses are direct from Jesus Himself. In this verse, Jesus tells us that we will have to give a direct account to Him for **"every idle word"** that we may speak in this life. He says that we will either be **"justified"** by the good words we have spoken in our lives, or be **"condemned"** by any of the bad words we may have spoken.

In other words, not only does God the Father want us to get our speech in order in how we relate to other people, but He is also going to be holding every single one us personally accountable with how we have spoken and expressed ourselves to other people in this life.

This is a very serious warning being given to us by our Lord – and how we talk and express ourselves to other people in this life should never, ever be taken for granted.

God has given each and everyone us a certain amount of power with the words that we can speak out to other people – and those words can either bring life or death to the person we are speaking to.

Not only will the kinds of words you speak out to others in this life determine how many good friends you may end up making or how good those personal friendships will end up being, but your own words are also going to be appropriately judged by the Lord Himself on your day of judgment with Him.

The Golden Rule will really apply to this part of our walk with the Lord. The Golden Rule says that we should treat others like we would want them to treat us. If you apply this rule to this particular topic, you could then say that we should **"speak to others in the way that we would want them to speak to us."**

Chapter 15: In the World – But Not of the World

Many of you have heard from your pastors the title of this chapter in that we are to be in the world, but not of the world in our walk with the Lord. Not only is this a very catchy phrase and saying, but this is also a rock, solid, God-truth that is coming straight out of our Bible.

Many Christians get a bit confused when they first hear this phrase and revelation. The first question they usually have is if God is calling me to do something worthwhile and noble in my call and purpose for Him down here on this earth, then why is God telling me not to become a part **"of"** this world? How can I complete my divine call in the Lord if I do not get actively involved in the world and with other people in general?

Jesus Himself went full scale into His surroundings once He received the Baptism of the Holy Spirit and then came out of the 40 day wilderness test with the devil. From there, He embarked on a major three and a half year miracle ministry before He went to the cross to die for all of us and our sins.

During those three and half years, Jesus was constantly preaching, teaching, healing and delivering people. At first glance, it looked and appeared as if He had become an actual part of the world with how much interaction that was going on between Him and everyone else that was around Him. But as you will see in the explanations below, God the Father does want us to become actively involved **"in"** the world so that we can fully accomplish all of His perfect will for our lives.

Another problem that some Christians have with this phrase is they misinterpret what God is trying to tell them when He is making the statement that we are not to be **"of"** the world. They think they should be retreating from life and everyone in general, and some of them end up becoming monks, hermits, and recluses, hiding away from as much of the world as they possibly can.

I believe God wants His people to become very active **"in"** the world so they can make it a much better place to live, work, and play in. How can you witness, save, teach, and help deliver other people if you are not **"in"** the world trying to reach and connect with them in the first place?

I believe this particular revelation from the Lord has two sides to it. It is like looking at a two sided coin. On the one side of the coin we are to be **"in"** the world. As you will see in one of the Scripture verses below, Jesus is telling His Father not to take us out of the world, since we all have a great commission and call from Him to try and save and help as many people as we possibly can.

We cannot **"reach"** the lost, the downtrodden, the helpless, the poor, the sinners, and the people who are being held in some type of captivity if we are not **"in"** the world trying to reach them with the message and gospel of our Lord and Savior.

This is what is meant by the Lord when He tells us that we still have to continue to be living **"in"** this world. We all have to be born into this world as a result of the curse of Adam and Eve, and until it is our time to leave and depart from this life, God will expect each and everyone of us to come and work for Him.

Once you enter into a full surrender with the Lord, He will then place you into His perfect will for your life. And once God places you into His perfect will for your life, then He will lead you into the divine plan and destiny that He has set up for your life. And in that divine destiny will be your call, your missions, your divine assignments, and the specific people that He will want you to work with.

Again, you cannot properly compete your call and all of your divine assignments for the Lord if you are not willing to get actively involved "in" the world to some degree and to some extent. This is the one side of the coin where we are supposed to be "in" the world.

However, this revelation from the Lord also has a flip side to it. There is a flip side to this same coin. Though we are to be actively involved **"in"** the world to the degree that God will lead us to, we also have to realize and be very aware that we are not to become too much of an actual part **"of"** the world.

As you will see in one of the verses below, God is telling us to keep ourselves **"unspotted"** from the world. In other words, He does not want us to become spotted, contaminated, and tainted by the bad and evil things of this world. And the only way that we can keep ourselves from becoming too spotted and contaminated from this world is not to get too deep and friendly with the ways of this world.

In other words, God is asking all of us to walk a very fine line between being actively and properly involved "in" the world so we can reach and help other people – but at the same time making sure that we do not fall too deep and too far into the world where we then start to fall into the actual evil, depravity, and corruptness of this world.

The best analogy I can give you on this so that you can fully understand what the Lord is trying to convey to us in this revelation is the **"fence analogy."**

Imagine a fence line running alongside your right side as you continue to walk on the straight and narrow path that God has you set up to walk on. The phrase and saying that will come off this fence line analogy that perfectly lines up with what the Lord is trying to tell us in this revelation is that we all should be **"staying on our side of the fence."**

On your side of the fence is the divine path that you are taking for the Lord, along with all of His righteous ways on how we are to act and behave in this life with ourselves and with other people in general.

On the other side of the fence are the paths taken by those who are either not saved, or the ones who are considered to be very carnal and fleshly type Christians, whose only goals and desires in this life is to get as much out of this life while they still can. Their only goals and ambitions in this life are to try and gain as much of the material and lustful things out of this life as they possibly can before their day in the sun is finally over.

We thus live in a dual type of world. On the one side of the fence is the side of God and the righteous way that He wants us to live this life. On the other side of the fence are the unsaved sinners and carnal Christians who are not living their life God's way, and they are out breaking any law and commandment they see fit so they can satisfy their cravings for the lustful pursuits of this life.

Once you become saved and born again by accepting Jesus Christ as your personal Lord and Savior, you are now in whole different ballgame. You are now on a whole different type of playing field. God the Father perfectly lays it out for each and everyone of us in the way that He has worded the following verse.

[19] I call heaven and earth as witnesses today against you, *that* I have set before you life and death, blessing and cursing; therefore choose life, that both you and your descendants may live;

Deuteronomy 30:19

In this verse, God is giving every single one of us a big choice to make in this life. We can either choose to follow God and His ways for living in this life and **"live"** – or we can choose to follow the wicked and evil ways of this world and **"die."** This verse is one whopper, all-or-nothing, black and white, straight-to-the-point verse direct from the mouth of the Lord Himself.

Notice God says absolutely nothing about any type of middle or neutral grounds with this proclamation.

Either we choose to follow God and live this life the way that He wants us to live it – or we can choose to follow the ways of this world and eventually bring down death and cursing upon us and possibly those who may be close to us.

Notice in this verse that God is telling us that we must **"obey His voice,"** which means that we have to follow directly after Him and all of His ways for us in this life, not after the ways of this world or anyone else in this world.

The Scripture Verses

Now here are 5 very good verses from the Bible that are giving us this specific revelation in that we are to be in the world, but not of the world.

I will first list each one of the verses one right after the other, and then I will point out and highlight several key words and phrases in these verses.

[19] If you were of the world, the world would love its own. Yet because you are not of the world, but I chose you out of the world, therefore the world hates you.
John 15:19

[14] I have given them Your word; and the world has hated them because they are not of the world, just as I am not of the world. [15] I do not pray that You should take them out of the world, but

that You should keep them from the evil one.
                                                    John 17:14-15

²⁷ Pure and undefiled religion before God and the Father is this: to visit orphans and widows in their trouble, *and* to keep oneself unspotted from the world.
                                                    James 1:27

¹⁵ **Do not love the world or the things in the world. If anyone loves the world, the love of the Father is not in him.** ¹⁶ **For all that** *is* **in the world**—the lust of the flesh, the lust of the eyes, and the pride of life—is not of the Father but is of the world. ¹⁷ And the world is passing away, and the lust of it; but he who does the will of God abides forever.
                                                    1 John 2:15

⁴ Adulterers and adulteresses! **Do you not know that friendship with the world is enmity with God? Whoever therefore wants to be a friend of the world makes himself an enemy of God.**
                                                    James 4:4

Notice in the first two verses that Jesus is specifically telling us that we are not to be **"of the world."** He then goes one step further in the third verse from James when He tells us that He wants us to remain **"unspotted"** from the world.

Jesus then perfectly wraps it up in the last two verses when He tells us that if we ever get to the point where we have become too friendly with the world and the ways of it, then we will literally become the enemy of God Almighty Himself!

When Jesus Himself is telling us that we will become His Father's enemy if we become too friendly and too attached to the ways and material things of this world

– you know we are dealing with a very serious warning from the Lord on this issue!

Jesus points out to us that all of the lustful pursuits and things of this life will eventually pass away when we die and cross over. In another verse, Jesus has already told us that what good will it do a man to gain all the wealth of this world as his possessions, but then lose his own soul in the pursuit and acquirement of all of that wealth. It will all have ended up being for naught when everything is all finally said and done.

Chapter 16: God is No Respecter of Persons

Part of the sanctification process that God the Father would like to start with each and everyone of us is to make sure that our minds get properly renewed according the knowledge and revelation that is in His Word. In other words, we have to learn how to develop right thinking in our minds and in our thought process. In order to get our minds properly renewed where we can start thinking right about things, the Holy Spirit will be moving very strongly to **put in** what He does want you to be thinking right about, and **taking out** what He does not want you to be thinking about.

One of the very first areas that you will really need to get a grip on in this area is to learn that God the Father is no respecter of persons. What this means is that every single man and woman He has ever created is on an equal footing with Him. What this means is that He has an equal and unconditional love for each person He has ever created and He is not going to be playing favorites with anyone.

As you will see in the Scripture verses I listed below, they are all telling us that God the Father is no respecter of persons and that He will not be showing any type of partiality or favoritism to anyone.

What this means is that God will work with each person who will properly come to Him with the same amount of intensity and to the same degree that He will work with anyone else. In other words, there will be equal treatment for everyone!

This means we will all have an equal chance to be able enter into God's perfect plan and destiny for our lives – and then allow Him to build that life up and take it into the specific directions that He will want to take it in.

Part of the problem in this area is that the Body of Christ is divided into one of two main camps. In the one camp is the born again Christian who has fully surrendered his entire life over to the Lord and is willing to enter into God's perfect plan and destiny for his life.

As a result of making this kind of full surrender to the Lord, God is now working and building up this person's life to its maximum capabilities and possibilities in this life. This fully surrendered born again Christian has a very active and powerful walk with the Lord as a result of being willing to come into this full surrender with the Him.

And then you have the second camp, which is where I believe most Christians are living in today – and that is out of the perfect will of God for their lives. In other words, they have never made that full surrender with the Lord where He would be the One to fully guide and direct their lives into the specific directions that He would want it to go in.

As a result of this extreme contrast between these two camps, you have Christians who are walking in this second camp, which is out of the perfect will of God for their lives, wondering why the fully surrendered born again Christian is getting all of the good activity and blessings in their lives and they are not getting anywhere in their lives with the Lord.

The fully surrendered born again Christians have meaning and purpose in their lives. They know where they are going with the Lord and they now have God's anointing, blessing, and favor operating in their lives so they can make it to the tops of the mountains God is asking them to climb for Him. And all of this positive activity is being brought into their lives as a result of being willing to fully surrender their entire lives over to God the Father for His direction and handling.

The Christians who are living and walking in the second camp are calling all of their own shots and running all of their own shows, and many of them are getting absolutely nowhere in this life as a result of trying to do all of this on their own.

As a result of these divided two camps in the Body of Christ, you have many Christians who are in this second camp being very jealous and envious of all of the good works and fruit that the fully surrendered born again Christian is producing for the Lord. But instead of trying to see the truth as to why these fully surrendered born again Christians are getting this kind of blessed activity with the Lord in the first place, they start getting mad at God and start accusing Him of playing favorites with a certain amount of His people, much like what siblings will do with their own natural parents if they think one of the other siblings is getting preferential treatment from one or both of the parents.

The Bible says that the truth will set you free, but you first have to be willing to see what that truth is and then fully understand it before it can start to work to set you free.

If you are not willing to see that fully surrendered born again Christians are receiving this kind of blessed and meaningful life from the Lord all as a result of making this full surrender with Him – then you will continue to stay stuck and grounded right where you are at, and you will continue to throw pity parties and blame everyone else for your miserable and unproductive life, including God Himself.

Bottom line – because the Bible tells us so – God the Father is no respecter of persons, and He will not be showing any type of partiality or favoritism to any man or any woman He has ever created.

What this means is that you will have no excuse on your day of judgment with the Lord as to why you did not have a more blessed, active, productive, and fruitful life for Him while living down here on this earth. You will have nobody to blame but yourself if you have chosen with your own free will to run your own life and call all of your own shots rather than turning your entire life over to God the Father for His direction and handling.

Now here are 4 very powerful and profound verses from the Bible that is giving us this powerful revelation from the Lord. The first verse is from the Original King James Version. This will be the verse that will give you the specific wording that God the Father is no respecter of persons. The other three verses are from the New King James Version.

³⁴ Then Peter opened his mouth, and said, Of a truth I perceive that **God is no respecter of persons**:
³⁵ But in every nation he that feareth him, and worketh righteousness, is accepted with him.
Acts 10:34-35 (KJV)

⁶ But from those who seemed to be something—whatever they were, it makes no difference to me; **God shows personal favoritism to no man**—for those who seemed *to be something* added nothing to me.
Galatians 2:6

¹⁷ For the LORD your God *is* God of gods and Lord of lords, the great God, mighty and awesome, **who shows no partiality nor takes a bribe**.
Deuteronomy 10:17

¹⁷ And if you call on the Father, **who without partiality judges according to each one's work**, conduct yourselves throughout the time of your stay *here* in fear;
1 Peter 1:17

As Christians, we all need to grab a hold of the profound revelation that is being given to us in these four verses. Think of what God is trying to tell all of us with this revelation – that every single one of us, with no exceptions, can be treated equally and fairly with the Lord in how He will handle our lives – but only if we are willing to enter into this full surrender with Him where He will now be the One to control and lead our lives in the direction that He will want them to go in.

If you are willing to enter into this full surrender with the Lord, He will now handle both you and what He wants to do with your life with the same amount of care, love, compassion, and intensity as He would with any other fully surrendered Christian. There are no exceptions to this revelation. There is an equal amount of unconditional love, support, and guidance from God the Father for every single Christian who is willing to enter into this full surrender with Him.

This means that every single Christian has an equal chance and an equal window to become everything that God is calling them to become in Him in this life – and to fully achieve everything that He wants them to accomplish in this life.

If you will not believe that God will treat everyone fairly and justly in this realm of the full surrender – then you will never make it to the top of whatever mountain God is calling you to climb for Him in this life.

In addition to the Christians who steadfastly and stubbornly refuse to commit and surrender their entire lives over to the Lord for His full handling – you then have many born again Christians who have made this full surrender with the Lord, but they are still continuing to remain stuck and grounded in their personal walks with the Lord.

And the reason some of these fully surrendered born again Christians are remaining grounded and stuck in their walk and calls with the Lord is because they have never been able to get over the mental hurdle of being able to believe in the revelation that is being given to us in these four verses in that God the Father is no respecter of persons, which will include every single one of them.

I have met many of these types of Christians in my own walk with the Lord. When I asked these people why they could not believe in this revelation since it is being given to us direct from the Bible itself – many of them have told me that it was because of some of the bad things that their own natural fathers had done to them in their past.

Even though they know this type of thinking is wrong since it is going against what the Bible is trying to tell us, there appears to be an emotional factor that comes into play, especially if there has been any type of severe abuse from their parents, especially the father.

When a child is born into a family, God has things set up in that the parents are supposed to properly love, nourish, and care for their child as they are growing into adulthood in the family. When that proper love, care, and nourishment is not there, and all the child ever hears or receives is verbal and/or physical abuse, then the child has a hard time learning how to trust anyone as they get older. They have been so beat up from all of this dysfunctional abuse, they even have a hard time in being able to trust in God Himself, even though they know God is all-perfect, all-loving, and is no respecter of persons.

Since they were not treated fairly and justly by their natural parents, they have a hard time in being able to believe that God will treat them equally and fairly like

He would anyone else. As a result of not being able to get this revelation properly worked into their mindset and way of thinking in this life, they end up remaining stuck and grounded in their own personal walks with the Lord, and they never climb or reach to all of the goals that God would have had in store for them in this life.

This is why it is so vitally important that each and every born again Christian believe and act on this revelation – that you are just as important to God as anyone else is, and that He will give you the same amount of time, care, and attention that He would give to anyone else.

To think that the one and only all-powerful God of this entire universe can personally single you out, and tell you from His Word that you are just as important and just as precious in His sight as anyone else that He has ever created since the beginning of our world – is enough to knock you right off the couch when you really stop and meditate on this revelation.

To those of you who are having a hard time in believing in this revelation – you will simply have to make up your mind whether or not you want to try and believe on it. If you do not, then you will never fulfill the divine destiny that God would have had in store for you in this life.

You only have one chance and one opportunity to fulfill the divine destiny to which God has called you to in this life.

You can either choose to believe that God has a great plan and a great purpose for your life, and that He will give you just as much time and attention to be able to fulfill that divine destiny as He would anyone else – or you can choose to believe that our God is not who the Bible says He is.

If you believe that the Holy Bible is truly the inspired and infallible Word of God – then you have to believe what the above 4 verses are trying to tell you. God cannot lie, and neither can His Word! This revelation is money in your bank if you can believe on it, ground on it, and act on it in this life.

If you can ground on this revelation as a major foundational truth in your walk with the Lord, God can then take full control of your life and remove all obstacles, barriers, and hindrances that will keep you from flying full force into the realm of His perfect will for your life, where an incredible adventure just lies waiting for you.

The choice is yours!

One other thing once you enter into this realm with the Lord where you are now walking and operating in His perfect will for your life – do not ever compare where your walk is going in the Lord to where anyone else may be going in their walk with Him. The calls and divine assignments that God will pass your way in this life are all relative.

What this means is that if God calls you to be a stay-at-home mom for the first 20 years of your marriage so that you can properly raise up your children in their earlier formative years, that call will be just as important as someone who is being called by God to become the next president of the United States.

The little finger is just as important as the right arm in the Body of Christ.

What matters with the Lord is not what He calls you to do for Him in this life – but what you do with the call that He hands out to you. Your job is to do the best job you can at whatever God will be calling you to do for Him on a daily basis.

God will be rewarding you for how well you work for Him, not for what He will actually call you to do. If you end up doing a better job for God raising up your children in the first 20 years of your marriage than what someone does with their call of being the next president of the United States – then you will be more highly rewarded once you enter into heaven than the one who may have received the bigger and heavier call such as being called to be the next president.

This is why the Bible tells us that many who are first in this world may end up being last, and those who are last in this world may end being first once we have all entered into heaven and everyone has gone through their own personal judgments at the Judgment Seat of Christ.

Once you have entered into this full surrender with the Lord where He will now be the One who will be in total control of your life and the direction it will now be heading – your job will be to the best job you can at whatever the Holy Spirit will lead you to do on a daily basis. If you can work this kind of bottom-line truth into your mindset, you will be less likely to become jealous of other Christians who may be walking in some of the more glamorous type calls than what you may be walking in.

Remember – every Christian has a vital and important part on God's team. The job of the teacher or the pastor is just as important as the job of the evangelist, prophet or apostle or even the cleaner or tea girl.

All that matters to the Lord is that you put the pedal to the metal for Him and try to accomplish, to the best of your abilities, everything that He will be calling you to do for Him in this life.

If you do – then you can leave this life knowing that you have not squandered and wasted your one and only chance to do something very meaningful for the Lord in this one earthly lifetime.
As a result, God will be highly rewarding you once you enter into heaven and meet Him face-to-face for your own personal judgment.

Chapter 17: The 9 Fruits of the Holy Spirit

As you will see in the Scripture verse I will give you in this chapter – there is one very special incredible verse that will tell you that God the Father wants to transmit and impart 9 specific fruits of the Holy Spirit up into our personalities.

God wants all of us to enter into a true sanctification process with Him so that He can begin the process of molding, shaping, and transforming us into the express image of His Son Jesus Christ. He wants to make us into a better and more holy people. He wants to transform us by the renewing of our minds. He wants to put right thinking into our thought process.

However, you will not be a passive robot in all of this. You have to be willing to work in cooperation with the Holy Spirit once He begins to start this sanctification process within you.

Your job will be to get into the Word to find out exactly what it is God is going to want to change about you. You will need to find out exactly what godly qualities God will want you to try and **"put on"** into your personality, and what qualities He will want you to try and **"put away."**

This chapter will be giving you all of the appropriate Scripture verses showing you exactly which qualities and attributes God will want to get worked into your personality, and which qualities He will want to pull out of you.

If you want to start off by keying on some of the more positive, godly qualities that God would really like to get worked into your personality – really study and meditate on these 9 specific qualities.

When God the Father purposely isolates and spells out 9 specific qualities that will be coming direct from His Holy Spirit – then He is really letting you know the extreme importance of these 9 specific fruits.

These 9 fruits are major fruits and qualities that are coming direct from God Himself – and every Christian should do the best they can to work with the Holy Spirit in getting all 9 of these fruits worked into their personality.

Here are the 9 fruits of the Holy Spirit listed one right after the other in a bolded, numbered format:

1. **Love**
2. **Joy**
3. **Peace**
4. **Longsuffering**
5. **Kindness**
6. **Goodness**
7. **Faithfulness**
8. **Gentleness**
9. **Self-control**

Now here is the specific verse from Scripture where these 9 fruits are being given to us by the Lord.

[22] But the fruit of the Spirit is love, joy, peace, longsuffering, kindness, goodness, faithfulness, [23] gentleness, self-control. Against such there is no law.

Galatians 5:22

Before I get into the appropriate commentary on each of these nine fruits, note the following:

The word "Spirit" is with a capital "S" – which means these 9 fruits are coming directly from the Holy Spirit, not from ourselves.

What this means is that God's love, God's peace, God's joy, and God's goodness can start to be transmitted up into our personality. These are His divine attributes and personality qualities that will start to move into the core of our personality.

Think about the ramifications of this – that God the Father Himself is allowing us to share in a part of His divine nature by allowing His Holy Spirit to transmit and impart these nine divine qualities right up into our soul and personality!

This is why God the Father is specifically telling us in this verse that these 9 fruits are coming directly from His Holy Spirit – so that we can all fully appreciate the magnitude of such an experience.

Jesus has already told us that He is the vine and we are the branches. The branches draw their life from the vine, not vice versa. Just as the branch draws its life from the vine, so too must we draw our life directly from Jesus. Jesus will release His divine life directly into us through the Holy Spirit in the exact same way that the vine will release the life of the tree into the branches.

In one short, but incredible powerful Scripture verse, God the Father is giving all of us an incredible revelation on what can go on behind the scenes in the spiritual realm for those who are willing to work with Him in this sanctification process.

Now I will go on to describe what each one of these nine fruits are all about and give you definitions from some of the different Bible Dictionaries and Commentaries, thereby making it easier for you to work with the Holy Spirit once He starts to move in on you to try and impart some of these divine qualities and attributes into the core of your personality.

1. Love

If I had to rank all of the above fruits in their order of possible importance, the quality of love would have to be number 1. And this is why it may have been listed as the first fruit in the above Scripture verse.

There are some very powerful and profound verses from the Bible on just this one quality alone, and it needs to have its own chapter to do it proper justice. Here are some of the different definitions on what love is from the different Bible Dictionaries and Commentaries:

1. **Unselfish, benevolent concern for another; brotherly concern; the object of brotherly concern or affection**

2. The self-denying, self-sacrificing, Christ-like love which is the foundation of all other graces

3. Unselfish, loyal and benevolent concern for the well-being of another

4. The high esteem which God has for His human children and the high regard which they, in turn, should have for Him and other people

5. To love, to have affection for someone; to like; to be a friend; the love of brothers for each other

One of the main messages that comes through loud and clear from studying our Bible is the extreme importance that God the Father is placing on that everyone learn how to love Him, love ourselves, love one another, and to even go as far as to be able to love our enemies and those who will try and hurt us.

However, our abilities as fallen humans to love one another is very limited. This is why it is so important for each and every Christian to work very closely with the Holy Spirit to get this fruit worked up into the core of our personalities.

It is only when the love of the Holy Spirit starts to flow and enter into our personalities can we even begin to love God, love ourselves, and love one another to the degree and to the intensity that God would really like to see from each one of us.

To those of you who will be entering into this sanctification process with the Lord – this quality should be listed as the number 1 quality you should really attempt to put on into the core of your soul and personality. The Holy Spirit will be moving on you very early and very quickly to get this quality imparted into your mind, soul, and emotions due to the extreme importance of it in your walk with the Lord.

You can be the greatest man of God and have some of the greatest gifts of God flowing through you – but if you are not walking with all of this in the spirit of love and humility, it will have all been for nothing.

2. Joy
In the rough and tough world we live in with all of the crime, disorder, and bad things that can happen to anyone of us at anytime, many Christians have lost a lot of their joy in the Lord as a result of some of the beatings they have taken in this life.

I remember I had a bank teller tell me one time that she very seldom sees people smiling anymore when they come in and do business with her. She says no one seems to be happy anymore and everyone seems to be carrying around the weight of the world on their shoulders.

Again, with the imperfections of our own fallen nature, and then you combine that with how people react differently to adversity – some Christians have literally had most, if not all of their joy in the Lord, knocked right out of them.

This is why the above verse from Galatians is so powerful and so needed by every single Christian today. In this verse, God is telling us that He can transmit some of His godly and divine qualities right up into the middle of us like filling up a new car with its first tank of gasoline. Many of God's people need a fresh infusion of His divine qualities due to the leaks that have occurred as a result of some of the beatings His people have taken during the course of their lives.

And the quality of joy is a much needed quality in this day and age. No matter how bad of a beating you may have taken in this life – God can still fully heal, deliver, and restore you if you are willing to work with Him in this healing process. And one of the things that God can fully restore in you is your joy in Him. And not only can the Lord fully restore what joy you used to have in Him, but He can also increase it to a much greater degree and intensity due to the wording in the above verse – with the quality of joy being one of the 9 specific fruits of His Holy Spirit!

Here are some of the different definitions of what real joy is all about:

- Great delight; gladness of heart
- The happy state that results from knowing and serving God
- That deep, abiding, inner rejoicing in the Lord
- To rejoice, to be glad
- Happy, joyful, cheerful, rejoicing, festive

Realize that God can transmit this divine quality right up into your personality – and this will be His joy, not your joy, once it starts to flow up into you. And once God starts to release His joy into your system, you won't be able to help but feel it. And once you are able to start feeling it again, it will become much easier for you to learn how to walk back in it in your own daily walk with the Lord.

The Bible says that the joy of the Lord is your strength.

This is why it is so important that every Christian have some level of God's joy operating through them in this life. Without God's joy operating in your life, things can begin to dry up. Nothing is ever fun anymore.

Everything can start to become a chore. Before you know it, you will want to start to withdraw from others and life in general.

The joy of the Lord can really give you an incredible surge of strength in your own daily walk with God – especially when you have to take on some really tough situations. This is why each Christian should work very closely with the Holy Spirit in not only getting Him to release His joy into their system, but to also keep it running through them on a very regular and consistent basis.

The Holy Spirit will do this for you if you are open to receiving this **divine infusion** from Him and are willing to work with Him to keep it properly flowing through you on a regular basis.

3. Peace
This is another major quality that we all need operating in our lives, especially with all of the uncertainty of this life and never knowing what is going to happen next.

Jobs are no longer as secure as they used to be. You never know when the company you work for may be bought out and your job will be gone in a flash. Half of all marriages are still ending up in divorce. We are all forced to constantly live under the threat of future terrorist activity, never knowing when or where the next attack will come from.

With all of this kind of heightened activity that we are all forced to deal with on a daily basis, it becomes very easy to lose your sense of peace, especially your peace in the Lord. Again, this is one of the 9 fruits of the Holy Spirit, and the Holy Spirit can really help you pick up the slack if you start losing your own sense of peace over some of the storm clouds that could come against you in this life.

Realize that the Holy Spirit has His peace to give to you and that He can give it to you in great abundance.

I have found that once His peace starts to flow up into your mind, soul, and emotions, it really is as the Bible says – a peace that surpasses all human understanding – especially when that peace comes in right in the middle of a severe storm cloud that you may be going through.

Here is how the quality of peace is described in some of the different Bible Dictionaries and Commentaries:

- The presence and experience of right relationships

- The tranquility of soul

- Sense of well-being and fulfillment that comes from God and is dependent on His presence

- The inner tranquility and poise of the Christian whose trust is in God through Christ

- Tranquility, rest, harmony, the absence of agitation or discord

The quality of peace should be one of the main qualities that you should try and get worked up into your soul through the Holy Spirit in the sanctification process. Without the peace of God operating in your life, you could become very easily rattled, shaken, tormented, and knocked right off your game in the Lord the first time any kind of adversity should ever come your way.

4. Longsuffering
One of the main definitions of the word longsuffering is that it is referring to patience. And patience is another sorely needed quality in the fast paced world in which we live in today.

Just watch people standing in line at the grocery store or at your local fast food restaurant and watch how short some people's fuses are today. Road rage is still a major problem on some of our highways. Look at someone the wrong way and they will want to try and take your head off. Many people have been killed or seriously injured because someone lost his temper over something that was very trivial.

With the fast-paced ways of our society, many people have had their fuses shortened up and it thus takes very little to set them off. As a result, many people have very little patience operating in their personalities today.

For Christians, this poses a major dilemma. One of the ways of our God is that He is a very patient and longsuffering God. His ways are not our ways. And one of the things you will find out very early on about His ways is that He works on a much slower time frame than we do. And unless you learn to adjust to His slower way of working things out, you will find yourself easily losing your patience with Him and how He wants to work things out in your life.

God operates on a much longer and slower time frame than we are used to operating in the fast paced world in which we live in. You will really have to work with the Holy Spirit on this particular quality to get it properly worked up into your personality. The reason for this is that your own impatience will start to act up and try to override the patience and longsuffering that the Holy Spirit will try and transmit to you. At times, it may become of battle of wills – your will against His will.

But once the Holy Spirit starts to try and manifest this quality up into your personality, then you have to try and move with it and allow it to get worked into your mind and emotions. If you do, then His patience will start to override your impatience, and before you know it, your fuses will start to lengthen and you will not lose your patience like you used to do.

Here are the different definitions for the word longsuffering:

- Forbearance, patience

- Patient endurance and steadfastness under provocation

- Forbearance under ill-will, with no thought of retaliation

- Patience, endurance, steadfastness and forbearance

- Forbearance under suffering and endurance in the face of adversity

- Ability to endure persecution and ill-treatment

With the way all of these definitions are reading, you can really see why we all need the patience and longsuffering of the Holy Spirit to start operating in our souls and personalities – especially when we are forced to face any kind of adversity. Sometimes it will be the patience and longsuffering of the Holy Spirit that will be the only thing that will give you the ability to last the entire length of a bad trial.

Learn how to ride and flow with the patience of the Holy Spirit in your daily life and walk with the Lord – and you will then be able to enter into a much more restful, peaceful state within your mind and emotions.

5. Kindness

As a result of more people being impatient, having short fuses, and with everyone always being in a hurry – many people have lost the ability to treat others with kindness and respect. A kind word, a kind action to another person can really do wonders for them.

When you really study the life of Jesus in the New Testament, you can really tell how kind He always was with other people in His dealings with them. Jesus is without question, the ultimate role model for all of us of someone who was fully walking and operating in all 9 fruits of the Holy Spirit.

The quality of kindness will go hand in hand with the quality of love. Once the Holy Spirit starts to transmit His love up into you, the quality of kindness will follow right along with it. It will then become much easier for you to be able to be kind to others once the love of God starts to flow more into your personality.

You cannot help but be more kind to others if God's love is flowing through you. This is why the quality of love has to be the main quality that you really concentrate on getting more of from the Holy Spirit.

Once the love of God starts to flow and operate through you to touch others, many of the other fruits of the Holy Spirit will then start to follow right after it in domino fashion.

Here are some of the different definitions of what real kindness is all about:

- Quality or state of being kind

- The steadfast love that maintains relationships through gracious aid in times of need

- Goodness of heart, serviceable, good, gracious, pleasant

- Love for mankind, hospitality, acts of kindness, readiness to help, human friendship, benevolence, taking thought of others

- Goodness in action, sweetness of disposition, gentleness in dealing with others, affability

- The ability to act for the welfare of those taxing your patience

As you can see from some of these different definitions, this is a very beautiful quality to have transmitted up into your soul and personality by the Holy Spirit. Not only will you be able to touch others with this godly quality, but you will also be able to touch yourself – because you will feel so much better about yourself if you can learn how to treat others with much more kindness and respect in your daily dealings and affairs with them.

6. Goodness
The Bible says that it is the goodness of God that will lead sinners to repentance and salvation. The quality of goodness is another real powerful quality to have operating through you.

This particular quality has a real drawing power to it. Not only does the goodness of God draw people direct to Him, but this fruit of goodness operating in a believer can also draw people direct to God through the actual believer.

Spirit-filled saints who are walking with many of these fruits operating through them are like a magnet. Many people who have been saved through an individual believer say that what drew them in was the love and goodness they saw shining through that believer.

Jesus says that we are to carry His light and let that light shine before men and not attempt to hide it. Part of His light are these 9 fruits of the Holy Spirit shining through an anointed believer. Nonbelievers are really drawn to someone who has some degree of these nine fruits manifesting through their personalities.

However, there is something extra special about the quality of goodness. Many Christians can effectively witness to others by just living right and being a good example and role model for others to follow. Many nonbelievers carefully watch and study some Christians because they know there is something really different about them.

One of the key qualities a nonbeliever will pick up on in a solid Christian is this quality of goodness. This quality has an ability to really get down deep into the core of a believer's personality. To those who really have this quality, you can tell that it is something operating deep down inside of them. This quality is not something that waivers like some of the other qualities can do. These people are good down to their very cores of their personalities. You can see it and feel it when you get around these types of people.

As a result of seeing this God-like goodness deeply ingrained into their personalities, there is an immediate drawing towards them. You feel totally safe being around them because you know you can totally trust them, and you know they would never deliberately hurt you.

Children are quick to sense and pick up on this quality in people who really have it. These types of Christians draw children and adults to them like magnets. This is why this particular fruit and quality is so important for each Christian to have. Because with it, you can easily draw many more people to the Lord.

If the goodness of God will lead people to repentance and salvation with Him – then the goodness of God operating through an anointed believer will have the ability to draw nonbelievers into salvation. And the goodness of God can be transmitted and worked up into your personality through the power of the Holy Spirit. You can have the actual goodness of God shining through you to reach others if you are willing to work with the Holy Spirit in this sanctification process.

Now here are some of the different definitions of what this quality is all about:

- Beneficence, ready to do good, love in action

- Kindness in actual manifestation, virtue equipped for action, a bountiful propensity both to will and to do what is good, intrinsic goodness producing a generosity and a Godlike state or being

- The word beneficence means the fact or quality of being kind or doing good

This particular quality is a very powerful fruit to have operating in your personality because of the drawing power it has in it. And the beautiful part about this fruit is that this quality is so pure in its goodness – it does not have any manipulative qualities within it.

In other words, a truly good person could not even begin to try and use you or manipulate you for their own personal gain because they are too good and righteous to even begin to think along those lines. This is why these kinds of people are so trustworthy and why so many people are drawn to them – because you feel so safe by just being around them.

7. Faithfulness

In the times we live in with half of all marriages still ending up in divorce, and with many people getting back-stabbed in the workplaces with people they thought they could initially trust – this particular quality is one that is really needed in our day and age. This quality is not only needed in our own personal relationship with God, but it is also needed in our own personal relationships with our friends and our families.

Once you are saved and have entered into a true personal relationship with the Lord – one of the first things you will really have to grab a hold of is holding fast to the Lord and staying faithful to Him for the rest of your eternal life. Once you are saved and have entered into a true personal relationship with the Lord, there is no turning back – ever!

This is what got the Jewish people in major trouble with God the Father back in the Old Testament. They could not stay faithful and loyal to Him on a consistent and regular basis. There were times that God the Father was literally calling them harlots and adulterers because they would not stay faithful to Him, especially when they kept chasing after other gods.

God the Father really holds this particular quality in high esteem, and this is one quality that He will really expect you to operate very strongly in – not only in your own personal relationship with Him, but also in your other personal relationships with your family and friends. In other words, He wants you to be faithful and loyal to your spouses, to your children, to your parents, and to your good friends.

Too many people are bailing out from their spouses and their children if they hit a few minor speed bumps in their marriages. Too many spouses are having affairs behind their spouse's back, thereby destroying all of the trust and faithfulness that may have been built up in the early years of their marriages. Too many fathers are bailing out of their marriages, and then forgetting and forsaking their own children – and sometimes for good, never wanting to see any of them ever again!

If God brings you a wonderful mate, wonderful children, and good and wonderful friends – then He will expect you to stay loyal and faithful to all of them in your own personal relationships with them. A true friend will stay by your side for life – through thick and thin and for better or for worse. Just as God will stay faithful to you in His own personal relationship with you – He will expect you to stay loyal and faithful in your own personal relationships with the other people in your life.

Now here are what some of the different Bible Dictionaries and Commentaries have to say about this particular quality:

- Fidelity which makes one true to his promise and faithful to his task

- Steadfast, dedicated, dependable and worthy of trust

- Steadfast, unchanging and thoroughly grounded in relation to the other

- Dependability, loyalty and stability

With the self-centered and materialistic world in which we now live in, where many people's only goals and ambitions are to get as much as they can out of this life while they still can – I am afraid this is one quality that is in very short supply. Most people are lucky if they manage to make 2 or 3 good, loyal, and faithful friends in this lifetime.

This is one quality that God the Father is really watching all of us on. He is watching who is going to stay true, loyal, and faithful to Him – and who will stay true, loyal, and faithful to the friends and family that are brought into our lives.

The flesh is strong – especially in the area of wanting to satisfy its lust for the material things of this life. This is why this quality is one of the 9 fruits of the Holy Spirit. We all need the faithfulness of the Holy Spirit worked into us to help us keep loyal to God, family, and friends.

8. Gentleness

Many men may draw back a bit from this next fruit, which is the quality of gentleness. Whether some of the liberals like it or not, Jesus was fully incarnated into a human flesh body – but this incarnation was done as a man – fully Man and fully God. He was not incarnated into the body of a woman, no matter how any liberal tries to spin this basic fact, with many liberals trying to make God gender neutral.

Since Jesus walked our earth as a man – the Son of Man – study His actions very carefully when you read the gospels and how He handled different types of people. There were times that He would engage and set people straight, like He did with some of the Scribes and Pharisees. But there were other times that He dealt with people very gently, with kindness and love. His gentle way of handling some of these people is what really jumps out at you when you really study how He handled different types of people.

Again, Jesus is the perfect role model for all of us to study and learn from – especially with how He handled people while He was walking down here on our earth. For men in particular, His actions and behavior towards others should be a major study for all of us and we should seek to pattern our own daily walk after Him. And one of the divine qualities that He had operating in Him with great abundance was the quality of gentleness.

The quality of gentleness is another major quality needed in our world today. So many people have been beat up and hurt in their dealings with other people – that just a gentle word, a gentle touch from another Christian can really open up the door for that person to be able to receive Jesus and His healing, saving, and deliverance power into their lives.

Once you really start walking in the Holy Spirit with His divine fruits operating and flowing through you – you will really be able to feel and sense when you should handle a certain person or a certain type of situation with more of a touch of gentleness rather than with any kind of stern rebuke or condemnation. There is a time for tough love – but there are also times that just a gentle and loving touch is all that is really needed to properly handle a certain situation.

The Holy Spirit will guide you in all of this. Just realize that the quality of gentleness is one of the 9 fruits of the Spirit, and this is one of the fruits that He would really like to get worked into your personality, especially in being able to use it when dealing with and helping out others.

Parents especially need this fruit operating through them, as it is very easy to get out of balance with the way you are correcting your children. Sometimes more of a tough love approach is needed, but at other times more of a gentle approach will be better suited for the situation.

If all your children ever hear from you are stern words of rebuke and criticism, and it is never properly balanced out with words and actions of love, kindness, and gentleness – then after a certain period of time your children will start to pull away from you, and they then will have no more desire to want to establish any type of good, solid, loving relationship with you.

Now here are some of the different definitions on the quality of gentleness:

- Mildness combined with tenderness

- Gracious, kindly disposition, controlled strength

- A disposition that is even-tempered, tranquil, balanced in spirit, unpretentious and that has passions under control

- A character that is equitable, reasonable, forbearing, moderate, fair and considerate

- Power and strength under control

- Willing to pardon injuries, correct faults. One who rules his spirit well

Not only will other people love and gravitate towards you more if you learn how to walk in this quality – but you will be at much more peace with yourself since you won't always have to be fighting and striving with others when trying to help them out.

9. Self-Control

Last, but not certainly least, is the quality of self-control. **This one is huge, and I mean huge!** Once you start to enter into a true sanctification process with the Lord – expect the Holy Spirit to move on you very early with this specific quality. The reason for this is that we all have a certain amount of character flaws operating in our personalities. There are some bad and negative qualities that will have to go.

The Bible tells us that our spirits and our flesh will war against each other in this life. Our flesh wants immediate self-gratification at all costs and will stop at nothing to try and get it. Our spirits know that some of our fleshly desires are not right for us and as a result, there will be a tug of war between the two – and sometimes it will be a major tug of war. And the only thing that will be able to control and curb some of the desires of our flesh is the quality of self-control.

Since we all live in a very self-centered and materialistic type world today, many people have very poor impulse control. If they see something they immediately want, they will do anything they can to try and get it. They will not be denied until they get what they are going after. These people are obviously very weak in the quality of self-control. This is why the Bible tells us that if we can learn how to really walk in the Holy Spirit, then we will not fulfill the lusts of our flesh.

Due to our fallen and sinful natures, all of us are weak to some degree in the quality of self-control. This is why God the Father made sure to have this fruit listed as one of the 9 fruits of His Holy Spirit. We all need God's self-control operating in our lives and in our personalities if we are going to have any hope in getting cleaned up and properly sanctified to the degree that He would like to get us to in this life.

If you do not have God's self-control operating through you – you will have very little victory over such things as bad tempers, judgmental and critical spirits, an unforgiving spirit, and vices such as smoking and the abuse of alcohol.

Once the Holy Spirit starts this sanctification process within you – be prepared for some major battles and tugs of wars with Him once He starts coming after some of the negative qualities operating in your personality.

But if you are willing to yield to Him and allow Him to start to work all 9 of these fruits into your personality – then you will find yourself starting to grow in ways and in areas that you never thought were possible in this life. His supernatural power in this area will blow you away once you see how far He can really take you to become the person that God would like you to become in Him in this lifetime.

Here are some of the definitions of what the quality of self-control is all about:

- Temperance, rational restraint of natural impulses

- Sober, temperate, calm and dispassionate approach to life, having mastered personal desires and passions

- Calls for a self-disciplined life following Christ's example of being in the world but not of the world

- Restraint or discipline exercised over one's behavior

The above definitions perfectly describe what God is looking for once He starts to work and transmit this quality up into our personalities. This specific quality is one of the major keys in being able to get any kind of victory over some of the lusts and desires of our flesh.

Chapter 18: The Power of Love

This chapter will serve as a follow up to our chapter titled, "The 9 Fruits of the Holy Spirit." In that chapter, I gave you the verse from Galatians where the Lord is telling us there are 9 specific fruits that He can transmit up into our personalities through His Holy Spirit. In this verse from Galatians, the very first quality that is listed as one of the 9 fruits of the Holy Spirit is the quality of love – and I do not think this was by accident!

As you will see in the Scripture verses I will list below, there is no doubt in my mind that the quality of love is the number 1 quality that God would like to get worked into our souls and personalities. Even nonbelievers, atheists, and agnostics can see the power of love and how it has the ability to change people and their lives when it is properly handled and walked out.

Hollywood has made tons of movies just on the power of love – especially the special love that can occur between a man and woman in a romantic relationship. Even hard, tough, grown men can be brought to tears when watching a real well made movie made about the power of love.

The quality of love is truly universal – as it literally transcends peoples, nations, and religions. Love is truly the universal language of this world, and people from all different walks of life recognize it for what it truly is and understand the power that is in it.

Then when you read and study the Bible – you see the major emphasis God the Father is placing on it when He tells us that He wants us to love Him, love ourselves, and to love one another.

So if the quality of love is recognized by all peoples and all nations, then why is it that throughout the course of human history there has been so many wars, so much hatred, so much crime, and so much inhumanity done to our fellow man? If everyone knows what love is, then how could so many people throughout the course of our human history commit the evil and atrocious acts they have committed?

Even in our present day and age people still have not learned from the past, as there is just as much hatred and evil operating in this world today as there has ever been. The Bible even tells us that the love of many will grow cold in the latter days, which means things are going to actually go from bad to worst in the coming years.

If man really knows what love is, then why can't more people act, operate, and walk in that love so we can all live in peace and harmony with one another? Why do so many people have to rob, rape, kill, plunder, and steal from one another? No matter what one's religious beliefs and ideologies may be – there is simply no excuse for some of the horrible barbaric acts of murder, assaults, abductions, robberies, and rapes that we see on an everyday basis.

As Christians, we all know that part of the answer as to why men cannot love one another in the way that God would really like from us is due to the fallen sin natures that we have all been born into this world with as a result of the curse of Adam and Eve. The Bible tells us that every single one of us has been born into this world in sin and iniquity. This is why Jesus had to come to die for all of us – because we have all sinned and have fallen way short of the glory of our God.

However, even born again believers have problems in being able to walk in love to the degree that God would really like in our everyday lives. We all know that God is expecting us to be able to walk in His love – but we still have problems in being able to love God, our families, our friends, and even own selves to the degree and intensity that He would really like from all of us.

We read in the Bible about all of the verses that God wants us to walk very strongly in this quality, but we still seem to fall way short of being able to actually do it in our real lives. If we all have the Holy Spirit living and operating on the inside of us, then why is it that we cannot seem to draw more of His love up into our personalities so that we can all walk with more of this quality operating in our lives?

I believe the answer lies in the previous chapter titled, "The 9 Fruits of the Holy Spirit."

Too many Christians are trying to walk in the quality of love operating out of their own strength, out of their own emotions, and out of their own flesh. Granted, God the Father wants us to do the best we can to try and put this quality into the core of our personalities. But our best is not going to be good enough in this area to get the job done with the way God would really like.

The reason for this is that we have all been born with these fallen, imperfect, and sinful natures. This means that we are not capable of walking in perfect love, no matter how hard we may try in our own natural strength. So what is the answer if we are not capable of walking in perfect love in the way that our Lord would really like for us to be able to do?

To those believers who are really wanting to learn how to walk in the real love of God in their lives – there is only one way to be able to do this – and that is to learn how to draw that love from the Holy Spirit.
And the only way that you can get the Holy Spirit to release His love into you as one of His 9 fruits is that you have to be willing to enter into a true sanctification process with the Lord where He can then begin to start the process of transforming you into the express image of His Son Jesus Christ.
There is no other way! There are no other shortcuts that you can take to get this accomplished. It is only when the very love of God Himself starts to flow into your personality can you even begin to love God, love yourself, and love other people to the degree and intensity that He would really like from you.

Once the Holy Spirit begins this sanctification process in your life – your job will be to learn how to live, walk, and operate in the divine qualities and attributes He will start to transmit into your personality.

Once the Holy Spirit starts to transmit His quality of love into the very core of your personality, your job will then be to learn how to walk in that love in your words and actions with others. Actually, once the Holy Spirit starts to transmit and impart His divine love into you, it will then become much easier for you to be able to love others in the way God wants you to be able to love them.

Once you start to feel God's love for His people, you won't be able to help yourself in feeling that same love for them since God's love will start to mesh with your own natural love. Once God's love starts to flow and mesh into what limited love you already have in your personality – then you will be able to start to love other people in the way that God had initially intended for all of us to be able to do.

The missing ingredient in all of this is obviously the love of the Holy Spirit. It is only when the Holy Spirit starts to release His love into your personality as one of His 9 fruits can you truly begin to love God, love yourself, and love other people in the way God intended.

Trying to love others with what limited imperfect love you may already have operating in you will never get the job done – either to your own satisfaction or to the satisfaction of God Himself. This is why Jesus has told us that without Him we can do nothing, especially in the area of being able to get properly sanctified in Him.

In this chapter, I will give you some of the best verses from Scripture on the quality of love, and why God the Father is placing such a strong emphasis that we learn how to walk in it in our personal relationship with Him, with ourselves, and with the other people in our lives. God the Father is really raising the bar on this one specific quality as you will be able to see with the way that He has worded some of these verses. He is making some extreme and radical statements with what He is expecting from all of us with just this one quality.

When you first read what these verses are telling us to do in reference to this particular quality, you will really be able to feel and sense your own shortcomings in this area. But again, realize this is where the Holy Spirit will be coming in big time. Just realize that God knows you cannot reach the level that He is really looking for – and that it will only be possible for you to reach this level only if the love of the Holy Spirit Himself is operating and flowing through you.

When you really study and meditate on the verses I will list below, you can sum all of them up in one simple statement. God is looking for you to be able to love in 6 different areas – all with the love of the Holy Spirit being available to you to help you out in each one of these areas. God wants you to be able to fully love in all 6 of these realms. You are to learn how to:

- **Love God**
- **Love yourself**
- **Love your family**
- **Love your friends**
- **Love your neighbors**

➢ **Love your enemies**

You will notice there are 6 specific areas that God will want you to really be able to love in. Bottom line – God will want you to love right across the board – from loving Him down to being able to love the worst of your enemies. The first 4 areas are much easier to learn how to do than the last two areas – especially the last one in being able to love your enemies and those who will try and hurt you in this life.

Loving most of your family and friends is very easy because of the strong natural bonds that we have already established with them. But learning how to love some of your neighbors who you have no real special bond with, or complete total strangers will be much harder for you to do, especially with the way that our world has become with so many more people keeping to themselves and being afraid to trust anyone.

However, this can be done with the help of the Holy Spirit. Once you start to feel the love of God Himself for some of these people, it will then become much easier for you to befriend some of these people and help them out when the need may arise.

Again, Jesus is the perfect example of someone who was always helping total strangers. When you study what He did as He was walking on our earth, He was always stopping and talking to people, along with helping, teaching, saving, healing and delivering some of these people when the need would arise. He was always there to meet their needs, especially their spiritual needs.

Just as Jesus was able to walk in perfect love in His words and actions with other people – so too can we learn how to walk in that same godly love if we will allow the Holy Spirit to enter us into this sanctification process where God the Father can then begin to work all 9 fruits of His Holy Spirit up into the very cores of our personalities.

Though we will never be able to love in the perfect way that Jesus can since none of us will ever become the fourth person of the Holy Trinity – we can still try to do the best we can in our dealings and relationships with other people.

Now I will give you some of the best and most profound verses from the Bible on the quality of love, how powerful of a thing it really is, and exactly what God the Father is looking for from each one of us in this area. I will break these Scripture verses down under their appropriate captions so you can fully grasp the revelation the Lord is trying to give you in this area.

1. Love is the Greatest of All the Virtues
These first two verses really set the stage on how high God is really ranking the quality of love. As you will see with the way these two verses are being worded, God the Father is placing the quality of love as number 1 in the entire scheme of things.

The first verse lists three specific virtues, with faith being one of them. And then it ends stating that love is the greatest of these three virtues – including being greater than faith itself. Just stop and think for a minute what God is trying to tell us with just this one statement in that having the love of God operating and flowing through us is even better and greater than having higher levels of faith in Him.

Without faith in God – we cannot connect to Him. Without faith in God – there can be no miracles. Faith is our lifeline to the Lord. Without faith in God, we would be spiritually dead in the Lord. So why would God say the quality of love is even greater than our lifeline to Him, which is our faith?

I believe God is trying to tell us something very important with this statement, and the apostle Paul perfectly captures what that something is in the second verse I will list below. Paul makes one of the most classic statements ever made on the importance of love and how this quality fits into the big picture as far as God is concerned.

Paul says that you can have the greatest gift of tongues, the greatest gift of prophecy, the greatest understanding of all the mysteries and knowledge of God, have the highest levels of faith in God, and do some of the greatest works for God – but if you do not have the love of God operating in your life, then all of this gifting, power, knowledge, and works in the Lord will all be for nothing! I repeat – all for nothing!

It will have all been for naught when you have to end up giving a full account of yourself to the Lord on your day of judgment with Him. Bottom line – all of your accomplishments in the Lord, and all of the good fruit you may have produced for the Lord in this lifetime will mean absolutely nothing to Him if you did not walk all of this out in the spirit of love.

This is why each and every Christian should make it their number 1 goal and priority in this life to learn how to walk in the love of God for their lives.

Nothing will touch other people more deeply than having the love of God shining through you and your life. With the quality of love being a universal language that everyone can understand and witness to – this quality, more than any other quality, will be the main one that can lead nonbelievers to salvation in the Lord, and lead other believers into a deeper walk with God. I do not think it is a coincidence that the quality of love is listed as the very first fruit of the Holy Spirit in the verse from Galatians on the 9 fruits of the Holy Spirit.

Here are the first two profound verses that will show us how important the quality of love really is in the big picture.

[13] And now abide faith, hope, love, these three; but the greatest of these *is* love.

1 Corinthians 13:13

13 Though I speak with the tongues of men and of angels, but have not love, I have become sounding brass or a clanging cymbal. [2] And though I have *the gift of* prophecy, and understand all mysteries and all knowledge, and though I have all faith, so that I could remove mountains, but have not love, I am nothing. [3] And though I bestow all my goods to feed *the poor,* and though I give my body to be burned, but have not love, it profits me nothing.

1 Corinthians 13:1-3

This last verse from Paul perfectly puts the quality of love in proper perspective for all of our lives, in that everything we do for the Lord has to be done in love.

2. Walk in Love

These next set of verses will tell us that we all have to learn how to **"walk in love,"** how to **"stir up love,"** and how to **"love from a pure heart."** They tell us that everything we do for God down here has to **"be done with love."**

These verses are all good, basic, foundational verses on the subject of love. Here they are:

5 Therefore be imitators of God as dear children. ² **And walk in love**, as Christ also has loved us and given Himself for us, an offering and a sacrifice to God for a sweet-smelling aroma.
                                    Ephesians 5:1-2

⁵ **Now the purpose of the commandment is love from a pure heart**, *from* a good conscience, and *from* sincere faith,
                                    1 Timothy 1:5

¹⁴ Let all *that* you *do* be done with love.
                                    1 Corinthians 16:14

²⁴ **And let us consider one another in order to stir up love and good works**, ²⁵ not forsaking the assembling of ourselves together, as *is* the manner of some, but exhorting *one another,* and so much the more as you see the Day approaching.
                                    Hebrews 10:24

⁸ Finally, all *of you be* of one mind, **having compassion for one another; love as brothers**, *be* **tenderhearted,** *be* **courteous**; ⁹ not returning evil for evil or reviling for reviling, but on the

contrary blessing, knowing that you were called to this, that you may inherit a blessing.

1 Peter 3:8-9

Simply put – God wants everything that we do for Him in this life to be done in love. We simply have to learn how to walk with His love operating in our lives. There is no other way to live this life but walking it out in the love of God towards Him, towards ourselves, and towards one another.

3. What Love Is

In my chapter on the 9 fruits of the Holy Spirit, I gave you the definition on love from some of the different Bible Dictionaries and Commentaries. For the sake of this chapter, I am going to go ahead and restate these definitions, and then add several more verses from Scripture on what some of the qualities that are in true love from a pure heart.

Here are some of the definitions on love from some of the different Bible Dictionaries and Commentaries:

- Unselfish, benevolent concern for another; brotherly concern; the object of brotherly concern or affection

- The self-denying, self-sacrificing, Christ-like love which is the foundation of all other graces

- Unselfish, loyal and benevolent concern for the well-being of another

- The high esteem which God has for His human children, and the high regard which they in turn should have for Him and other people

- To love, to have affection for someone; to be a friend; the love of brothers for each other

Now here are two very good verses on what is found in true love:

¹⁸ There is no fear in love; but perfect love casts out fear, because fear involves torment. But he who fears has not been made perfect in love.
1 John 4:18

⁴ **Love suffers long** *and* **is kind; love does not envy; love does not parade itself, is not puffed up;** ⁵ **does not behave rudely, does not seek its own, is not provoked, thinks no evil;** ⁶ **does not rejoice in iniquity, but rejoices in the truth;** ⁷ **bears all things, believes all things, hopes all things, endures all things.** ⁸ **Love never fails.** But whether *there are* prophecies, they will fail; whether *there are* tongues, they will cease; whether *there is* knowledge, it will vanish away.
1 Corinthians 13:4-8

This last verse from Paul is a real mouthful. True love will always be kind. True love will never flaunt itself for attention. True love will never be jealous of others and their accomplishments. True love will always be thinking of others and their welfare. True love will never rejoice or wallow in evil and sin.

The first verse from John states that there is no fear in love. Those who are trying to love you by trying to rule over you in fear do not truly love you in the way God has intended. Those husbands who are physically and/or verbally abusing their wives in an effort to try and control them with fear are not operating in true love, contrary to what they may be thinking in their warped and debased minds.

They verbally and/or physically beat their wives down and then pick them up, and then tell them how much they love them so they can keep on perpetuating this cycle of violence and abuse. This is not true love – this is pure evil!

The above verse from John says that perfect love will cast out all fear. If these men truly loved their wives, they would not be physically or verbally abusing and violating them in the ways they have been. These kind of men are an abomination to the Lord – and what they call love, God calls pure evil.

So many people's idea of love for another is to try and manipulate other people for their own personal gain and profit. The last verse from Paul says that true love will never think of evil, much less ever do evil to another – and that it will not seek its own, which means it will never attempt to love another person for their own personal gain, profit, or ego.

As a result of all the contamination that is in this fallen world, many people have lost the ability to truly love other people in the pure way that God has intended. This is why all Christians need the sanctifying work of the Holy Spirit started in their lives – so God can begin to get them cleaned up in their thinking and in the way they act towards others.

4. Loving God

Now that we know that love is the greatest of all the virtues and qualities and that God wants all of us to learn how to walk in His love – exactly where is the love to be aimed at?

The very first thing your love should be aimed at and centered on is direct to God Himself! God wants to establish a one-on-on, intimate, personal relationship with each one of us – and in this personal relationship God will want you to truly learn how to love Him from your heart and from your soul.

These next set of verses are all very intense in the way they are being worded. God is using maximum intense wording in the way that He is expressing Himself on this issue.

The first two verses are telling us that God wants us to love Him with all of our hearts and with all of our souls. In other words, God wants you to love Him with maximum intensity from your mind, heart, and emotions.

In the first verse I will show you, Jesus is telling everyone that the greatest of all the commandments of God the Father is that we learn how to love God with all of our mind, with all of our soul, and with all of our heart. When Jesus is telling us that this is the greatest of all of God's commandments – then you know the extreme importance that the Lord is placing on just this one commandment.

The other verses are telling you that God wants you to press in and seek after Him with all of your heart and with all of your soul – which again means to seek after Him with all of your mind, heart, and emotions.

These two types of verses fit perfectly together with one another. If you truly love God with all of your heart and with all of your soul – then you will want to press in and seek after Him with that same kind of intensity from your heart and soul.

Many Christians say they love God, but they really do not prove it to Him by pressing in and seeking after Him in their daily walk with Him. If you are really in love with God, then you will have a strong natural desire to want to seek after Him and include Him in every part of your daily life.

Our God is a God of maximum intensity. The Bible says that His love for us is like a consuming fire. In the same way, God would like to have that love returned back to Him with some level of intensity from our mind and our heart. This can be done with the help of the Holy Spirit. The Holy Spirit can begin to transmit His divine love into your personality as one of His 9 fruits so you can then start to learn how to love God in the way and with the intensity that He would really like. Again, all of these verses are major foundational verses on the love that God would like all of us to have for Him in our own personal relationship with Him.

[36] "Teacher, which *is* the great commandment in the law?"

³⁷ Jesus said to him, "'You shall love the LORD your God with all your heart, with all your soul, and with all your mind.' ³⁸ This is *the* first and great commandment.
Matthew 22:36-38

⁶ And the LORD your God will circumcise your heart and the heart of your descendants, to love the LORD your God with all your heart and with all your soul, that you may live.
Deuteronomy 30:6

¹³ And you will seek Me and find *Me,* when you search for Me with all your heart.
Jeremiah 29:13

²⁹ But from there you will seek the LORD your God, and you will find *Him* if you seek Him with all your heart and with all your soul.
Deuteronomy 4:29

¹² Then they entered into a covenant to seek the LORD God of their fathers with all their heart and with all their soul;
2 Chronicles 15:12

⁸ and tore the kingdom away from the house of David, and gave it to you; and *yet* you have not been as My servant David, **who kept My commandments and who followed Me with all his heart**, to do only *what was* right in My eyes;
1 Kings 14:8

In 1 Kings 14:8, God the Father is paying a very big compliment to King David, who ended up being the greatest King that Israel has ever had. He says that David followed after Him with all of his heart – which again is denoting someone who was following God with maximum intensity, maximum love, and maximum loyalty.

If you are truly in love with God, then you will spend some type of regular quality time seeking after Him, His ways, His knowledge, and His direct involvement in every aspect of your life.

God will become your best Friend, your best Lover, and your one and only true loving Father. This is why Jesus is referred to as the Bridegroom and we as His bride. This analogy that God is giving us is showing us the kind of intense and passionate love that He wants all of us to have in our own personal relationship with Him.

5. Loving Yourself
In addition to loving God and others, God also wants us to learn how to love ourselves. This is one area where you can really get out of balance on, with many people either going to one extreme or the other.

In the very self-centered society in which now live in, many people have gone to the one extreme of being totally narcissistic – which means they are only concerned about their own personal well-being and their own agendas to the exclusion of anyone else. The world totally revolves around them and their own personal agendas, and they will do everything and anything they can to try to get their own way on things.

Most of these types of people are incapable of bonding or loving anyone else but themselves. We all know people who are like this.

Then you have the other extreme – where some people literally want to annihilate their own personalities. They start misinterpreting certain Scriptures verses on what it means to die to one's self, thinking that God wants them to completely forget about themselves and focus entirely on serving Him and others to the total exclusion of their own selves.

When Jesus tells us that we are to die to ourselves, I believe He is trying to tell us that we are to enter into a full surrender with Him so that He is fully free to guide our lives into the perfect will of God the Father.

When you enter into a true full surrender with the Lord of your entire life – you are putting to death all of your desires, all of your goals, and all of your wants as to how you should live this life. You are now turning the reigns of your life over to God the Father so He can start to fully lead you down the divine path that He has set up for your life.

Dying to one's self does not mean that you try and totally wipe out or annihilate your personality with you who are in God. God wants to build you up in His grace, power, and knowledge. He does not want to try and destroy who you really are in Him. There are some sects in the Body that are still into self-mortification type practices such as self-flagellation.

It is just my own personal opinion that you do not have to engage in these types of extreme practices. You do not have to beat yourself into submission to God. All God is looking for is that you be willing to lay down your entire life for Him so that He can fully take over the reins of your life and lead you into the perfect plan and destiny that He has set up for your life.

The real answer in learning how to be able to love yourself in the way that God would really like is probably right in the middle of these two extremes.

The Holy Spirit will always be there to help keep you in balance with the way you are loving and treating yourself. Just realize that you have to stay on top of this part of the game – always making sure that you do not start to get too full of yourself and start sliding down to the one extreme of becoming too narcissistic and self-centered.

But you also have to make sure you do not start sliding down to the other extreme – where you start to begin to totally forget about yourself and start becoming a doormat for anyone and everyone who will want to try and use you for your goodness and generosity. Once you start to slide down into this type of extreme realm, other people will see it, and they will then try to start taking advantage of you in any way they can.

With all of the physical and verbal abuse that goes on behind closed doors in many marriages and families throughout the entire world – many people have had all of their healthy levels of self-confidence and self-esteem beat right out of them. They only do not love themselves anymore; they do not even like themselves anymore.

After hearing how no good they are, how stupid they are, how unworthy they are, and how they will never amount to anything worthwhile in this life – pretty soon they start believing in the lies of their enemy. And once they start believing in those lies, they will then start to lose all sense of healthy self-worth as to who they really are in the Lord.

For those types of people who are living and operating in unacceptable low levels of self-confidence and self-esteem – the first thing God the Father will do with you once you enter into a full surrender with Him is to start to show you who you really are in Him and the real treasure and beauty that you really are in His eyes.

The Bible says that God the Father is no respecter of persons. What this means is that every single one of us is on an equal footing with God, and that He loves each and everyone of us equally and unconditionally – which also includes you!

The Holy Spirit will really help you out in this area if you are open to receiving His help. He will show you who you really are in Christ, that you are not a nobody, that you are a somebody – and that God loves you and cares for you just as much as He loves and cares for anyone else in this life.

Really study and chew on the wording of the verses I will now list. The two key words in these verses are the words **"as yourself."**

In other words, God wants you to love yourself to the same degree and with the same intensity as you would love anyone else. God is not excluding you from this equation – He is including you. This is why He is specifically using the words **"as yourself"** in each one of these verses. Here they are:

³⁸ This is *the* first and great commandment. ³⁹ And *the* second *is* like it: '**You shall love your neighbor as yourself.**'

Matthew 22:38-39

¹⁴ For all the law is fulfilled in one word, *even* in this: "**You shall love your neighbor as yourself.**"

Galatians 5:14

¹⁸ You shall not take vengeance, nor bear any grudge against the children of your people, but you shall **love your neighbor as yourself**: I *am* the LORD.

Leviticus 19:18

I personally believe that you really cannot begin to love other people in the way that God would really like if you cannot learn how to first love yourself. This is why God is specifically using the words to love others as you would love yourself, with all of these words being in the same sentence.

6. Loving Others

God not only wants us to be able to love Him and love ourselves – but He now wants us to be able to love one another.

When God says that we are to love one another, that we are to love others, that we are to love our neighbor – I believe you can bottom-line these statements saying that God wants you to be able to love all of the members of your own family, your personal friends, your neighbors that live around you, and then any total strangers you may ever run across. In other words,

God wants you to be able to love everyone across the board of your life.

Remember, this is the second greatest commandment next to loving God Himself. This is how important this commandment is in the eyes of God. Can you imagine what would happen to this world if everyone would really obey and walk out these two specific commandments?

Here are six key verses spelling all of this out loud and clear.

¹⁷ **'You shall not hate your brother in your heart.** You shall surely rebuke your neighbor, and not bear sin because of him. ¹⁸ You shall not take vengeance, nor bear any grudge against the children of your people, but you shall **love your neighbor** as yourself: I *am* the LORD.

Leviticus 19:17

³⁴ A new commandment I give to you, that you love one another; as I have loved you, that you also love one another. ³⁵ By this all will know that you are My disciples, if you have love for one another."

John 13:34

¹² This is My commandment, that you **love one another** as I have loved you.

John 15:12

¹¹ Beloved, if God so loved us, we also ought to **love one another.**

1 John 4:11

⁷ Beloved, let us **love one another**, for love is of God; and everyone who loves is born of God and knows God.

1 John 4:7

¹⁴ We know that we have passed from death to life, because we love the brethren. He who does not love *his* brother abides in death. ¹⁵ Whoever hates his brother is a murderer, and you know that no murderer has eternal life abiding in him.

1 John 3:14-15

The last two verses from 1 John are making some maximum intense statements. The first verse says that he who cannot love his brother does not truly know God. In other words, God will not know you if you cannot learn how to love other people in your walk with Him.

The very last verse then takes it one extreme step further when it says that he who cannot love his brother abides in death, and that he is actually considered a murderer in the eyes of God, and as a murderer, he does not have eternal life abiding in him. This is about as intense of a warning direct from God Himself that you can receive on this topic.

I believe the main reason God is really laying down the gauntlet on the way that He has worded these last two verses is because if we cannot learn how to love God and love other people in this life – then we will never be able to live in harmony and unity with others. And if we cannot live in harmony and unity with other people down here on this earth, then God will not want us living up in His heaven causing strife and discord among His other children.

This is why it is so important that each and every Christian work very closely with the Holy Spirit in this sanctification process – so that we can all learn how to love God, love ourselves, and love all other people in the way that He would really like for us to be able to do.

With our own natural love not being enough to really grow in this area due to our fallen and imperfect natures – we all have to learn how to rely on the Holy Spirit so we can get Him to release His divine love into us and through us so we can begin to reach and touch others with that love.

7. Loving Your Enemies

Without any question, one of the hardest commands that the Lord has given us is that we have to learn how to love our enemies. And when He says our enemies, He is including the worst of our enemies.

How can you truly love someone who has raped you, who has severely abused you in your marriage, who has murdered someone in your family in cold-blood, or who has abducted and killed one of your children like what we see so much in the local news with pedophiles still being allowed to run rampant across this country?

It is one thing to be able to forgive this type of criminal, and then let him go into the hands of God for His vengeance, payback, and justice. But it is quite another thing to be able take a leap into this realm and actually try and love this person in the way that God would really like for us to love him.

So how can this realistically be done with some of the really bad and evil people who are still walking on this earth? I only have two possible answers for you on this issue.

One – we simply have to rely on the love of the Holy Spirit to be transmitted and imparted into us as one of His 9 fruits. I do not think most of us have this kind of love to give to someone who is simply pure evil with some of the horrible and barbaric crimes we have seen committed in recent years. You are simply going to have to learn how to ride and flow with the love of the Holy Spirit to be able to love these types of evil people in the way that the Lord would really like.

For most of us, our own natural love is not going to take us very far in this realm. This is why it is so important for each and every Christian to get this sanctification process started in their life – so God can begin to allow His Holy Spirit to release these 9 powerful fruits and qualities into the cores of our personalities.

Second – the only way you can even begin to try and do this with the worst of your enemies is that you have to attempt to see things from God's point of view and perspective. In other words, you are going to have to learn how to see your enemy through God's eyes and how He looks at them. And this is where it really gets deep and intense.

The most perfect example of someone truly loving His enemies in the way God the Father would really like is Jesus Christ Himself. After Jesus had been beat to a pulp before His actual crucifixion, and then nailed to a cross to die a slow and torturous death over a 6 hour period – Jesus makes one of the most mind-blowing statements ever made on being able to love and forgive your enemies.

Before He dies, Jesus speaks out and tells His Father to forgive all of those who had just got done crucifying Him to that cross because they really did not know what they were doing!

[34] Then said Jesus, Father, forgive them; for they know not what they do. And they parted his raiment, and cast lots.

Luke 23:34

This statement by Jesus is speaking volumes of revelation on just this one issue. You can tell by the words and tone of Jesus' statement, that He was really feeling the love of God for these people, even as they watched and jeered as He was dying on the cross.

In other words, Jesus was still loving all of these people even after they had just got done committing the worse crime that the world has even seen or will ever see again – crucifying the living Christ!

The Bible says that we are to think like Jesus and act like Jesus. We now have the mind of Christ as born again believers. This means we are to imitate Jesus in our words, in our thoughts, and in our actions in our walk with the God the Father.

If you carefully study the actual wording in the above verse, you might be able to pick up some deeper revelation as to how Jesus could have possibly made this kind of extreme statement after He had already been nailed to the cross and was experiencing the most extreme pain imaginable. The clue might be in the words "**… for they do not know what they do.**"

They obviously knew what they were doing by committing this horrible act against Jesus – but the angle Jesus might be seeing all of this from is they really did not know what they were doing in the big-picture, eternal scheme of things. If they really knew that there was a God and a devil, and a heaven and a hell, and that being cast into hell will be for all of eternity – some of them might have thought twice before engaging in such a horrible and evil act.

Some of God's prophets and seers who have been given actual visions of what hell is really like all have come back with some of the same information. Some of them were allowed to talk with people who were actually down there. And many of them have said that if they had only known that there really was a hell, and that their evil and wicked lifestyles would have led them down there, that they would have never done what they did to get themselves thrown down in there. If you look at all of the evil and wicked people in our world who have committed acts of pure, cold-blooded murder and who seem to have no real remorse for what they have done – they all know they will end up in jail if they ever get caught. Yet this still does not deter some of them from committing some of these evil and horrible acts.

But what they really don't know is if there is a hell or not – and whether or not they will get dropped down into it the minute they die and cross over.

If they really knew what was waiting for them on the other side and how horrible of a place hell really is – some of them might have thought twice before committing some of their evil acts.

This might have been what Jesus was referring to when He made the above statement in that they really did not know what they were doing – for if they did, and they knew it would get them thrown down into hell for all of eternity, they may have thought twice before actually doing it.

I do not know if this kind of deeper revelation will be enough for some of you to really be able to love an evil and vicious criminal who may have killed or hurt one of your own. This is a very deep area, and you will have to be led by the Holy Spirit to really be able to love an enemy who has viciously wronged either you or a close loved one.

But if you are able to step outside of your box for just a minute and see how this evil criminal fits into the big picture, and that he will go straight to hell if he does not get saved and get his sins forgiven before he dies – then maybe you will be able to see him in the same light that Jesus was seeing those who were crucifying Him – and love him with the love of God, just as Jesus was doing while He was hanging on that cross to die for all of us.

Maybe the love of God can flow into you because you will then see that some of these evil people really do not know what they are doing in the eternal scheme of things by choosing with their own free wills to commit some of their horrible and evil acts.

But nonetheless, God the Father would like all of us to be able to do this by the way that He has worded the following two Scripture verses. Here are the two main verses, with the words coming directly from Jesus Himself that we learn how to be able to do this:

[44] But I say to you, love your enemies, bless those who curse you, do good to those who hate you, and pray for those who spitefully use you and persecute you, [45] that you may be sons of your Father in heaven; for He makes His sun rise on the evil and on the good, and sends rain on the just and on the unjust. [46] For if you love those who love you, what reward have you? Do not even the tax collectors do the same? [47] And if you greet your

brethren only, what do you do more *than others?* Do not even the tax collectors do so? [48] Therefore you shall be perfect, just as your Father in heaven is perfect.

Matthew 5:44-48

[27] "But I say to you who hear: Love your enemies, do good to those who hate you, [28] bless those who curse you, and pray for those who spitefully use you. [29] To him who strikes you on the *one* cheek, offer the other also. And from him who takes away your cloak, do not withhold *your* tunic either. [30] Give to everyone who asks of you. And from him who takes away your goods do not ask *them* back. [31] And just as you want men to do to you, you also do to them likewise.

[32] "But if you love those who love you, what credit is that to you? For even sinners love those who love them. [33] And if you do good to those who do good to you, what credit is that to you? For even sinners do the same. [34] And if you lend *to those* from whom you hope to receive back, what credit is that to you? For even sinners lend to sinners to receive as much back. [35] But love your enemies, do good, and lend, hoping for nothing in return; and your reward will be great, and you will be sons of the Most High. For He is kind to the unthankful and evil. [36] Therefore be merciful, just as your Father also is merciful.

Luke 6:27-36

Notice in the last part of the second verse it says that God Himself is kind and merciful to the unthankful and the evil. This may be why Jesus is telling us to love our enemies – because He and His Father love everyone, including all evil sinners.

Jesus ends the first verse above telling us that we should all strive to be perfect like our Father in heaven is perfect. If God can love these evil and unthankful sinners, then He wants us to try and be able to do the same thing in our walk with Him.

8. Be Doers of the Word

Now that you know from the above Scripture verses that God wants you to love Him, love yourself, and love everyone else across the board of your life – including any enemies you may have – now God wants you to be able to show that love in your actions to others.

There are a ton of verses in the Bible about how God wants you to act towards others. I will leave you with a few good verses showing you the importance that we all learn how to be actual doers of the Word and not just hearers in reference to being able to show love to others in our words and actions.

[22] But be doers of the word, and not hearers only, deceiving yourselves.

James 1:22

[17] But whoever has this world's goods, and sees his brother in need, and shuts up his heart from him, how does the love of God abide in him?
[18] My little children, let us not love in word or in tongue, but in deed and in truth.

1 John 3:17-18

[10] Love does no harm to a neighbor; therefore love *is* the fulfillment of the law.

Romans 13:10

[17] A friend loves at all times,
And a brother is born for adversity.

Proverbs 17:17

[16] By this we know love, because He laid down His life for us. And we also ought to lay down *our* lives for the brethren.

1 John 3:16

[13] Greater love has no one than this, than to lay down one's life for his friends.

John 15:13

All of these verses are perfectly showing us what true love can really do in our relations with others. Just as Jesus was willing to lay down His entire life for all of us in order that we be able to be brought back to Him and His Father – God and Jesus are wanting all of us to love others with that same kind of intensity and loyalty – even to the point of being willing to sacrifice our life to save someone else's life if that kind of need should ever arise.

Chapter 19: Letting Go of your Past

Once you become saved and born again, the Bible tells us that we have now become new creations in Jesus Christ. Our slates have now been wiped fully clean, and we have now been given a brand new start in this life if we are willing to properly work with the Lord and allow Him to raise us up in His knowledge, grace, and power.

Making Jesus Lord over your life means that you are now willing turn the reigns of your life over to Him, and He will now lead your life into the specific directions He will want it to go in. You are now no longer your own. You have been bought back by God the Father at the price of His Son's shed blood. You now belong to God and Jesus and no one else in this life – which includes yourself, your family, and your best friends! Once you enter into this full surrender with the Lord, one of the first things God may do with many of you is to take you back in your past so He can begin to clean up any wreckage that may have occurred. Before you can really move forward into the divine destiny that God has in store for you in this life, you first may have to deal with some specific things that may have occurred in your past.

The reason for this is because too many Christians are bound up in their past – and as a result, they cannot fully live in their present.
Before you can really start to move forward in your divine destiny with the Lord – you will first have to learn how to let your past fully go.

Jesus Christ and the apostle Paul make two very profound and life-altering statements in the two verses I will give you in this chapter. For many, these two specific verses will determine whether or not you will be able to fully succeed in the divine call that God has placed on your life.

As a result of the curse of Adam and Eve that is still in full operation on this earth, we are all forced to be born into a fallen and cursed world. We are all stuck having to deal with the reality of pure evil in our lives through the activity of demonic spirits and bad and evil people who have chosen with their own free wills to live this life out on the dark side. As a result, every single one of us will get hurt to some degree and to some extent in this life. There is no getting around it. And for many, some of these hurts will end up being extreme and traumatic.

Every minute of every day someone is getting murdered, robbed, raped, abused, or abducted. We literally cannot go one day without some kind of this activity being reported on our local news channels. Jesus Himself said that a certain amount of tribulation and persecution would always come our way in this life. This is why the Bible tells us that we have to learn how to become good soldiers of Jesus Christ and learn how to put on and apply the real armor of God for our lives.

We have all been born into a war zone as a result of the curse of Adam and Eve – and unless you learn how to walk in the power and anointing of God for your life – some of these torpedo shots may knock you right out of your divine call in the Lord, if not possibly knock you right out of this life for good through an actual early physical death.

All of us to some degree have issues from our past that have to be properly dealt with before we can really proceed to walk into the perfect plan of God for our lives. Some Christians are so bound up with some of the things that has happened to them in their past – that they literally cannot get off the couch to start living again, much less ever fully fly into their divine destinies for the Lord.

Many of God's eagles have had their wings totally broken and decimated with some of the torpedo shots they have taken. Many of them are living on anti-depressants and pain killers because they can no longer handle the stress, pain, and heartache of this life.

Before an eagle of God can really start to fly into the heights that God has in store for them in this life – that eagle has got to break off any chains that may be holding them back. These chains are keeping some of God's eagles grounded. And for many of God's eagles – some of these chains are things they are still holding onto from their past. Jesus has said that He has come to set the captives free – and one of the main areas that we all have to be set free from is some of our wrong thinking that may have arisen out of some of the bad things that may have occurred in our past.

As you will see in the two verses I will list below, Jesus and the apostle Paul are telling us that we have to learn how to let go of our past. Jesus says that anyone who is trying to move forward in his walk and call for God – but keeps looking back – is not fit for the kingdom of God.

Paul says that the one thing he makes sure to do in his walk with the Lord is to forget those things which are behind him and press forward into those things which now lie ahead of him. Once you put these two verses together, one right next to the other, you get perfect revelation from the Lord on this issue.

Bottom line – you have to learn how to let fully go of your past before you can start to proceed full steam ahead in your divine destiny for the Lord. If you do not learn how to let your past fully go – you will stay stuck and grounded right where you are at, and you will never fully accomplish everything that God would've had in store for you in this life.

And that will be an eternal regret that you will carry with you once you enter into heaven and the Lord shows you how much more you could have accomplished for Him in this life had you allowed Him to unchain you from your hurtful past. The choice is yours.

You can either choose to stay fully bound up in your past, continue to throw pity parties and blame everyone and everything for your miseries – or you can choose to rise up and make a brand new fresh start with the Lord by choosing to fully surrender your entire life into His hands – and then work with Him to get your past fully cleaned up so that you can then start to fully live in the

present again, and then fly into the divine destiny that He has already planned out for your life.

For many of you who are severely bound up with things that may have occurred in your past – realize that God will give you an ample and reasonable amount of time to get your past cleaned up.

Many of you will need an inner healing from the Lord on certain issues. Though the two verses I will list below state that God wants you to let go of your past so you can fully fly into what He has in store for you in this life – God will not expect some of you to make this kind of quantum leap overnight, especially if some of your past hurts have been extreme and traumatic.

One of the things I have found out in my own personal journey with the Lord is what happens after you initially enter into this full surrender with Him. What God will do with you is take you back in your memory lane and bring back up to your remembrance many things that have occurred in your past.

The reason He will do this is so you can learn from your past. He will show you where He was at and where He was not at on certain things. He will show you some of the good things you did and some of the bad things you did so you can learn from those past mistakes and not repeat them in the future.
He will show you how He has been behind the scenes the entire time, and how He eventually ended up working out some of the bad things for His and your own good with the way some of these things ended up working out.

He will show you the extreme consequences of not fully following Him in this life, and that some of the bad things that may have happened to you were as a result of you making your own decisions without consulting Him first – not being aware of the dangers that were around that corner you were getting ready to turn into.

When God does begin to do this kind of deeper inner work with you – go with Him on it. Let Him show you the truth on many of the different matters of your past. If you do, then His truth will start to work to help set you free – no matter how bad some of the things may have been in your past.

God can fully heal you and break off any past chain if you are willing to believe that He can do it for you.

Some of God's people are bound up with false chains of guilt as a result of some of the sexual molestations that may have occurred in their dysfunctional families. God can fully break these types of chains off you, no matter how bad or how severe you think they may be.

The Holy Spirit is the Master Surgeon. He is the One who will be getting down deep into where these hurts and pains are located. If you are willing to work and cooperate with Him during this inner healing process, He will be able to cut out and completely take away most, if not all of the hurt, pain, and trauma associated with some of these painful events.

I will end this chapter with some of the specific areas the Lord will target once you open up to Him to get your past cleaned up so you can start to fully live again in your present.

But here is the point you will really need to grab a hold of off the wording of these two Scripture verses. God will take you back in your past for a reasonable length of time so you can directly deal with certain issues and problem areas He will want to target. But after that time and season has past – you will then need to let your past fully go and concentrate and focus on the present and future as to where God will now be taking you.

There will simply come a day and time that you will have to let your past and all of the hurts from your past completely go. If you don't – you will stay stuck, grounded, and paralyzed in your walk with the Lord. You will never able to fly off the edge of that cliff into the freedom and adventure that God has in store for you in this life unless you first learn how to let your past fully go.

This principle is a basic 101 principle that each and every single Christian has got to get worked into their mindsets. This basic principle could be one of the major determining factors as to whether or not you ever fly off that cliff into the divine path that God has set up for you to follow in this life.

Many of God's eagles never learn to fly with the wings that He has given them because they could not get unbound from the chains of their hurtful past. As a result, many of God's eagles will lose their one and only chance to leave their mark in this world in the divine destiny that He has set up for their lives. I believe this is why the Bible says that many are called, but few are chosen.

Many of God's people are being called to come up into His higher calling for their lives – but many of them are not being chosen because they simply could not let go of their hurtful past.

The choice to learn how to let your past fully go so you can start to fully live again in your present is an individual choice for each believer. Not even God Himself will override your free will in this area. All God can do is give you the knowledge from His Word that this is what He really wants from you, with all of it being for your own good. And then God will take you back in your past for a reasonable amount of time so you can get all of your loose ends cleaned up and tied up.

But after that time is up, God will then expect you to make a very important decision for your life. Will you now let your past fully go so you can fly into the divine destiny that He has set up for your life – or will you choose to stay stuck and grounded, wailing in the misery of your past?

Each Christian will have to make this choice for themselves. This is why the Bible says that we are transformed by the renewing of our minds. You have to learn how to develop right thinking in your thought process with how you think about and view things. And one of the first basic things you will need to learn to think right about is how to fully let go of your past.

Learn how to let fully go of your past with the help of the Holy Spirit – and then you can step from the dugout out onto the real playing field where the real action is really at with the Lord!

Now I will go to the two Scripture verses that will give us this powerful and life-changing revelation.

The Scripture Verses

Luke 9:62 is coming directly from Jesus Himself.

[62] But Jesus said to him, "No one, having put his hand to the plow, and looking back, is fit for the kingdom of God."

Luke 9:62

Notice Jesus says that **"no one"** who keeps looking back on his past is fit for His kingdom. The words **"no one"** is an all-inclusive word. It means all of us – no exceptions.

In other words, Jesus wants all of us to get a grip on this revelation and get it properly worked into our mindsets so we can all plow straight ahead into the calls and divine destinies that He has in store for us in this life.

The second verse is coming from the apostle Paul. Paul really puts this revelation in proper perspective in relation to the big picture. Here is how he puts it:

[12] Not that I have already attained, or am already perfected; but I press on, that I may lay hold of that for which Christ Jesus has also laid hold of me. [13] Brethren, I do not count myself to have apprehended; but one thing *I do,* forgetting those things which

are behind and reaching forward to those things which are ahead, [14] I press toward the goal for the prize of the upward call of God in Christ Jesus.

Philippians 3:12

Notice Paul starts out the second part of this verse with the words **"but one thing I do."** And then from there he goes into the revelation of not looking at what is behind him, but looking and reaching forward for those things which now lie ahead of him. The words **"but one thing I do"** is being put in the context of something that he is really making sure that he does on a regular and consistent basis.

This particular revelation is one that you will really have to stay on top of and not let get away from you. It's very easy to start falling back on all of the bad things that may have occurred in your past, and then use that as an excuse to start feeling sorry for yourself, or to justify some of the irrational things you may be doing.

Just because your parents may have physically abused you does not give you the right to physically abuse your own children. Just because one of your dysfunctional parents may have been an alcoholic does not mean you have to become an alcoholic yourself.

Then notice Paul ends this verse really putting everything in proper perspective when he says that what he wants to press forward on is the **"upward call of God."** God the Father has a specific plan and destiny for each person who will come to Him and fully surrender their entire lives into His hands. But you will never be able to press forward and fly into this upward and high calling unless you first learn how to let go of your past.

Both of these verses perfectly and beautifully capture this basic 101 principle. This particular principle is, without any question, a major, basic, fundamental principle that each and every Christian has to get worked into their mindset and way of thinking in this life. For many, it will be the difference as to whether or not they fully accomplish everything that God has set out for them to do in His perfect plan for their lives. Here are some specific areas from your past that you can expect the Holy Spirit to move in on very strongly if any of these are in your past and background.

- **Broken marriages**
- **Sexual abuse of any kind**
- **Physical abuse**
- **Extreme verbal abuse**
- **Being a victim of any kind of crime**
- **Dysfunctional families**
- **Death of a close loved one**
- **Any type of financial disaster**

All of these are serious torpedo shots that can knock many of us straight to the ground, especially if some of this has occurred when you were at a young age. When dealing with people who have been seriously hurt or injured like what you see with victims of any kind of crime or sexual or physical abuse – the first thing God will ask you to do is to fully forgive the person who has wronged or injured you, no matter how bad and how vicious that wrong may have been.

Chapter 20: Be Anxious for Nothing

You simply have to learn what kinds of things you are to think about and focus on in order to really be able to fly as a powerful and anointed eagle of God.

In this chapter, I will give you a very profound revelation that God the Father would like to get worked into your mindset and way of thinking. This revelation is once again coming from Jesus and the apostle Paul. In the three Scripture verses I will give you in this chapter, Jesus is telling us that we are to do the following with Him:

1. **Be anxious for nothing**
2. **That we are not to have an anxious mind**
3. **That we are not to worry about our lives and what will happen tomorrow**

I remember when I first saw these verses; I wondered how anyone could learn to be anxious for nothing with all of the bad things that could hit anyone of us at anytime. How can you be anxious for nothing when:

1. **You have just lost your job and you will now have to find another one**

2. **You have just come out of a messy and painful divorce and you will now have to start all over again**

3. **Your spouse has just been diagnosed with terminal cancer and they only have 6 more**

months to live

4. You have just caught your spouse cheating on you

5. You just found out that you son or daughter has become highly addicted to crack cocaine or meth

6. You have just become the victim of a crime such as a rape, robbery, or an assault

I could go on and on with all of the adverse things that could hit anyone of us at anytime with the full force of a hurricane. As a result of the curse of Adam and Eve that is still in full operation on this earth, we are all stuck with having to battle various types of storm clouds from time to time. And for some, these storm clouds will be downright vicious, nasty, and traumatic. Every minute of everyday someone is getting knocked straight to the ground with a vicious torpedo shot. How can anyone learn to be anxious for nothing in the way Jesus would really like from us in the sea of uncertainty that we are all forced to live and swim in – never knowing what is going to happen to us two minutes from now, much less what is going to happen tomorrow or in the days following?

I will first start out by giving you the three verses from Scripture where Jesus is telling us that this is something that He would really like all of us to learn how to do. I will then end this chapter with some comments on how we can possibly learn how to get this type of right thinking worked into our mindset and way of thinking – even if we are forced to have to deal with a major storm cloud.

Be Anxious For Nothing

This first verse from the apostle Paul really sets the stage on this specific piece of revelation.

> ⁶ Be anxious for nothing, but in everything by prayer and supplication, with thanksgiving, let your requests be made known to God; ⁷ and the peace of God, which surpasses all understanding, will guard your hearts and minds through Christ Jesus.
>
> **Philippians 4:6**

Paul gives us a major revelation in this verse with how we can be anxious for nothing with the words that come right after he initially makes this statement. Notice he says that we are to make all of our requests known to God in prayer – and if we do, then the peace of God can enter into us to guard our hearts and minds through Jesus.

In other words, if you have been hit by a severe storm cloud – go to God the Father in prayer and tell Him exactly what you will need to handle the problem. If you do, then God will hear your prayer loud and clear, and He will then move to help you handle the storm cloud.

Once you know that God is now on the job to help you take care of this severe storm cloud – then the peace of God will start to flow into your thinking and emotions because you know that God will now help you solve the problem or crisis you are now facing.

This is why Paul is using the words that the **"peace of God, which surpasses all understanding"** will now enter into you to guard your heart and mind from getting all worked up and out of control.

Once you go to God the Father in prayer to ask for His help to handle a serious problem or situation, then His peace will be able to start to flow into you. And once His peace starts to flow into you, then you will feel His peace starting to calm you down – even right in the middle of the worse kind of storm cloud you could imagine yourself falling into.

I have heard testimony after testimony of people who have fallen into the worse kinds of storm clouds you could possibly imagine – and then all of sudden they would feel the peace of God come into them after they had prayed and committed the problem into the hands of God. They had no idea how long it would take for God to resolve the problem. They had no idea as to how God was going to handle the problem. All they knew was that God had heard their prayer and that He would now handle the problem for them.

Once this fact was really grabbed by their minds and their spirits, then the peace of God was able to enter into them. And once the peace of God entered into them, and then they were able to calm down and be anxious for nothing – exactly like what this verse is telling us to learn how to do.

This verse is telling us that the peace of God will actually "guard" our hearts and our minds. To guard means to protect. What this means is that

the peace of God can help you be anxious for nothing.

Once you feel the peace of God come into your mind, into your thinking, and into your emotions – then you won't be able to help but feel anxious for nothing – even right in the middle of a severe storm cloud.

So in one powerful and profound verse, God is telling us to be anxious for nothing – but at the same time He is telling us exactly how to be able to do this – and that is by going to Him in prayer and telling Him exactly what you will need to handle the problem, and then fully commit and surrender the problem into His hands for His direct handling.

Once you have fully surrendered the entire problem into God's hands, then He will release His peace into your mind and emotions so He can calm you down and help you to be anxious for nothing.

Do Not Have An Anxious Mind
This next verse will perfectly connect to the above verse from Paul. This next verse is coming direct from Jesus Himself. Here is what He has to say about learning how to remain calmer in how we look at things in this life.

[29] "And do not seek what you should eat or what you should drink, nor have an anxious mind. [30] For all these things the nations of the world seek after, and your Father knows that you need these things. [31] But seek the kingdom of God, and all these things shall be added to you.
Luke 12:29-31

This verse is a major power verse! This verse really puts everything into proper perspective in how we should view this life, and what we should all be striving for and seeking after in this life.

Notice that Jesus is specifically telling us that we are not to be anxious about the basic necessities of our life. Without food or water, we will literally die. Our bodies cannot go very long without proper nourishment. Yet Jesus is telling us not to worry about these basic things.

The key words in this verse is the last sentence where Jesus tells us to concentrate and focus on seeking after the kingdom of God. If we do, then God the Father will make sure to add all of the basic things that we will need to survive and live in this world.

Seeking after the Kingdom of God means that you are to seek directly after God Himself in order to establish a good personal relationship with Him – and then seek after His perfect plan and destiny for your life.

If you make God number 1 in your life by seeking after Him and His perfect plan and destiny for your life – then God will make sure that you have every little thing you will need to perfectly walk out your call for Him.

In this divine support that you will be getting from the Lord will be all of the money that you will ever need to accomplish His perfect will for your life, all of the good friends you will need, all of the favor you will need so that certain doors and opportunities can open up for you to take you to the next step, and the spouse you will need to walk and share the journey with if it will be in His perfect will that you get married in this life.

This verse from Jesus should be burned into every believer's memory bank – as it perfectly sets the stage as to what is most important in this life and shows us exactly what we should be striving for and seeking after. This verse shows us that our top priority has to be with God and with what He wants to do with our lives. If we make the Lord and His perfect will for our life our top priority and goal in this life, then God will give us everything else we will ever need to be able to live and work for Him in this life.

Notice Jesus says that "all" these things will be added to us if we seek after His kingdom as our number 1 priority.

The word **"all"** is a maximum intense word. The word **"all"** means that God will give us everything we will need to live and work for Him – not just some or part of what we will need!

Many Christians are not getting some of their basic needs met because they are in direct violation of this basic spiritual truth. God is not number 1 in their life. They are not seeking after God to get to know Him better. They have not entered into a true personal relationship with Him. They have not fully surrendered their entire lives into His hands so that He can place them into His perfect plan and destiny for their lives.

Notice Jesus starts the last sentence out with the word **"but."** **But** first seek the kingdom of God – and **then** all of the basic things you will need in this life will be given to you.

Once you fully understand this basic truth and get it properly implemented into your life – then you will no longer have an anxious mind, since you will know that God has your life fully and soundly in the palms of His hands and that He will now be working everything out for His and your own good.

Do Not Worry About Your Life
This last verse will perfectly wrap up what the above two verses are trying to tell you. If you no longer have need of having an anxious mind because you are now seeking after God and His perfect will for your life, then this means you can now take the last and final step – and that is not to worry about your life and the direction it is now going since God is now in total control of your life.

God is now the Captain of your ship. God is now at the helm of your ship, and He will now be the One to direct your life in the direction that He will want it to go in. Once you fully grasp this revelation, then you will no longer need to worry about your life and have an anxious mind – because you know now that God has everything in good stead with how He will be working and handling your life.

The burden and stress of trying to figure everything out has now been taken off your back. God will now be leading you into the specific jobs He will want you to have in this life. He will now be leading you to the spouse He will want you to marry if it is in His perfect will that you marry in this life. He will now lead you to the friends that He will want you to have in this life. Too many Christians are still trying to work out all of the above issues out of their own flesh and intelligence. As a result, they end up marrying the wrong people, end up taking the wrong jobs, and end up hooking up with the wrong friends.

By the time they reach mid-life, their house of cards all of a sudden comes crashing down on them. Their marriages end up in divorce, and they either lose their jobs, or they feel totally unfulfilled in the jobs they are now working in. They then end up realizing they should have followed God's divine plan for their lives rather than following their own dreams and aspirations.

If you will follow God and His perfect plan for your life – then much, if not all of the stress, anxiety, and burden can be lifted from your life. As a result, you can then learn how to be anxious for nothing and learn how to relax and enjoy this life with much more vigor and vitality in the way that God would really like. Study this next verse very carefully. This verse is loaded with major revelation.

[25] "Therefore I say to you, do not worry about your life, what you will eat or what you will drink; nor about your body, what you will put on. Is not life more than food and the body more than clothing? [26] Look at the birds of the air, for they neither sow nor reap nor gather into barns; yet your heavenly Father feeds them. Are you not of more value than they? [27] Which of you by worrying can add one cubit to his stature?
[28] "So why do you worry about clothing? Consider the lilies of the field, how they grow: they neither toil nor spin; [29] and yet I say to you that even Solomon in all his glory was not arrayed like one

of these. ³⁰ Now if God so clothes the grass of the field, which today is, and tomorrow is thrown into the oven, *will He* not much more *clothe* you, O you of little faith?
³¹ "Therefore do not worry, saying, 'What shall we eat?' or 'What shall we drink?' or 'What shall we wear?' ³² For after all these things the Gentiles seek. For your heavenly Father knows that you need all these things. ³³ But seek first the kingdom of God and His righteousness, and all these things shall be added to you. ³⁴ Therefore do not worry about tomorrow, for tomorrow will worry about its own things. Sufficient for the day *is* its own trouble.

Matthew 6:25-34

Jesus could not have put it more perfectly than by the way He has worded this longer verse. He gives 3 major analogies with the birds, the grass, and the lilies of the fields. All three of these are being perfectly held up and supported by God the Father. And if God the Father is upholding and keeping these three perfectly alive, then He will do the same for each and everyone of us since we are obviously of much more value to Him than they are.

If you can really grab a hold of this revelation and get it worked into your mindset and way of thinking, then you can achieve what the last part of this verse is trying to tell you to do – and that is to not worry about your life and what tomorrow may bring because you know that God now has every little detail of your life held perfectly in His hands.

This leaves you with either one of two choices. You can either learn how to fully trust God with every aspect of your life and learn how to be anxious for nothing because you know everything

is totally in His hands down to the very smallest detail of your life – or you can choose to worry about anything and everything driving you and everyone else around you crazy.

Chapter 21: Godliness with Contentment is Great Gain

Once again, the apostle Paul comes in with a very powerful revelation that really has application for everyone in this day and age. This is another good mental principle that each Christian should seek to get worked into their mindsets and way of thinking in this life.

For those of you who live outside of South Africa, I live in South Africa. I feel that our country is the most blessed country in this world as a result of our country being founded on the principles of true Christianity.

Though we still have many problems with some of the things that are going on in our country, we still feel that God's hand is on this country and will continue to stay on it until the gospel has been preached to the rest of the world and the [5]Rapture has occurred.

As a result of being the most blessed country in the world, many in our country have fallen prey to the spirit of greed and materialism. I am afraid with all of the material blessings bestowed upon our country by our Father, some of His children have become spoiled

---

[5] The Bible talks about being caught up

Then we who are alive *and* remain shall be **caught up** together with them in the clouds to meet the Lord in the air. And thus we shall always be with the Lord.

1 Thessalonians 4:17

in the luxuries of this life, and now many of His own love the world more than they love Him.

Money, power, and material wealth has ruined many lives, not only in our country, but throughout the rest of the world as well. The Bible tells us that it is not the money itself that will corrupt and ruin a person and his life, it is the love and abnormal pursuit of that money that will ruin a person and his life.

There is no question that any significant amount of money that may fall into your hands is an incredible initial high. Once any kind of significant money falls into your hands, the first thing that will come into your mind is what you can buy with all of this money. Your mind will go nuts with all of the material things you think you may really need and will want to buy with this money. Many people who have won big jackpots but have gone completely broke within 4-5 years. Millions of dollars were completely wasted on foolish purchases and unwise investments.

People have killed one another over money. Many people have lost their marriages and their good relationships with their friends and other family members over disputes over money and how to properly handle it. Money will change some people's personalities for the worse, making them forget where they have initially come from and who their real friends are in this life. Hollywood is littered with the casualties of what fame, money, and power can do to someone if that amount of money and fame is not properly handled.

Once again, the Word of God comes to our rescue as to how we should be looking at money and the material things of this life. God the Father has made sure that He put in the appropriate verses in His Word that will show us how we are to look at money and the material blessings that we can receive from Him in this life.

God loves to bless His children with some of these types of material blessings – but what each Christian has to do is to keep all of this in proper perspective with the big picture, and not let any of these material blessings draw us away from God and with what He wants to do with our lives.

Many pastors and churches have been ruined with the sudden influx of money and then the improper management of that money. Everyone always starts out with the best of intentions, but somewhere along the line people just get stupid and out of control with large sums of money.

Other churches have developed an unhealthy fear of losing whatever money they already have flowing through their churches.

I believe that some of these churches have gone too far to the seeker-sensitive side in their sermons and messages for fear of losing money from some of the flock they might offend if they preach all sides of God's Word.

The fear of losing money is driving them as to what they should preach about on Sundays instead of being guided and led by the Holy Spirit

as to what they should be preaching about. As a result, some of our churches are out of balance with some of their teachings, and they are withholding some very valuable knowledge their flocks need to hear from God's Word.

If God is calling you and anointing you to build and pastor a church – then trust and have faith in God that He will keep you properly funded and supported. Do not let the fear of man and the fear of losing money from your flock keep you from preaching and teaching what God wants you to preach about on a weekly basis.

If God cannot properly support you in the running of your church – then there is something wrong with your situation and you need to ask God to find out exactly what some of the problems and barriers are that is preventing you from receiving the right amount of money to help keep you afloat.

I listed a verse in this chapter that tells us that we are to first seek after the kingdom of God – and if we do, then everything else that we will need to survive and function in this world will be given to us by God the Father.

However, once God does start to release some of these material blessings into your life, you will really have to work to stay on top of this part of your game with Him and not let any of this money, wealth, and material possessions go to your head and start to pull you away from Him and what He wants to do with your life.

You always have to remember where all of this money is coming from in the first place. All of this money is coming directly from God. It is not coming from yourself or from the world in general, even though the rest of the world will try and tell you otherwise. Stay humble with whatever blessings God will bestow upon you as a result of the good works that you have already done for Him to-date.

Once you really enter into a full surrender with the Lord where you are now seeking Him and His perfect will for your life, then sooner or later some of the money and material blessings from God will start to be released into your life. And once this starts to happen, you are really going to have to ground on the types of verses I will list in this chapter.

The apostle Paul once more very beautifully puts everything in proper perspective in the way that he has worded several of the verses in this chapter. In the verses I will list below, he says that:

1. **Godliness with contentment is great gain**
2. **To be content in whatever state you may be in**
3. **To be content with the things you already have**

For many in our money-hungry society, these particular qualities are not operating in their lives and mindsets. They cannot be content with the things they already have because they cannot stop thinking of what they are going to buy next. No matter what they buy or how much they buy, it never seems to satisfy or fulfill them – so they are always on the lookout for that next new toy or investment.

As a result of always wanting bigger and better things, these types of people have a hard time in being content with whatever state they are already in since they are never satisfied with what they already do have. As a result, they live in a lot of mental turmoil and they end up being totally miserable with all of their wealth and possessions. Hollywood is living proof that money, power, and material wealth will not buy you true happiness and fulfillment in this life.

As Christians, we already know that the key and secret to being able to find true inner happiness is by establishing a close, intimate, personal relationship with the Lord.

Once you really start to walk in the Holy Spirit and start to draw much closer to God in your own personal relationship with Him – you will find a very funny thing starting to occur in your life. You will find that your love and desire for money and material possessions will grow smaller and smaller.

All of a sudden your new house, your new car, your new wardrobe, and all of those new toys just do not seem to matter much to you anymore. The initial infatuation with some of these bigger material possessions seems to want to fade. You stop wanting to think about the next new thing you could buy.

All of sudden, you start to become very content with what you already do have. You start to see how blessed you already are in the Lord, and your desire for wanting bigger and better things seems to want to wane. You start to realize what is most important in your life and where you should be setting your priorities at in this life.

As you start to draw closer to the Lord in your own personal relationship with Him, the Holy Spirit will start to illuminate your mind as to what is most important in this life. Once this starts to happen, He will start to draw you closer to God and further away from material things.

The closer you start to draw to the Lord in this life, the further away you will start to get from the ways and material possessions of this world – especially in the obsessive and abnormal pursuits of money, power, and fame.

Once all of this starts to occur, then you will able to live and dwell in the states that Paul is talking about in these verses. You will then start to become much more content with the material possessions you already have.

You will start to become much more content with whatever state you may be currently in as you realize that your happiness and state of well-being is founded and rooted in your personal relationship God and Jesus – not with the material possessions you already have in your life.

You start to realize that drawing closer to God and seeking after His perfect will for your life is more important than anything else you could desire or seek after in this life. Once the Holy Spirit starts to open up your eyes, you begin to see what should really matter the most in this life.

If you could sum up the three most important things that you should be seeking after in this life, I think you could sum it up in these three types of pursuits:

1. **Seek to establish a close, intimate, personal relationship with the Lord**

2. **Seek to establish close, intimate, personal relationships with your family and friends**

3. **Seek to accomplish the perfect will of God for your life**

If you start seeking after God, family, and friends to deepen and better your personal relationships with each one of them – and then top it off by seeking to accomplish whatever God wants you to do for Him on a daily basis – then the lure and desire for money and material possessions will start to wane and they will no longer rule your life.

Jesus could not have put it any better when He said that you could not serve both God and mammon in the parable of the Unjust Steward. The word **"mammon"** in this parable means wealth and riches. This is why Jesus also said that it is harder for a rich man to enter into the kingdom of heaven than it is for a camel to pass through the eye of a needle.

The abnormal love of money, and the abnormal and obsessive pursuit of trying to acquire more of that money, is what have led so many people to total ruination. This is why these specific verses from the apostle Paul are so important for each and every Christian to really grab a hold of and burn into their memory banks, so that we do not ever forget what is most important in this life and where we should all be setting our priorities at in this life.

When you really study the wording in these three verses, the Bible is once again putting everything in proper perspective in relation to the big picture and how we should be looking at this life and what our goals and aspirations should be centered on.

Bottom line – all of the money, material possessions, titles, awards, plaques, and trophies you may have acquired in this life will not be going with you when you die and cross over to enter into heaven.

The only three things that you will be taking with you when you cross over to be with the Lord is the personal relationship that you have established with Him down here on this earth, the personal relationships that you have established with your saved loved ones, and all of the accomplishments, works, and fruit that you have achieved for God while doing His perfect will for your life.

Jesus says that you will be rewarded for your good works and labors that you do for Him while down here on this earth. Works will not get you into heaven, as you can only be saved by His grace through your faith, but any good works that you do for God in this life will be appropriately and highly rewarded once you enter into heaven.

However, nothing else will cross over. I repeat, nothing else will be crossing over with you once you enter into heaven. They will all be left in the dust to rot and perish. That nice big house, that nice new car, all of those beautiful clothes, and all of the money you may have stored up in your retirement accounts will not be going with you to the other side.

In other words, no suitcases will be needed to be packed on your deathbed when you get ready to cross over to meet your Lord and Savior.

Paul saw all of this very clearly, and this was why he was able to word the following verses so eloquently and perfectly.

I will go ahead and put each one of these verses under three separate captions, and then point out certain key words and phrases so you can get these words of knowledge and wisdom ingrained and imparted into your storehouse of knowledge that you are building up in the Lord.

Be Content with Such Things As You Have
This first verse from Hebrews really hones in on learning how to be content with such things as you already have. The key word in this verse is the word **"things."** I believe God is targeting our material possessions and things with the way He has worded this specific verse.

⁵ Let your conduct be without covetousness; *be* content with such things as you have. For He Himself has said, "I will never leave you nor forsake you."
Hebrews 13:5

Notice this verse links the word **"things"** in with the phrase of letting your conduct be without covetousness – which means not wanting or desiring what other people may have by way of material possessions and goods that you may not have.

When you start seeking after God and His perfect will for your life, then God will start to bring in the material things you will need to operate in your calls and divine assignments for Him. I believe God is trying to tell all of us to learn how to be content and happy with whatever He does bring in your life and not moan and complain with what He does not bring into your life.

Though we are all equal in the eyes of God, we are not all equal in the way material goods and possessions are distributed out in this life. Some people will make more money than others will. Some people will live in the bigger and fancier houses.

This is why God is starting off the above verse by stating that you are not to covet what other people may have that you do not have. Remember – what your neighbor may have that you do not have will not be going with them once they die and cross over to the other side.

Be Content in Whatever State You Are in
In this next verse, the apostle Paul takes it one step further. In addition to learning how to be content with whatever material goods and possessions you may already have in the Lord – Paul is now stating that we must also learn how to be content with whatever state we may find ourselves in.

For many in the type of world we live in today, this one is really a hard one to get worked into their mindset and way of thinking. Many people are constantly complaining about their current lot and state of affairs. They are always looking for that better and bigger thing, that new romance, that new job, that new friend, that new thrill, that new promotion, etc.

These types of people have never learned how to stop and enjoy what they already do have. They have not appreciated what God has already done for them. They are always looking out at the horizon wondering when things are going to get bigger and better for them.

Granted, God wants us to continue to grow in His knowledge, grace, and power. And in that growth process there will be new advances, new things, new adventures, new opportunities and new promotions that will occur during the course of our lives. But we even have to keep all of this in proper balance and perspective.

If we are always concentrating and focusing on what God may do for us in our futures – we will never be able to fully enjoy what He has just done for us in our present. Paul was really able to see and grasp this piece of revelation from the Lord.

He found a major spiritual secret in being able to find true, inner peace and happiness in the Lord in this life – and that spiritual secret is learning how to be content and happy in whatever state you may be at with God right now in your present set of circumstances.

If you cannot find happiness, joy, peace, and contentment in the Lord with what He has already done for you in your present – then you will probably not be able to find it with whatever He will want to do for you in your future, since you will always be looking for that next, new, big thing that you think will make you happy, content, and fulfilled.

Then when God does bring you up into the next level with the next round of rewards – you are once again looking off into your future wondering what God can do for you next instead of living in and enjoying your present. This is why Jesus says that we are not to worry about tomorrow and what tomorrow may bring. If we are always looking off onto tomorrow and what tomorrow may bring, we will never be able to fully appreciate and live with what we already have today.

Here is this most profound verse:

[11] Not that I speak in regard to need, for I have learned in whatever state I am, to be content: [12] I know how to be abased, and I know how to abound. Everywhere and in all things I have learned both to be full and to be hungry, both to abound and to suffer need. [13] I can do all things through Christ who strengthens me.

Philippians 4:11-13

Notice Paul says that he has learned to be content in **"whatever state"** he is currently in. He then further expounds on this by saying that he has learned how to be content when things are going good and when things are going bad. He also says he is content no matter where he is at.

In other words, Paul is covering the entire board on this issue. He has learned the secret to being content and happy in the Lord requires that you learn how to be content no matter what your present set of circumstances may be.

The word **"abased"** in the above verse means to be degraded or humiliated – to be lowered or brought down. He is covering one end of the spectrum to the other when he says that he has learned to be content when things may be at their lowest levels in his life, and when things may be at their highest level when he uses the words **"abound"** and **"full."** In other words, he has learned how to be content whether he is abounding or abasing.

Material things do not mean much to God. Your happiness and contentment in this life is found directly in the quality of your personal relationship with God and Jesus.

The better the quality of your personal relationship with God and Jesus, the happier and content you will find yourself becoming in this life. It really is that simple – and Paul found that secret out very early on in his walk with the Lord.

Paul then ends this verse by stating that he can do all things because Jesus can give him His strength to weather any storm cloud or adversity that could come his way. This was probably another reason why Paul was able to find this secret in being able to be content in the Lord no matter what his present set of circumstances were. Even in the middle of the worse type of storm cloud imaginable, Paul found out that the Lord was always there to help him weather and get through any storm cloud that life or the devil could throw his way.

And boy, did this guy have to go through some severe storm clouds in his life. He is perfect living proof that you can go through some real severe adversity in your life, and yet still keep your head and act together in the Lord. If Paul made it through some of the severe trials and tribulations that he personally encountered in his life, then all of us can make it through whatever storm clouds we may have to face in this life.

This one verse from Paul is loaded with major revelation. Study and meditate on this particular verse, and get these spiritual secrets worked and imparted into your mindset and way of thinking so you can learn to get them implemented into your personal walk with the Lord.

Godliness with Contentment is Great Gain
This last verse from Paul really puts the icing on this entire cake. In addition to learning how to be content with whatever things we may already have and in whatever state we may be in with the Lord – Paul now adds one more factor to this equation. He adds that we are to walk in **"godliness"** in addition to learning how to be content.

In one, simple, little sentence – he puts all of it together in the following verse and says that **"godliness with contentment is great gain."** This phrase is so catchy; I decided to use it as the title of this chapter.

The word **"godliness"** in some of the different Bible Dictionaries is defined as:

- **Holy living**

- An attitude and style of life that acknowledges God's claims on human life and seeks to live in accordance with God' s will
- To be devout, reverence to God manifested in actions

Someone who is godly has godly traits and qualities built up into their personality.

What Paul is trying to tell us in this one powerful sentence is that it is a great thing and a great gain if you can learn how to be content with whatever you may have, with whatever you may get, with whatever state or current situation you may be in – and then to walk out this state of contentment with godly character and qualities manifesting through your personality.

Learning how to be godly in your walk with the Lord is once again all part of the sanctification process that God would like to start with each one of us. As God starts the process to transform you into the express image of His Son Jesus, then you won't be able to help but to become more godly in your personal walk with Him.

Here is the verse. Notice the comments Paul makes about those who are not godly and some of the fleshly things these kinds of people are operating in.

[3] If anyone teaches otherwise and does not consent to wholesome words, *even* the words of our Lord Jesus Christ, and to the doctrine which accords with godliness, [4] he is proud, knowing nothing, but is obsessed with disputes and arguments

over words, from which come envy, strife, reviling, evil suspicions, ⁵ useless wranglings of men of corrupt minds and destitute of the truth, who suppose that godliness is a *means of gain*. From such withdraw yourself.
⁶ Now godliness with contentment is great gain. ⁷ For we brought nothing into *this* world, *and it is* certain we can carry nothing out. ⁸ And having food and clothing, with these we shall be content. ⁹ But those who desire to be rich fall into temptation and a snare, and *into* many foolish and harmful lusts which drown men in destruction and perdition. ¹⁰ For the love of money is a root of all *kinds of* evil, for which some have strayed from the faith in their greediness, and pierced themselves through with many sorrows.

The Good Confession
¹¹ But you, O man of God, flee these things and pursue righteousness, godliness, faith, love, patience, gentleness.

1 Timothy 6: 3-11

This entire verse is a real mouthful! Notice Paul makes two specific comments about money and wealth in general. He says that the love of money, not the money itself, is the root of all kinds of evil – and then he says that those who are always trying to become rich in this life fall into a bad temptation and snare which will end up drowning them in destruction and perdition. These are some very harsh and strong words!

This verse will line up with what Jesus has said in that it is harder for a rich man to enter into the kingdom of God than it is for a camel to pass through the eye of a needle. Paul even makes the charge that the love of money has caused some to stray from their faith in God. Is he saying that some can lose their salvation over this issue with God?

It is very interesting in this verse that Paul is comparing learning to be content with what we already have with those who are constantly pursuing the money and wealth of this world. He ends this most powerful verse by telling us that we should all be pursuing godly things in our walks with the Lord, such as building up godly character and building up our levels of faith, love, patience and gentleness in the Lord.

Then right in the middle of this verse he really puts everything in proper perspective when he points out that we have brought nothing into this world and we will carry nothing out of it when we do die and cross over. **Again – no suitcases will need to be packed on our deathbeds.**

Chapter 22: Slave to None – Servant to All

Once again, the apostle Paul comes in with a very powerful revelation on how we should look at ourselves in respect to our relationship with the Lord and in our relationships with other people in our life. There are two very powerful and profound verses from 1 Corinthians that are telling us that we have now been bought back at a price as a result of Jesus dying on the cross for all of us.

When you put these two verses together, one right next to the other as you would two pieces of a jigsaw puzzle – the revelation comes through loud and clear from God the Father on exactly how we should be looking at our relationship with Him and the other people in our life.

These two verses will tell us:

1. **Not to become slaves of men**
2. **That we are free from all men**
3. **We are to be servants to all**

Put all of this together, and you can bottom line this revelation in one simple statement. We are to be a **slave to none and a servant to all.**

Once you become saved and born again by accepting Jesus Christ as your personal Lord and Savior, God and Jesus will now become your true Lord and Master in this life and the life to come. You no longer even belong to yourself, much less belong to anyone else in this life.

In the first two verses I will list below, Paul is telling us that we are not to become slaves to other men. He says that we have now been made free from all other men in this life. Yet at the same time, he tells us that we are to be a servant to them all so that we might win the more of them to the Lord.

What this is telling us is that we really have to keep this piece of revelation in proper perspective. Though no man or no woman owns us in this life, God will still want us to work very closely with Him in serving others in this life. What this means is that we will all have to try and work together in some type of unity and harmony with one another so we can all accomplish what God wants us to get done in this life.

In some of the other verses I will list in this chapter, God is telling us that we are to be subject to rulers and governing authorities, that we are to obey those who rule over us, and that we are to submit ourselves to the ordinances of man for His sake.

What this means is that we are to honor and work with our bosses in the work place, with our political leaders in public office, with the president of our country, and with your parents if you are still under-age and still living at home with your parents.

The best way to look at this piece of revelation is like looking at a two sided coin. On the one side of the coin, you now belong to God and Jesus. You do not belong to any one man, woman, country, political leader or to even yourself. God has bought you back at the price of His Son's death on the cross and He, and He alone, is now your Lord and Master in this life and the new life to come.

As a result, God the Father will now be the One leading your life in the direction that He will want it to go in. He will now be the One to lead you to the jobs that He will want you to have in this life, to the people He will want you to help, to the spouse He will want you to marry, and to the friends that He will want you to have in this life. Through the Holy Spirit, God the Father will perfectly lead you every step of the way with the perfect life that He now has planned out for you.

Neither you or anyone else in your life has the right and authority to control and lead your life from the moment you become saved and born again – and have fully surrendered yourself to God and His perfect plan and destiny for your life. This right and authority now belongs to God the Father – and no one, I repeat, no one will usurp His authority in this area of your life. God the Father now has total control over your life and He will now be the One to call all of the shots in your life. This right no longer belongs to you or anyone else in this life. Your divine destiny now belongs to God the Father.

However, there is now the flip side to this coin. Though God will be personally guiding you every step of the way with what He will be doing with your life, you are still going to have to work in unity and harmony with other people in this life.

If God leads you to a specific job that He will want you to take, but you cannot respect and subject yourself to those who will be in charge over you, then you are not going to be able to survive in that job, and as a result, you will have just taken yourself right off a major step that God had just planned out for you and your life. Some Christians have problems with taking orders from anyone, especially from those who are in some type of authority over them. They have very little respect for those in authority over them and they thus do not last very long in most of the jobs they take.
As a result, God constantly has to go to plans B and C for them in order to try and help keep them afloat. As a result, they end up walking in more of God's permissive will for their lives rather than in God's perfect will because they keep walking right off the steps that He keeps leading them to climb.

When it is all said and done, and their life is totally reviewed up in the Judgment Seat of Christ, they will be shown what more they could have accomplished in this life had they just learned to settle down and work in harmony and unity with some of the bosses and supervisors that God was initially leading them to work with in the first place.

Each step that God will lead you to climb in this life is a vital and important step as you climb up your personal ladder of success in Him. And in some of these steps will be the specific jobs that God will be wanting you to take for Him. And in these jobs, God will be expecting you to work in harmony and unity with your bosses and the other employees. God will want you to become a team player, even if things are not being run smoothly and efficiently in the day-to-day operation of the job.

Get yourself thrown off one or more of these particular steps because you could not work with those in authority over you, and you could get yourself thrown right out of God's call for your life. This is why it is so important that you get this particular piece of revelation firmly and solidly worked and planted into your mindset and way of thinking in this life. It could mean the difference as to whether or not you fully accomplish all of what God has in store for you in this life.

However, the reverse is also true on all of this. As you will see in one of the verses I will list below – God will also be looking at those who will be in authority over you. This verse says that masters are to give to their servants what is just and fair, knowing they have a Master in heaven who will be watching over all that they do.

This means that all bosses and supervisors better be treating their fellow employees with respect, kindness, and fairness in their dealings with them or they will have to answer to God Himself on their day of judgment with Him.

However, as we already know, not everyone who is in authority over you will be treating you fairly and justly. If this should happen to any of you, then you will need to go to God the Father in prayer and ask Him how you should handle the problem you may be having. With many people operating out of their flesh in this life, many who are in positions of authority and power have let a lot of this power go straight to their heads. As a result, they have abused many of those who are working underneath them.

This kind of scenario happens across the board in just about every situation you can imagine. It can happen in any type of work environment or in families where one or both of the parents start to either abuse one another or some of their children. It can happen in boyfriend-girlfriend relationships or even in best-friend relationships.

Many of these relationships can deteriorate over time down to very dysfunctional levels. If or when this should ever happen to any of you – go to God the Father and ask Him how you are to handle this and whether or not it is time for you to cut the cords and break free from the relationship. Sometimes God will ask you to stay a little while longer. Other times He will either ask you to leave, or He will move in and make some type of change Himself to get you out from under someone else's demeaning dictatorship.

Let's look at this powerful testimony. A friend of mine's husband came under some severe abuse from a new boss that came to work for his company. He had been with the company for a long time and he was only 5 years away from being able to retire. He did not want to quit, but he couldn't take for much longer the severe abuse his new boss was throwing at him.

My friend then went into the gap with God the Father behind the scenes – and God literally moved within a space of 12 hours to set this man completely free from the abusive boss he was working under.

When he went into work the next morning, one of the higher-ups called him in and told him they were going to transfer him to another shift because they did not want him leaving or getting fired from this new boss.

Complete and total deliverance was given to this man within 12 hours after he had been under this man's abusive rule for about 6 months – and this was all as a direct result of his wife going in the gap with God the Father behind the scenes for his deliverance!

If any of you have fallen into any kind of dysfunctional and abusive relationship with any of your parents, spouses, bosses, or friends – go to God the Father and ask Him how you should handle the problem.

You have now fallen into a battle situation and you will now need to get your orders direct from God on how to handle the situation. Though God wants us to be a servant to all – this does not mean you have to become a submissive doormat and punching bag for someone else's dysfunctional and psychotic behavior.

Many women are being physically abused by their boyfriends or husbands. Many young girls are being sexually abused by their fathers or someone who is close to their family. Many bosses are sexually harassing some of their female co-workers. This kind of abnormal and abusive behavior is totally unacceptable in God's eyes and He will help you to properly deal with it if you approach Him in prayer. You can also plead the Blood against Physical Abuse.

However, on much smaller matters, there will be times that you will just have to turn your cheek and let the matter go. You are going to have to know when to engage and when to just let certain matters go as best as you can. But realize that God does have limits with His own patience, and He will move in with a very strong hand to get you delivered out of something if someone you know has started to get out of control with how they are interacting with you.

Now I will give you the specific verses from Scripture that deal with this very profound truth.

Slave to None – Servant to All
These first three verses will really hit the nail right on the head. They will specifically tell us that we are **"not to become slaves of men"** and that we are **"free from all men"** – but at the same time we are to be a servant to all so that we might win the more of them to God and Jesus.

These verses will also tell us that we are to remain with God and His calling on our lives. The last verse I will list makes an extremely profound statement when it says that we **"are the Lord's"** and as such, we are to **"live to the Lord"** and that we are to **"die to the Lord."**

Bottom line – we belong to the Lord, and we work and live for Him, and Him alone in this life – and no one else!

These first three verses are major power verses. Here they are:

²³ You were bought at a price; do not become slaves of men.
²⁴ Brethren, let each one remain with God in that *state* in which he was called.

1 Corinthians 7:23-24

¹⁹ For though I am free from all *men,* I have made myself a servant to all, that I might win the more

1 Corinthians 9:19

⁷ For none of us lives to himself, and no one dies to himself. ⁸ For if we live, we live to the Lord; and if we die, we die to the Lord. Therefore, whether we live or die, we are the Lord's.

Romans 14:7-8

In three very powerful verses, God the Father is giving all of us full and complete revelation on how we should be viewing this life in respect to our personal relationship with Him and with the other people in our life.

Be Subject to Rulers and Authorities

These next four verses will help keep the above three verses in proper perspective. Though God is telling us that we belong to Him and no one else in this life – we still have to be able to work in unity and harmony with other people, and the only way we can do this, especially in the workplace, is that we have to be willing to be subject ourselves to those who will rule over us in some way.

These next set of verses will tell us that we have to be willing to be subject to rulers and authorities, to those who will rule over us in some way, and to every ordinance of man. These verses will tell us that this will be including Kings and Governors, which means the presidents and political leaders of our countries. When the Bible says that we are to obey those who will rule over us, I believe God is telling us to respect and obey those who are in positions of leadership and authority in our lives such as our bosses, the CEO's of the company you may work for, the direct foremen or supervisors you may be reporting to, and to any other leader of any other group or organization you may be working for.

Jesus did not try and overthrow the Roman government when He was walking down here on our earth – and unless God is leading you to dethrone a dictator who has got completely out of control with what is happening in your work place – God will expect you to do the best you can to get along with everyone else that you will work with, and to obey all of the rules that your superiors would like you to abide by.

Here are 4 very good verses on this issue.

3 Remind them to be subject to rulers and authorities, to obey, to be ready for every good work, ^{2} to speak evil of no one, to be peaceable, gentle, showing all humility to all men.
Titus 3:1-2

^{17} Obey those who rule over you, and be submissive, for they watch out for your souls, as those who must give account. Let them do so with joy and not with grief, for that would be unprofitable for you.
Hebrews 13:17

^{13} Therefore submit yourselves to every ordinance of man for the Lord's sake, whether to the king as supreme, ^{14} or to governors, as to those who are sent by him for the punishment of evildoers and *for the* praise of those who do good. ¹⁵ For this is the will of God, that by doing good you may put to silence the ignorance of foolish men— ¹⁶ as free, yet not using liberty as a cloak for vice, but as bondservants of God. ¹⁷ Honor all *people.* Love the brotherhood. Fear God. Honor the king.

1 Peter 2:13-17

13 Let every soul be subject to the governing authorities. For there is no authority except from God, and the authorities that exist are appointed by God. ² Therefore whoever resists the authority resists the ordinance of God, and those who resist will bring judgment on themselves.

Romans 13:1-2

The last verse gives us a very solemn warning when it says that we will have to answer to God on our day of judgment with Him if we have not sought to obey those in authority over us. It says that if we resist and disobey our leaders – then we are disobeying God Himself, since God is the One who will be deciding who gets these types of leadership positions in the first place.

These verses are also stressing the importance that we all try and get along with one another when it says we are to honor the king, to love the brotherhood, to honor all other people, to speak evil of no one, and to learn how to be peaceable, gentle, and showing humility to all men.

If more people could learn how to abide by some of these basic principles and truths, many of our workplaces could become much more fun and pleasant to work in.

Masters – Treat Your Servants Just and Fair

Just as God the Father was targeting all of us who will be working under some type of rule from our bosses and supervisors in the above verses – these next two verses from the Lord will be targeting all of those who will be ruling over us.

God says that those who are in any type of leadership position over us should be making sure they treat all of us just and fair. The words **"just and fair"** are two very intense words when you really look at how they apply in our workplaces. Many bosses, CEO's, foremen and supervisors are not treating a lot of their workers just and fair. They are playing favorites with certain people and running roughshod over others. Many have let their positions of leadership and authority goes to their heads. As a result, none of their fellow workers want anything more to do with them. From there, communication will start to shut down and productivity will eventually end up suffering as a result. To all of you who are in supervisory positions in your jobs – grab a hold of what these next two verses are trying to tell you.

4 Masters, give your bondservants what is just and fair, knowing that you also have a Master in heaven.
Colossians 4:1

^{27} Do not withhold good from those to whom it is due,
When it is in the power of your hand to do *so.*
Proverbs 3:27

Notice the last part of the first verse when it says that you have a Master in heaven who is watching how you handle your position of leadership. If you are not treating your employees fairly and justly, then you will have to answer to God Almighty Himself on your day of judgment with Him.

Treat your employees like you yourself would want to be treated – with fairness, honesty, respect, and kindness. If you do, then you will be loved by them and they will want to work harder for you. And if they will want to work harder and better for you, then you will end up becoming much more productive and profitable on your end of the job.

What goes around will eventually come around. Sow good seeds in your work environment and you eventually will reap a nice harvest. Sow bad seeds of arrogance, fear, and intimidation and you will eventually reap corruption, death, and destruction.

Saddam Hussein is a perfect example of someone who ruled his people in every wrong way imaginable. He completely abused all of the power that was given to him and he ended up losing everything that took him years to build – and all of this was completely lost in a matter of days!

Satan, Hitler, and all of the Saddam Husseins of this world have eventually fallen, and so will you if you are not treating your employees fairly, justly and honestly. Remember – God the Father is watching you very closely with how you treat all of those who are working under you!

Any type of leadership position given to you by God is a big promotion and a nice blessing. The Bible says that to whom much is given, much more will be expected. Do not lose sight of this big picture and what really matters the most at the end of your day and eventually at the end of your life. You will eventually be judged by God Himself with how you have handled your job and with what kind of working relationship you had established with all of those who had worked under you.

Submission in Your Marriage
For those of you who are married, this next verse will tell you how God wants you to interact with one another. In this verse, it says that wives are to submit to their husbands. God says that the husband is the head of the wife. He then says that Jesus is the head of the church, and just as the church is supposed to be subject to Jesus, wives are to be subject to their husbands in the same way. God is thus giving us a proper chain-of-command that is operating in His kingdom.

However, just because God has told us that wives are supposed to be subject to their husbands does not give the husbands the right to abuse their wives. This verse ends with a very strong warning in that husbands ought to love their wives as their own bodies. In other words, you should love your wife as you would love yourself, which is part of the second greatest commandment in that you are to love one another as you would love yourself.

If you will love your wife in the way that God would really want you to love her – you will not be physically and/or verbally abusing her. You will treat her like the God-given treasure that she really

is. If your wife has been given directly to you by God, then you have been given one of the greatest blessings that God can bestow upon you in this life.

I know there are some Christians and other false religions that think this give them some type of spiritual right to be able to abuse and totally control their wives. But this view is wrong, and nothing will trigger the release of God's wrath and anger on you and your life than forcing Him to watch you verbally and physically beat your wife into complete and total submission to your will and warped desires.

Behind closed doors in many marriages across this world you see this dysfunctional and psychotic behavior occurring with alarming frequency. The way some men treat and abuse their wives is a crime of the highest order in the eyes of God – and there will be hell to literally pay for some of them once they meet their Maker and they are forced to give an account of what they have done to their wives during the course of their married lives.

When God says for husbands to love their wives, He means for you to love them in a godly way, not in an obsessive and compulsive way where your only desire is to seek to bend them to your will and way of thinking.

Here is the verse from our Lord which really puts all of this in proper perspective.

²² Wives, submit to your own husbands, as to the Lord. ²³ For the husband is head of the wife, as also Christ is head of the church; and He is the Savior of the body. ²⁴ Therefore, just as the church is subject to Christ, so *let* the wives *be* to their own husbands in everything.
²⁵ Husbands, love your wives, just as Christ also loved the church and gave Himself for her, ²⁶ that He might sanctify and cleanse her with the washing of water by the word, ²⁷ that He might present her to Himself a glorious church, not having spot or wrinkle or any such thing, but that she should be holy and without blemish. ²⁸ So husbands ought to love their own wives as their own bodies; he who loves his wife loves himself.

Ephesians 5:22

For many Christians, this verse has been a rather controversial one. But if every Christian man and woman would learn how to love and treat others in the godly way that God would like us to, then there would be no one getting out of balance with the way the Lord has worded this verse.

For those of you who would like a good, detailed chapter on learning how to love others in the way God would like you too, we have another chapter in this book titled, "The Power of Love." In this chapter, I give you some of the key verses from the Bible on the kind of love that God would like to see all of us walk and live in.

Chapter 23: Be Slow to Anger

With the very fast paced way of living that many of us are forced to live with in this country – stress has become a major factor in many people's lives. As a result of the increase in stress in many of our lives, many people are now turning to anti-depressants, drugs, or alcohol to help try and calm themselves down and to help take their minds off all of the stress and uncertainty of this life.

For the people who will not attempt to rely on drugs, alcohol, or anti-depressants to help them handle the high levels of stress they are forced to deal with on a daily basis – many people are then forced to deal with the side effects that high levels of stress can have on you.

And one of the main side effects that high levels of stress can have on you is that it will shorten up your fuses. You will find yourself losing your temper with much more frequency and over things that you normally would have never lost your temper over. You will also find yourself losing your temper much more quickly than you ever had in your past.

As a result, we have some time bombs walking our streets and driving on our highways that are just ready to go off at the slightest bit of provocation. Road rage is still a major problem on some of our highways. Accidentally cut someone off, or drive too slow for someone else's taste, and they will start honking, yelling, and cussing at you, and in some of the more extreme cases, they will literally try and chase you down, all over something that was very trivial to begin with.

To those of you who watch your local news everyday – there is case after case of people who have lost their tempers over something completely stupid and trivial, and as a result, they have either hurt themselves or hurt other people.

Parents, in some cases, have literally beaten their children to death over minor disputes or over a child that was crying too long. Boyfriends have beaten up or killed their girlfriends over jealous disputes. Parents have physically fought with one another or with some of their coaches at some of their child's athletic events over minor disputes over a coach's decision, or over a bad call made by the referee or umpire.

In all of these cases – the lack of self-control over one's temper has caused some of these people to explode with rage and violence where they will literally strike out at the person that have set them off. This same scenario keeps repeating itself over and over again on a regular-daily basis throughout the entire world.

Even some Christians are operating with very short fuses. They are constantly yelling at their spouses, their children, and their co-workers. As a result, many of their family and friends want nothing more to do with them and all they do is tolerate them as best as they can.

Many marriages that have started out on a good and loving note have severely deteriorated over the years because one or both of the spouses have lost all reasonable control over their bad tempers. They have verbally and sometimes physically beat the love right out of their marriages. As a result, many people have lost their marriages, their relationships with their children, and their good friends. No one wants anything more to do with them, and they all end up being totally alone, depressed, and miserable – all because they could not keep proper control of their bad tempers.

For those of you who are having problems with keeping proper control of your bad tempers in the high stress world in which we all live in today – realize that there is help for you in this area from God Almighty Himself. Per the chapter that we have titled, "The 9 Fruits of the Holy Spirit," there are two very powerful fruits and divine qualities that the Holy Spirit can start to transmit up into the core of your personality. These two fruits are the fruits of peace and self-control.

Unless you have the peace of the Holy Spirit operating in your mind and emotions – you are going to have a very hard time in handling all of the stress this life can throw at you.

You have to have a strong supernatural source of peace flowing through you, and you cannot get this kind of supernatural peace from your own emotions, or from your own mental makeup due to your own imperfections. This kind of strong supernatural peace can only be received direct from the Holy Spirit Himself. This is why the Bible

tells us that these 9 fruits are from the Holy Spirit – not from us.

The other fruit from the Holy Spirit that you are really going to need to combat this problem is the fruit of self-control. Unless you have the self-control of the Holy Spirit Himself flowing and operating through you, then you will find that your own level of self-control is not going to be good enough to give you complete victory in this area, especially if you have had this problem operating in you for a long time and it has now become a conditioned habit.

The first thing you are going to need to do is to find out what the Word of God has to say on this matter. In this chapter, I will give you 9 very good verses from the Bible on what God's opinion really is on being quick-tempered and having a short fuse.

As you will see in the Scripture verses I will list below, God the Father is telling us:

- **To be slow to anger**
- **To be slow to wrath**
- **To cease from anger**
- **Not to be quick-tempered**
- **Not to let the sun go down on your wrath**
- **To overlook a transgression against you**

Jesus Himself has told us to turn the other cheek when warranted. Many of the things people are losing their tempers over are completely unacceptable in the eyes of God. There is a time to engage, but there is also a time not to engage. I believe there is something called righteous wrath, righteous anger, and righteous indignation. There are times that you can lose your temper, and rightly so.

God the Father really let it blow with some of the judgments He pronounced back in the Old Testament against certain groups of people – but every time God the Father would lose His temper, it was always for a very good reason. The Bible tells us that God the Father is slow to anger, but if you manage to hit the end of His fuse – watch out!

It was also the same with Jesus when He was walking on our earth. Jesus did not mince any words when attacking some of the Scribes and Pharisees for their hypocritical behavior. He also did not hold back when the money changers were trying to use His house of worship as a place to try and sell their goods to do business.

You have to know when to engage with righteous anger and when not to. The Bible says that God the Father is slow to anger, and as such, He wants all of us to be the exact same way in our dealings with ourselves and with other people.

As you will see in one of the verses I will list below, God the Father says that it is to our own glory and to our own benefit that we learn how to overlook transgressions that are made against us. In other words, it will be very pleasing to Him if we can learn how to let certain matters go that are not worth the time and energy to get all bent out of shape over.

The Bible tells us that it should be our aim in this life to be well-pleasing to the Lord – and losing your temper over anything and everything is not being well-pleasing to Him.

I will first start off by giving you some of the better verses from the Bible that deals with the issue of having a bad and quick temper. I will then end this chapter with a 2 step process that you can use if you really want to work with the Lord in trying to defeat and put to death this bad character flaw in your personality.

The Scripture Verses

Here are 9 very good verses from the Bible on what God's opinion is on those who have bad and quick tempers.

[11] The discretion of a man makes him slow to anger,
And his glory *is* to overlook a transgression.

Proverbs 19:11

[32] *He who is* slow to anger *is* better than the mighty,
And he who rules his spirit than he who takes a city.

Proverbs 16:32

[19] So then, my beloved brethren, let every man be swift to hear, slow to speak, slow to wrath; [20] for the wrath of man does not produce the righteousness of God.

James 1:19

[29] *He who is* slow to wrath has great understanding,
But *he who is* impulsive exalts folly.

Proverbs 14:29

[8] Cease from anger, and forsake wrath;
Do not fret—*it* only *causes* harm.

Psalms 37:8

[19] *A man of* great wrath will suffer punishment;
For if you rescue *him,* you will have to do it again.

Proverbs 19:19

[28] Whoever *has* no rule over his own spirit
Is like a city broken down, without walls.

Proverbs 25:28

[17] A quick-tempered *man* acts foolishly,
And a man of wicked intentions is hated.

Proverbs 14:17

[25] Therefore, putting away lying, "*Let* each one *of you* speak truth with his neighbor," for we are members of one another. [26] "Be

angry, and do not sin": do not let the sun go down on your wrath, [27] nor give place to the devil. [28] Let him who stole steal no longer, but rather let him labor, working with *his* hands what is good, that he may have something to give him who has need. [29] Let no corrupt word proceed out of your mouth, but what is good for necessary edification, that it may impart grace to the hearers. [30] And do not grieve the Holy Spirit of God, by whom you were sealed for the day of redemption. [31] Let all bitterness, wrath, anger, clamor, and evil speaking be put away from you, with all malice. [32] And be kind to one another, tenderhearted, forgiving one another, even as God in Christ forgave you.

Ephesians 4:25-32

Notice in the last verse that it says not to let the sun go down on your wrath. This is very good advice for all married couples who like to carry some of the arguments of the day into their beds at night.

This last verse also says that we will grieve the Holy Spirit Himself if we have a lot of bitterness, anger, and wrath operating through us. We are to learn to forgive others, just as God the Father has now forgiven all of us through the Blood that His Son has shed on the cross for all of us. If God can fully forgive all of our trespasses, then we can learn to fully forgive others who will trespass against us. And if we can learn to forgive others, then we will be less likely to lose our tempers every time someone trespasses against us in some way.

Notice God says that those who cannot be slow to wrath are not producing the righteousness of God in their lives. He says those who are impulsive and lose their tempers easily and quickly are foolish and are exalting **"folly."** The word **"folly"** means a **"lack of** understanding and a lack of rational conduct – foolishness."

In other words, in God's eyes, you are showing Him complete foolishness and a complete lack of understanding in what you are losing your temper over. You are looking like a complete fool and idiot to both Him and to other people with some of the trivial and foolish things you are losing your temper over. Most of the time people are not laughing with you, they are laughing at you.

The verse from Proverbs 19:19 say that a man of great wrath will suffer punishment. Sooner or later, your bad temper is going to get you into serious trouble. You are going to either lose it with the wrong person or in the wrong situation, and when that happens, there will be severe consequences. For some, it will literally mean having an early departure from this life.

Flip off the wrong guy on the highway who may have just cut you off – and he may be the last person you will ever see alive again in this life!

The verse from Proverbs 25:28 says that a man who has no rule over his spirit and emotions is like a city that is broken down without any walls. In other words, you will have no protection from either God or your enemies if you engage with the wrong person at the wrong time. You are leaving yourself wide open to demonic or human attack if you are not going to learn how to control your temper with how you react and respond to others – especially with those who will attempt to cross you in someway.

In the second verse above from Proverbs 16:32, God is saying that those who are slow to anger are better than the "mighty" and he who can take a city. By the way God has worded this verse; you can tell how big of a thing it really is to Him that we learn how to control our emotions, especially our emotions of anger and wrath.

Once God's peace and self-control starts to flow into your personality through His Holy Spirit – then it will become much easier for you to keep control of your bad temper.

The Bible says it is by the power of the Holy Spirit that you will put to death the deeds of your body – and one of the deeds of the flesh and body that you will definitely want to put to death is a lousy, foul, and bad temper.

This is a powerful, supernatural type of help and work that you can receive direct from the Holy Spirit Himself if you are open and willing to work with Him on this as part of your sanctification process in the Lord.

Chapter 24: Pride will come before the Fall

As part of the sanctification process that God would like to start with each one of us – one of the first things that God will be doing, through the power of the Holy Spirit, is to either take out or prevent certain types of negative qualities from entering into our personalities.

Without question, one of the major negative qualities that God will be moving very strongly on to either prevent it from being able to enter into us to any significant degree, or to literally knock it right out of us if it has moved too far up into our personalities, is the negative quality of pride.

This cancerous, lethal, and destructive quality, probably more than any other negative quality, has brought down more kingdoms, toppled more empires, caused more wars, destroyed more marriages, ruined more friendships, and led more criminals into our jail systems than all of the other negative qualities combined and put together. The spirit of pride has to be the absolute king of all the negative and destructive qualities that can enter into our personalities – and no one is safe and immune from it. All Christians, young and old, super saint or not, have got to keep a sharp eye on this negative quality, and do everything they can not to let this spirit get a foothold and grip into their personalities and mindsets.

As you will see in the one of the Scripture verses I will list below, the spirit of pride will always come right before destruction and a major fall. Even unbelieving heathens are aware of this basic truth from our Bible. The saying that **"pride will come before the fall"** is an universal truth understood by everyone. But as understood and hated as this quality is by most people, many still succumb to its enticing and seductive nature, and many end up losing everything as a result of the consequences of wallowing in it for too long of a period of time.

For the record, I believe there is a good kind of pride and a bad kind of pride. Many Christians, after reading what some of the verses from the Bible has to say about this toxic quality, try to remove all sense of pride from them and their lives. As a result, they end up reducing a lot of their own natural joy in the Lord. Webster's Dictionary, and some of the other different Bible Dictionaries describe this good kind of pride as follows:

- **Proper respect for one-self, self-respect**
- **A reasonable or justifiable self-respect**
- **Sense of one's own dignity and self-worth**
- **Delight or satisfaction in one's own or another's achievements**

If your child comes home and tells you that he has just received straight A's on his report card, your first natural and instinctive response will be to want to tell them "how proud" you are of them and what they have just accomplished. If your husband comes home and tells you he has just received a nice promotion and pay raise at work for the good job he has been doing – again, your first natural response will be to want to tell him how proud you are of him and his efforts to try and make a better life for your and your family.

This is the good kind of pride. There is nothing wrong in having this good kind of pride for what your children may be able to accomplish, and for what you may accomplish in your own work for the Lord in this lifetime. I believe that God Himself wants us to have this good kind of pride for the blessings and opportunities He may bring our way in this life.

If God has just blessed you with a nice new house, there is nothing wrong in being proud of that house and wanting to take good care of it. If God has blessed you with a wonderful marriage with a beautiful mate and beautiful children, there is nothing wrong in taking pride in all of them and what they may accomplish for the Lord in this life.

This good kind of pride that you may have in the actual work that you are doing for the Lord and with whatever blessings He may want to pass your way in this life all help to contribute to your own personal joy in the Lord. It helps to give you a nice sense of approval, and it also helps to motivate you to want to keep pressing further on with the Lord in whatever He has called you to do for Him in this life.

However, as with anything else that may start out good, there is always the danger of possible excess. What starts out as a simple and a humble type of pride can start to grow into something much more deadly if a person does not properly keep on top of it.

One of the 9 fruits of the Holy Spirit is the fruit of self-control. Not only will you need to use your own self-control to help keep a proper grip and lid on this quality from getting out of control in your personality – but you will also need the self-control of the Holy Spirit Himself to help you keep proper control of it, especially for those who are called by God to move into any type of leadership roles within His Body.

In the verses I will list below, you will see two key words being repeated several times. These two key words are the words **"pride"** or **"proud,"** and the word **"haughty."**

Webster's Dictionary, and several of the different Bible Dictionaries describe the negative kind of pride as follows:

- **An unduly high opinion of oneself**
- **Exaggerated self-esteem, conceit**
- **Haughty behavior resulting from arrogance**
- **An improper and excessive self-esteem known as conceit and arrogance**
- **A sin of attitude and of the heart and spirit**
- **A puffed up and inflated ego**
- **Boasting and high-mindedness**
- **A conceited sense of one's superiority**
- **Highly exalted in attitude, opposite from the virtue of humility**

All you have to do is compare the two different sets of definitions of the good kind of pride versus the bad kind of pride to see what the real differences are between the two of them.

What gets some Christians into major trouble with the Lord is falling and entering into the second category mentioned above. What can start out as a humble, justified, and reasonable kind of self-respect for one's self and one's own efforts and accomplishments in the Lord can quickly deteriorate and descend down into the bad kind of pride where one starts to lose all sense of who they really are in the Lord.

The other key word that you will see listed in the verses below is the word **"haughty."** Here is what Webster's and some of the other Bible Dictionaries have to say about this negative quality:

- **Showing great pride on oneself and disdain**
- **Contempt or scorn for others**
- **Proud, arrogant, supercilious (disdain or contemptuous)**
- **An arrogant spirit**

As you will see in the Scripture verses below, the Lord is using some very intense and strong language when describing this negative quality. Not only does God call pride an actual sin in His sight, but He goes one step further and calls it an actual **abomination**!

As I have stated several times in some of my other chapters, whenever God the Father is using the word **"abomination"** to describe what He is thinking about something – He is using the most extreme and intense word that He possibly can to let all of us know, without any other possible interpretation, that we are to have no part of the activity He is describing as an abomination. We are to avoid it like the plague.

When God puts the qualities of pride and haughtiness in this abomination category – you know that He is giving all of us a very serious warning on this issue. In the Scripture verse below where God the Father is telling us that pride and a haughty spirit will come before destruction and a fall – He is giving all of us major revelation. The history of our world, and what we see on a daily basis throughout the entire world, are all showing us this piece of revelation in actual operation.

The history of our world is littered with the casualties that this negative and demonic quality and mindset has caused. It literally, and I mean literally, has completely toppled and destroyed kingdoms, countries, nations, alliances, companies, marriages, and good friendships.

Probably the greatest fall that has ever occurred coming from this one negative quality may end up being the story of how Satan fell from heaven. The Bible only gives us partial information about this story.

As you will see in the three Scripture verses I will give you below on how Satan managed to get cast out of heaven – the quality of pride was definitely one of the main causes that led to his own personal downfall in the Lord.

And to think that he was then able to get one-third of the rest of the angels to get cast out of heaven right along with him! I repeat – one third of all the angels who were living with him in heaven were also cast out – and they have now all permanently lost their place in heaven for all of eternity!

There is no more saving grace for Satan and all of these fallen angels. And to think that all of them were born and created up in this perfect heavenly environment – and then to throw it all away – all because one angel thought he could literally overthrow God Almighty Himself. Not only has this got to be the height of pure arrogance and pride, but it also has to be the height of pure stupidity!

As you will see in one of the Scripture verses below, Satan was one of the highest of all the angels God has ever created. He was allowed to literally walk on the mountain of God the Father Himself. He thus had to know how awesome and how powerful God the Father really is and that there was no way that anyone could ever begin to try and overthrow Him.

If God is all-powerful and there are no other Gods in existence, then anyone with half a brain can deduce that God cannot be defeated or overthrown. But Satan obviously was blinded by something else from being able to see this simple and logical truth – and that something else was probably the spirit of pride and arrogance that he had operating in him by the time he started to reach this point of no return. I believe this is why God is telling us in this particular verse that the spirit of pride will come right before the fall – as pride is what will start to blind you as to what the real truth of a matter is.

A perfect example has to be the fall of Saddam Hussein in Iraq. All this man had to do was to let the UN inspectors complete their investigation into his country for weapons of mass destruction that were never found – and he could have easily retained full control of his built up, corrupt empire. But his pride got in the way.

He had to show the world that he could stand up and defy the strongest military might in the world. As a result of letting his pride get in the way and cloud his better judgment on giving into the UN inspectors, he literally lost his entire kingdom in just a matter of a few days!

He literally went from living in the most lavish and expensive living quarters that anyone could possibly live in to being found at the bottom of a hole in the ground all disheveled and unkempt.

We are talking about someone falling from the highest peak of a mountain as king and ruler of an entire country to the lowest depths that anyone can possibly fall to in this life – behind the bars of a jail losing all of his freedom, all of his wealth, and all of his contact with his family and friends.

You have all heard many preachers talk about Joseph going from the pit to the palace. Saddam Hussein managed to do just the opposite. In a matter of just a few days, he literally went from the palace to the pit.

Saddam Hussein, Adolph Hitler, Joseph Stalin and all the rest of the despotic and evil dictators who have ever ruled on this earth will all go down as major history lessons for all of us showing us what pride, arrogance, and a haughty spirit can do to a person and his life.

It will first completely destroy a person's soul and spirit, and then it will eventually destroy and ruin the rest of what life they still have left. And then for many of them, they will end up being cast into the most horrible place imaginable when they die and cross over – hell itself, and then eventually into the Lake of Fire and Brimstone after the Millennium has taken place, where the Bible says that the smoke of their torment will ascend forever and ever.

The fall of Satan and all of these evil rulers in this world will serve as major examples of how deadly the spirit of pride can be, and how it can completely destroy a person and his life much the same way that an incurable cancer can invade and attack a person's physical body. Once a cancer has spread too far into a human body where medical treatment can no longer stop it, the infected person will die shortly thereafter. It is the exact same way with the spirit of pride.

Once pride starts to seep into someone's personality to any significant degree – it has to be dealt with and neutralized with the help of the Holy Spirit. If it is not, then it will continue to grow and spread through that person's personality and mindset.

From there, it will start to seep into their emotions, actions, and behaviors. And once this negative quality starts to manifest into their actions and behaviors, then their judgment will start to cloud. And once their sense of proper judgment starts to cloud up, they will no longer be able to separate truth from error. The only truth they will be able to see is what they perceive the truth to be, not what God's real truth is, or what anyone else may try and tell them what is right.

They eventually end up becoming their own little god, thinking they have all of the answers to everything and that the entire world revolves around them and what they are trying to achieve and accomplish. They are no longer willing to be accountable to anyone else in their life, including God Himself.

They have forgotten and forsaken all of their true friends in this life. They have forgotten where they have come from, and they feel they no longer need any of God's help or guidance to get them to where they are going. They are now totally self-sufficient and they think they can literally conquer the world through their own efforts and wisdom.

And then sooner or later it happens – they fall – and they end up losing everything they have managed to build up over all of those years due to their own stupidity and imperfections.

This scenario not only happens with rulers of different countries, but this same scenario also describes what happens to CEO's of major companies, to managers, to supervisors, to foremen and to anyone else in any type of leadership position. With any type of position of leadership comes power and authority, and with power and authority comes the possibility of pride and corruption.

Many people end up becoming criminals in this life as a result of too much of the wrong kind of pride operating in their personalities.

Their pompous, arrogant, conceited, know-it-all attitudes convince them that they are smart enough to be able to get away with breaking any law they see fit just to satisfy their own lusts and desires – even if it means committing cold-blooded murder.

Their inflated sense of pride and ego tells them they are too smart to get caught by the law, and then again, it happens. They are caught as a result of their own stupidity and imperfections, and many of them end up never seeing the light of day for the rest of their earthly lives.

And all of this was as a direct result of the spirit of pride and arrogance they had operating in their mindsets and how they thought about things. This is why the Bible tells us that we have to be transformed by the renewing of our minds. We have to learn how to develop right thinking in our thought process.

As a result of some of these people never learning what to think right about in this life, many of them have either died before their time may have really been up, or they have ended up spending a good portion of their adult lives behind bars in an eight-by-six foot cell.

When God the Father says that pride will come before a **"fall"** – He is giving all of us a major warning that some of these falls could end up being be very severe. For many, it will mean an early departure from this life. For others, it could mean a certain amount of time behind bars, the destruction and dissolution of their marriages, or possibly losing their jobs and the good pay they were making.

There are many different things that we can "fall" from. As a Christian, do not ever tempt your fate with God the Father with what He is personally doing with you and your life. Stay humble and accountable in your walk with the Lord.

If you don't, and pride starts to enter your personality to any significant degree with the Lord – God will be coming after you with two-by-fours and baseball bats upside your head to keep this deadly quality from becoming a part of your mindset and way of thinking in this life.

I have personally seen the Lord body slam several people to the mat when they got too far away from Him and started to get too big for their britches as a result of too much pride starting to seep up into their personalities.

God has His ways of humbling and chastening you, and He will not be putting up with any of His own getting too far away from Him – especially in the area of pride, arrogance and haughtiness. He has already lost a third of His angelic host to this deadly quality, and He will do everything He possibly can not to lose any more of His children to this deadly sin and abomination.

Now here are some very powerful verses from Scripture giving you what God's opinion really is on this deadly sin and abomination.

Pride is a Sin and an Abomination
These first two verses perfectly set the stage for all of us as far as what God the Father really thinks of this negative spirit and quality that could infect anyone of us at anytime. God is specifically telling us in these

two verses that anyone who has become too proud in his own heart is committing a sin and an abomination in His sight!

Burn these two verses into your memory banks, and make sure you never, ever let this deadly spirit get a foothold into your mind and heart.

⁴ A haughty look, a proud heart,
And the plowing of the wicked *are* sin.
Proverbs 21:4

⁵ **Everyone proud in heart *is* an abomination to the Lord;**
Though they join forces, none will go unpunished.
Proverbs 16:5

Once again, God the Father could not make things any more clear. Not only is the spirit of pride a definite sin in His eyes, but He is now taking it one step further and calling it an actual abomination in His sight.

God has now drawn a major battle line in the sand on this one particular negative quality with the way He has worded these two verses. And He is letting all of us know, loud and clear, that He will not want any of us to have any part of this destructive spirit that will not only destroy our personal lives down here on this earth, but will also destroy and sever the personal relationship that we can have with Him.

God is Afar From Those Who Are Proud
This next verse will now take it one step further. Not only is God calling those who are proud an abomination before His very eyes – but this next verse will now tell us that God is **"afar"** from those who are

proud. And when God says that He is becoming **"afar"** from you – you are in big trouble!

What this means is that your personal relationship with the Lord can be severely affected and possibly severed if you do not start to see the errors of your ways with this deadly quality. God will start to pull away from you in your own personal relationship with Him if you do not start to get yourself straightened out with Him on this issue of becoming too proud in your own heart.

If you have fallen into any kind of serious pride with the Lord, you still have some time to see the errors of your way and get back into right standing with the Lord. God will be willing to fully forgive you if you are willing to see that too much pride has entered into your mind and heart, and then be willing to confess and repent before Him from this deadly sin.

Humble yourself and get this sin confessed, forgiven, and removed from your soul before God is forced to take some kind of corrective action with you. He will only give you a certain amount of rope to run with before He pulls you in and takes the appropriate corrective actions to literally, and I mean literally, knock this deadly sin and abomination right out of your soul and spirit.

Here is the verse giving us this solemn warning:

[6] Though the LORD *is* on high,
Yet He regards the lowly;
But the proud He knows from afar.
Psalm 138:6

There is nothing worse that can occur in your walk with the Lord than to have Him start to pull away from you in your own personal relationship with Him. This particular verse is giving all of us a major warning and should be taken very, very seriously.

Pride Will Come Before the Fall
These next two verses will now put the icing on the entire cake on this one particular sin. In addition to God calling pride a sin and abomination in His sight, and then telling us that He will start to pull away from us in our own personal relationship with Him – He is now giving us one more final dire warning in these next two verses.

In the first verse I will list below, God is telling us that **"pride goes before destruction"** and a **"haughty spirit before a fall."** In the second verse, He states that **"before destruction the heart of a man is haughty."** In other words, the spirit of pride and haughtiness can lead to a destructive type of fall.

Again, Satan and Saddam Hussein are two perfect and classic examples of one man and one angel completely falling and losing everything they had built up over their years of living in heaven and on this earth – and they literally lost all of it in just a matter of a few days.

They have both fallen from the top of a major mountain down to the very bottom of that same mountain. They have both gone from the palace to the pit in one fell swoop! That's how far and how fast someone can fall if they have been operating in the spirit of pride to any significant degree for any length of time.

You can either choose to climb to the top of a mountain operating under a full surrender with God the Father where He will be the One to lead you up that mountain by His Holy Spirit – or you can choose to attempt to climb that mountain all on your own, operating under your own knowledge, wisdom, and pride.

Jesus has already told us that if we try and build our house all on our own efforts without any of God's help or guidance, that we will end up laboring in vain when it is all said and done.

Saddam Hussein managed to build up his entire empire all on his own efforts and pride – but that same pride ended up being his downfall, and he literally lost everything that took him years to build up – and all of it was lost in a matter of just a few days. His dramatic fall is a perfect example of what Jesus is trying to tell us with this statement. Saddam's efforts and accomplishments in this life all ended up being in total vain.

The story of Satan in particular should also serve as a major history lesson for all of us on what can happen to someone if the spirit of pride gets too far ingrained into their heart and mindset.

If one of God's highest created angels can literally fall from the top of a heavenly kingdom in the presence of God Almighty Himself – then anyone of us can fall in the exact same way if we do not stay on top of our walk with the Lord – especially in the area of our sanctification with the Lord where He is trying to mold, shape, and transform us into the express image of His Son **Jesus Christ**.

These two verses in particular should be memorized by all Christians, as God the Father is giving all us a major revelation with the statements being made in both of these verses. Here they are:

[18] Pride *goes* before destruction,
And a haughty spirit before a fall.
[19] Better *to be* of a humble spirit with the lowly,
Than to divide the spoil with the proud.
Proverbs 16:18-19

[12] Before destruction the heart of a man is haughty,
And before honor *is* humility.
Proverbs 18:12

In the first verse, God is telling us that we will be better off hanging out with the more lowly and humble type of people in this life rather than trying to hang out with the type of people whose only goal in this life is to acquire more material wealth and riches. What wealth and riches you may be able to acquire in this life will all rot and perish the minute you die and cross over. Not once ounce, not one penny will be crossing over with you on your deathbed.

Let No One Glory in Men
These next 5 verses will add very nicely to all of the verses listed above. What happens to someone once the spirit of pride starts to enter into their personality is

that they will then start to seek after their own glory. It now becomes all about them and them alone.

Christians who have fallen into this type of pride trap will not only start to try and steal the glory from anyone else who may be attempting to compete against them – but they will also try and steal the glory that would only be due to God Himself!

These next four verses are again, very strong words and revelation being given to us by the Lord, with all of it being for our own good. Here they are:

[29] that no flesh should glory in His presence.

1 Corinthians 1:29

[21] **Therefore let no one boast in men**. For all things are yours:

1 Corinthians 3:21

[7] Do not be wise in your own eyes;
Fear the LORD and depart from evil.
[8] It will be health to your flesh,
And strength to your bones.

Proverbs 3:7-8

[17] But "he who glories, let him glory in the LORD." [18] For not he who commends himself is approved, but whom the Lord commends.

2 Corinthians 10:17

[23] Thus says the LORD:
"Let not the wise *man* glory in his wisdom,
Let not the mighty *man* glory in his might,
Nor let the rich *man* glory in his riches;
[24] But let him who glories glory in this,
That he understands and knows Me,

That I *am* the LORD, exercising lovingkindness, judgment, and righteousness in the earth.
For in these I delight," says the LORD.
Jeremiah 9:23-24

All 5 of these verses are laying it out very plainly and very clearly. We are not to glory in ourselves or to any other men and women in this life – and we are not to glory in our own accomplishments, in our own strength, or in any of the riches and wealth that we may have acquired in this life. The only Person that we are to glory to in this life is to the Lord Himself.

The fourth verse puts it very nicely when it says that we are not to commend ourselves for our own good works. Any commending that will be of any matter and value to us will be what the Lord will want to commend us for, not what we may want to commend ourselves for, or what anyone else may want to commend us for.

In other words, the only Person you should really be trying to impress and seeking approval from in this life is God Himself, since He will be the only One who will be judging and rewarding you when everything is all finally said and done on your life.

It's really quite amazing how many people in our materialistic, greedy, and self-centered society are only working and living for whatever glory, fame, and notoriety they can get from other people in this life instead of trying to work direct for God and His seal of approval for what they are doing with their lives.

Stay Humble in Your Walk With the Lord

If God the Father does not want us walking with any kind of bad pride operating in our personalities, then what would be the exact opposite of having this kind of bad pride? These next 4 verses will tell you.

All 4 of these verses are telling us that we should be clothed with humility, that things should be done with a lowliness of mind, and that we should humble ourselves in the sight and under the mighty hand of God the Father. In other words, we all have to learn how to walk with a humble spirit and a humble mindset in our thoughts and in our actions towards ourselves, towards God, and towards all other people.

Here are 4 very good verses from the Lord giving us this piece of revelation:

[5] Likewise you younger people, submit yourselves to *your* elders. Yes, all of *you* be submissive to one another, and be clothed with humility, for
"God resists the proud,
But gives grace to the humble.
1 Peter 5:5

[3] *Let* nothing *be done* through selfish ambition or conceit, but in lowliness of mind let each esteem others better than himself.
[4] Let each of you look out not only for his own interests, but also for the interests of others.
Philippians 2:3-4

[10] Humble yourselves in the sight of the Lord, and He will lift you up.
James 4:10

⁶ Therefore humble yourselves under the mighty hand of God, that He may exalt you in due time, ⁷ casting all your care upon Him, for He cares for you.

1 Peter 5:6

Notice that if you are willing to walk with this kind of a humble spirit in this life that God will lift you up and properly exalt you to some type of degree when the time is right.

In the type of materialistic, greedy, and competitive world that many of us are forced to live in today, trying to develop a real spirit of humility is a tall order. But God the Father, through the sanctifying work of the Holy Spirit on the inside of you, can work this kind of a humble spirit into your personality if you are willing to work with Him on it. This can be done, even in the type of competitive world we live in today if you really want God to help you in this area.

The Fall of Satan

As I stated in the beginning of this chapter, probably the greatest casualty of someone falling from this bad kind of pride operating in their personalities has to be Satan himself. The verses I will list below only give us partial information and knowledge as to what actually had occurred. We will have to wait until we get to heaven to get the rest of this story.

But these Scripture verses do give us enough information to get a basic understanding of what happened in his story, and what caused him to completely fall from grace in the first place with our Lord and Savior. When you really stop and think about this fallen angel's story, it really is beyond belief!

To think that God the Father gave him and the rest of these fallen angels a chance to literally make it up into His third heaven where He lives at compared to what the human race has to go through. We all live for trying to make it into this heaven. Satan and the rest of these fallen angels were all born into this perfect heaven. They had it all right from the very beginning – and yet they still blew it!

They had God, they had His perfect heaven in which to live and work in, and they also had no other corrupting influences trying to come against them until Satan chose to rebel against God the Father after a certain period of time. What will be very interesting to find out is how long of a period of time it took before Satan started to corrupt in his personality, with the spirit of pride and lust causing him to want to try and rebel against God.

To think that all of these fallen angels had an equal chance and opportunity to make it in this perfect heavenly environment. All they had to do was keep their act together, stay humble and accountable in their walks with the Lord, do things God's way and stay out of trouble – and they all could have lived happily ever after for all of eternity in this perfect heavenly paradise. But for whatever reason, all of this was simply not enough for some of them. They had to have it all, and Satan apparently made some kind of a futile attempt to elevate and exalt himself above the throne of God Himself.

Since they were all living in God's presence in this third heaven for who knows how long – they all had to know that there was no other god or gods in existence, and that this one and only God was all-powerful and that He could not be literally overthrown. To have this kind of knowledge right at the beginning, and then to tempt their eternal fates by trying to literally overthrow this one and only Almighty God is totally beyond comprehension.

Satan and all of these angels was either just plain stupid to begin with, or the spirit of pride was so blinding them, that they could no longer see the truth in certain matters and they thus thought they had a real chance to be able to literally overthrow our God. I have to believe that these fallen angels had the initial intelligence and knowledge to begin with to fully understand how the big picture was all set up with God the Father. I do not think they started out with any kind of major stupidity from being able to see this obvious truth.

But somewhere along the way pride entered in, and once it did, it started to blind and corrupt them. And once that corruption started to take place within their own natural personalities, it did not take long for them to malfunction to the dark side and then make an attempt to try and overthrow the Lord.

As a result of this treasonous and rebellious act, God the Father had no other alternative but to cast all of these abominable angels out of His presence for all of eternity – never, ever to be given another chance to be able to get back in!

Just stop and ponder and think on the eternal consequences of this one angel's rebellion against God – to be forever banished from the only environment they had probably ever known. And all of this occurred as a result of one angel's failure to keep his act together with the Lord!

For whatever reason, Satan let the spirit of pride and arrogance seep into his mindset and way of thinking. And once this spirit of pride and arrogance got to the point of starting to blind him to the big picture truths they were all living with – then it was only a matter of time before he would literally decide to act on it and go for all the marbles himself.

And once he made his final and fatal move with the Lord that was going to be it. God pulled the plug, and he, and all the rest of the angels who tried to rebel with him, were all forever cast out of this perfect heavenly environment. Satan and all of the rest of the fallen angels who rebelled with him are now lost for all of eternity – and their final destination will be the Lake of Fire and Brimstone where they will all be thrown into at the end of the Millennium Kingdom with Jesus. And to think that the catalyst that caused all of these events to occur was the spirit of pride! This is why the Lord is specifically telling us in the above verses that pride will come before the fall – and in this case, we are talking about the most extreme kind of fall imaginable – falling from heaven itself with no chance of ever being able to make it back in!

This is why all Christians have got to stay on top of this particular negative quality. If the spirit of pride can take out one third of the entire angelic host from the third heaven where God lives – then it can do the exact same thing to all of us living on this lower plane of existence. And we see it happening every single day down here on this earth.

Day in and day out, someone who has let the spirit of pride get the best of them is committing acts of murder, robbery, rape, adultery, thefts, scams, corporate fraud, and mismanagement of funds and money, etc. As a result of the spirit of pride totally blinding them, they think they are perfectly justified in committing some of these evil acts to begin with. And then to top it off, they think they are too smart to ever get caught by the criminal justice system. And for some, they will get away with some of these crimes and never be caught by the law in this lifetime. But then they forget one simple little thing.

It will only be a matter of time before they physically die and cross over – and when they do, they will all have to meet God the Father Himself for a personal judgment. And for many of them, this judgment will be causing the greatest fall of all if they have not been saved before they had died – the fall into the pits of hell, and then eventually the fall into the Lake of Fire and Brimstone after the Millennium has taken place, where they will then spend the rest of their eternal lives with Satan and all the rest of his fallen angels.

To watch this kind of scenario play itself out, day in and day out, is just gut wrenching. To think that so many of these people have become so blinded by their own pride and arrogance that they will no longer listen to God or anyone else who may want to try and help them out. Unbelievable!

Now here are the two main verses from the Old Testament giving us this story about Satan and how he managed to completely fall from the love and grace of God the Father. The third verse is from the Book of Revelation, which will tell us that a third of the heavenly angels were also cast out with Satan.

[12] "Son of man, take up a lamentation for the king of Tyre, and say to him, 'Thus says the Lord GOD:
"You *were* the seal of perfection,
Full of wisdom and perfect in beauty.
[13] You were in Eden, the garden of God;
Every precious stone *was* your covering:
The sardius, topaz, and diamond,
Beryl, onyx, and jasper,
Sapphire, turquoise, and emerald with gold.
The workmanship of your timbrels and pipes
Was prepared for you on the day you were created.
[14] "You *were* the anointed cherub who covers;
I established you;
You were on the holy mountain of God;
You walked back and forth in the midst of fiery stones.
[15] You *were* perfect in your ways from the day you were created,
Till iniquity was found in you.
[16] "By the abundance of your trading
You became filled with violence within,
And you sinned;
Therefore I cast you as a profane thing
Out of the mountain of God;
And I destroyed you, O covering cherub,
From the midst of the fiery stones.
[17] "Your heart was lifted up because of your beauty;
You corrupted your wisdom for the sake of your splendor;
I cast you to the ground,
I laid you before kings,
That they might gaze at you.

¹⁸ "You defiled your sanctuaries
By the multitude of your iniquities,
By the iniquity of your trading;
Therefore I brought fire from your midst;
It devoured you,
And I turned you to ashes upon the earth
In the sight of all who saw you.
¹⁹ All who knew you among the peoples are astonished at you;
You have become a horror,
And *shall be* no more forever."

Ezekiel 28:12-19

The Fall of Lucifer

¹² "How you are fallen from heaven,
O Lucifer, son of the morning!
How you are cut down to the ground,
You who weakened the nations!
¹³ For you have said in your heart:
'I will ascend into heaven,
I will exalt my throne above the stars of God;
I will also sit on the mount of the congregation
On the farthest sides of the north;
¹⁴ I will ascend above the heights of the clouds,
I will be like the Most High.'
¹⁵ Yet you shall be brought down to Sheol,
To the lowest depths of the Pit.
¹⁶ "Those who see you will gaze at you,
And consider you, *saying:*
'*Is* this the man who made the earth tremble,
Who shook kingdoms,
¹⁷ Who made the world as a wilderness
And destroyed its cities,
Who did not open the house of his prisoners?'

Isaiah 14:12-17

³ And another sign appeared in heaven: behold, a great, fiery red dragon having seven heads and ten horns, and seven diadems on his heads. ⁴ His tail drew a third of the stars of heaven and threw them to the earth. And the dragon stood before the woman who was ready to give birth, to devour her Child as soon as it was born.

Revelation 12:3-4

Satan was called Lucifer before he rebelled and was cast out of heaven. Lucifer means **"light bearer."** The name Satan means **"adversary."** As a result of his fall from heaven, Satan goes from being a light bearing, anointed cherub to now being an enemy of God Almighty Himself!

Also notice that Satan was not born evil or wicked. The first verse says that he was the seal of perfection, that he was full of wisdom and perfect in beauty, and perfect in his ways from the day he was actually created by God. The Bible also tells us that he was literally allowed to walk on the mountain of God Himself, and that he might have been able to walk very close to where God's actual throne is located. And then it happened – sin and iniquity was found in him. The Bible does not tell us how long of a period of time there was from the time that he was walking right before God until he started to sin and transgress.

The nature of the sin appears to have been something to do with the trading opportunities that the Lord must have given to him. The above passage tells us that somehow violence started to rise within him as a result of the abundance of those trading opportunities. The word "abundance" is telling us that Satan must have been very profitable with these trading opportunities.

My guess is that all of this wealth and success must have started to go to his head.

The very first part of the first verse says he was covered with precious and valuable stones, and then it goes on to state what each one of these stones were. He was thus walking in some kind of significant wealth and prosperity. This verse also tells us that he had a certain number of sanctuaries under his rule, as it says that he then ended up defiling a certain number of his own sanctuaries by some of the sins and iniquities he was committing.

Besides letting some of this wealth and prosperity start to get the best of him, the first verse then tells us that pride definitely started to enter into him when it says that his heart was **"lifted up"** because of his beauty. From that position, it then says that his wisdom started to get **"corrupted"** – and all of this was starting to occur as a result of the initial **"splendor"** he was walking in.

Put all of the above together, and it would appear that God the Father greatly blessed this angel with a profitable trading business and a significant amount of wealth and prosperity. But as a result of all of this significant abundance, pride started to enter in – and he then started to focus and concentrate too much on his own beauty, knowledge, wisdom, and his own glorious splendor.

The second verse then takes us one step further into what happened next. It was bad enough that Satan was starting to corrupt from all of the wealth and prosperity that God had initially blessed him with. But then he had to see if he could start to expand and enrich his own personal territory. And what does he try and target next – the throne of God Almighty Himself! The wording in the second verse then tells us that Satan literally wanted to exalt his own personal throne above the throne of God. And not only did he want to personally exalt his throne to this unreachable height, but then it states that he wanted to **"be like"** the Most High God Himself! Not only are we talking total, complete, and open rebellion against God – but now we are talking complete and utter blasphemy against the Lord, to literally think that he could become like God Himself!

And no sooner does Satan reach this point of no return with the Lord that he then gets cast right out of heaven! The first verse tells us that Satan was then cast out of heaven as a **"profane thing"** and that he shall be **"no more forever."** In other words, Satan no longer exists in the eyes of God. He is now totally lost forever and he will never, ever have another chance to get back into the good graces of our Lord and Savior. When God the Father says you no longer exist in His eyes as far as He is concerned when He says you shall be **"no more forever"** – God is pronouncing the most extreme judgment that He possibly can on a created being.

And to think that this created angel went from being a beautiful, wise, perfect, and anointed cherub to being cast right out of heaven with God telling him that he will no longer exist in His eyes. **We are talking about a created angelic being falling from one of the highest mountain peaks anyone could ever hope**

to walk on down to the lowest level that anyone can be cast down into.

At this time, Satan is still allowed to roam in the air in the second heaven. But once Jesus comes back to set up His Millennium Kingdom, Satan will first be cast into what is called the Bottomless Pit. And then after the 1000 year Millennium Kingdom has ended, Satan will then be cast into the Lake of Fire and Brimstone where he will then remain forever and ever with the rest of his fallen angels and the rest of all unsaved humanity that has ever lived.

And not only did Satan manage to get himself thrown out of the third heaven, but the third verse above also tells us that he somehow managed to get a third of the angels to get cast out right along with him when it says that his tail **"drew"** a third of the stars from heaven and threw them down onto the earth. I think the key word to focus on is the word **"drew"** – that Satan somehow managed to draw a third of these angels into his plan and scheme to try and exalt himself and his own personal throne above the throne of God.

To think that this one highly intelligent and beautiful angel could corrupt to such an extreme degree to where he thought he could literally overthrow our God the Father – and then to think that he could try to become just like Him – has got to be the greatest miscalculation and blunder any created being has ever made.

For the life of me, I simply cannot understand how Satan could have become so blinded and so deluded to think that this was even a possibility to begin with.

Once you examine and analyze all of the above facts of this angel's downfall – there can be no question that the spirit of pride had to have played a major part in his own personal corruption and eventual downfall.

I believe that his spirit of pride was so blinding and so distorting his view of the big picture, that he literally thought he could get away with trying to overthrow the Lord Himself – much in the same way that Saddam Hussein thought he could stand up and engage with the strongest military might in the world. Again, another major miscalculation and blunder as a result of the spirit of pride totally blinding him as to what the real truth was that was staring him right in the face. I believe this is why God is telling us in the above verses that the spirit of pride, haughtiness, and arrogance will come right before the fall and destruction of one's own personal life.

This is why the Lord is really sounding the alarm with the way He has worded all of the above verses. When God the Father says that the spirit of pride will come right before a fall – you know He is trying to give all of us a major warning that this deadly spirit has to be stopped dead in its tracks before it even has a chance to wrap itself around our mind and way of thinking.

The spirit of pride has to be dealt with very early on before it starts to grow too far and too big into our thought process. This is why the Lord is really emphasizing that each and every Christian enter into this sanctification process with Him so the Holy Spirit can start to take control and help you stay on top of your game as you continue to grow in the grace, knowledge, power, favor, and blessings of the Lord.

God blessed Satan with incredible amounts of wealth and authority – and look what happened – he could not stay humble and appreciative of those blessings. And once he started to take his eyes off the real source, God the Father, he then started to look on his own beauty and on his own wisdom, literally to the point that he thought he could become like God Himself.

Though we can all look at this story from the outside and wonder how anyone could have been so stupid to think they could become like God Himself or to try and literally overthrow Him – realize that once this spirit gets a real foothold into your mind and thought process – it has a very subtle way of being able to alter and distort your view and perception of reality. And once it has grown into any kind of full fruition in your mindset, you can become totally blinded to any kind of real truth.

Now here is another good verse to burn into your memory banks.

27 Do not boast about tomorrow,
For you do not know what a day may bring forth.
² Let another man praise you, and not your own mouth;
A stranger, and not your own lips.

Proverbs 27:1

Chapter 25: Choose Your Friends Carefully

For those of you who have really entered into a true Spirit-filled, fully-surrendered walk with the Lord where He is now leading your life in the direction that He will want it to go in – one of the first things that you will find happening is that God will start to prune out the people that He does not want in your life and start to bring in the people that He does want in your life. As you will see in the Scripture verses I will list below, the Bible tells us to **choose our friends very carefully** in this life. These verses will tell us that he who walks with wise people will become wise himself, but that he who keeps company with fools will be destroyed. The Bible tells us that we are not to be unequally yoked with unbelievers that we are to stay away from people who cause divisions and offenses, and to withdraw from every brother who walks disorderly.

This does not mean that we cannot work with the lost, the downtrodden, and the people who need to find God and His message of eternal salvation. When Jesus came to our earth in the flesh, He always went after the sinners and the outcasts. But when Jesus went after these sinners, it was always for the express purpose of getting them saved and cleaned up.

Jesus did not chase after everyone. He ripped on the Pharisees and many of the high-ranking Jewish leaders. Some people are open to be helped, others are not. The Bible tells us to stay away from people who are considered to be **"dogs,"** and to beware of people who are **"evil workers."**

One of the first things that God will do with your life once you come into a full surrender with Him is to start to set some boundary lines. He will now decide the path that you will follow in Him. He will now be leading you into the specific jobs that He will want you to have in this life. If you are single and have not married yet, He will lead you to the mate that He will want you to marry if it is in His perfect will that you get married in this life.

And once those boundary lines start to go up – one of the first things that God will do is to decide who is going to be coming into those boundary lines and who will be going out. In other words, God will be deciding who your true friends are going to be in this life and who will not.

The main reason God will be helping you to choose who your true friends are going to be in this life is because His ultimate and highest aim for you is to transform and sanctify you. In other words, He wants you to spiritually grow and mature in your walk with Him.

The Bible tells us that we are transformed by the renewing of our minds. God's ultimate aim for us is our sanctification – where He starts to begin to mold and transform us into the express image of His Son Jesus Christ.

The main reason that God will start to take out the friends in your life that He does not want you to have is because some of these people may be negative influences in your life. They may not be open to growing and maturing in the Lord like you will be, and all they will do is try and hold you back when you start your own spiritual journey and growth in the Lord.

They will start criticizing and making fun of you and all they will end up doing is stunting your growth in the Lord.

God will not be putting up with this, and He will thus be taking all of these bad and negative influences out of your life very early on once you enter into this full surrender with Him. For those of you who are married and have children – it is the same thing when you do not want your children hanging out with other children who you know would be a bad and negative influence on your child.

You know that if your children start hanging out with the wrong type of crowd, they can become very easily corrupted in a very short period of time. As a result, you will become very protective with your children, and you will watch them very closely when they are old enough to start choosing who their friends are going to be.

It is the exact same way with God the Father! This is why God will be moving very early on to take out these negative influences in your life. Once this starts to happen, you have to go with the program or you could cause God to start pulling back on you. And once that starts to happen, you could then start to backslide and everything could then start to shut down.

If you will allow God to prune out the people that He does not want you to have in your life – then what He will start to do is to bring in the people that He will want to have in your life. I call these types of friends **"God-friends."** These people will be other good, godly, Spirit-filled Christians who are truly walking in good stead with the Lord and they will now be the people that He will want you to share your walk with!

As you will see in the Scripture verses listed below – you will need other good, solid, Christian friends in your life to help you grow in the Lord. The Bible tells us that we can only "know in part." No one has all of the answers to everything. By sharing your walk with other good, solid, Christian friends, you can each help each other out in your pursuit of the knowledge and ways of God.

You will know some things about God they may not know, and they will know some things that you may not know. You thus are able to help contribute to each other's storehouse of knowledge in the Lord.

One of the verses listed below state that two friends can help sharpen each other up like **"iron sharpens iron."** Just like one piece of iron can make the other piece of iron extremely sharp by rubbing up against it – two solid Christian friends can also have the same type of positive effect on one another by sharing their own personal walks in the Lord with one other.

By having other good, solid, Christian friends to share your journey with – you will literally accelerate your spiritual growth and development in the Lord because you will have more than one source in which to feed and learn from. You will be learning about God from all of your own personal adventures and experiences with Him – but you will also be learning more about God from all of your other friend's personal journey and experiences with Him.

How many of these types of God-friends can you expect God to bring into your life? Only God will be able to answer that for each and every one of you. Some may only get one or two to start off with, others may get 5 or 10. Let God make the decision as to how many and when they will be brought into your life.

What I have learned is that it is not the quantity or amount that comes in – it is the quality. You are much better off having just one or two good, solid, quality friends as versus 10 or 15 that are not as good quality friends as the one or two may be.

Every Christian is operating at different levels of spiritual development with the Lord. God knows best as to who would be best suited for you at the level of spiritual development that you are currently operating at with Him. When God does bring in these types of special God-friends to share your journey with – they will be real treasures! These God-friendships will be anointed by God Himself due to the quality feedings and interaction that will occur in them.

Sadly, what you will find out very early on, is just because someone may be a saved and born again Christian does not mean this person has their act together in the Lord. Some people have become too judgmental and too critical in their walks with the Lord. Some have become too arrogant and pompous, thinking they have all the answers to everything. They will tend to look down on anyone else who is not operating at the knowledge levels they are operating at. Some have become so flaky in their walks with the Lord, that they have lost touch with reality and you won't be able to connect with any of them.

God knows best as to who will be best suited for you at your current level of spiritual development with Him – so let Him guide you to the ones that He will want you to connect with. I have seen God do this so many times for others, that I literally consider it a miraculous piece of work – especially as to how He gets you to meet some of these people in the first place. Some of these chess moves are quite incredible, as most of these people will be total strangers to you until God moves in to match the two of you up.

The other thing that could occur besides God matching you up with total strangers is that He may move on someone else you may know, but that you are not particular good friends with. That person then gets saved and plugged in, and then they find out that you too are saved and plugged in – and now a good God-friendship can start to build up as you now have something in common with one another to start to build a good solid friendship with.

This could be another member in your family, someone that you may work with, a friend who you may have known from your past, or someone you may see at church from time to time but never really talked with. The possibilities are endless as to where these people may come from. These God-friends can come from anywhere and at anytime – so keep your radars up, as you never know when God may move to bring one of them into your life.

Choose Your Friends Carefully

This verse should literally be burned into your memory banks so that you never, ever forget this basic fundamental command from the Lord! Here it is:

[26] The righteous should choose his friends carefully,
For the way of the wicked leads them astray.
Proverbs 12:26

Notice this verse is specifically telling us that if we do not choose our friends very carefully in this life, that we could end up choosing the wrong type of people to become friends with, and they can then end up leading us astray from God and with what He wants to do with our lives. Many of God's people have lost their calls in Him because they chose to hang out with the wrong type of people.

Benefits of Choosing Good God-Friends

Here are six very interesting verses showing you why God does want you to have other good, solid, Christian friends to share your walk with.

These six verses will show you that there is safety in the multitude of counselors, that plans can go awry without having other people to hash things out with, that war is waged by having wise counsel with others, that learning is increased by listening to wise counsel, and that if you cease to listen to wise counsel – that you will start to stray from being able to acquire more knowledge in God.

[14] Where *there is* no counsel, the people fall;
But in the multitude of counselors *there is* safety.

Proverbs 11:14

[5] A wise man *is* strong,
Yes, a man of knowledge increases strength;
[6] For by wise counsel you will wage your own war,
And in a multitude of counselors *there is* safety.

Proverbs 24:5-6

[18] Plans are established by counsel;
By wise counsel wage war.

Proverbs 20:18

[22] Without counsel, plans go awry,
But in the multitude of counselors they are established.

Proverbs 15:22

[20] Listen to counsel and receive instruction,
That you may be wise in your latter days.

Proverbs 19:20

[27] Cease listening to instruction, my son,
And you will stray from the words of knowledge.

Proverbs 19:27

Once you turn the reigns of your life over to God for Him to fully handle, He will now make sure that you get matched up with the right kind of people that you can become true God-friends with.

As Iron Sharpens Iron

This next verse is extremely fascinating as it tells us that two friends can help sharpen each other up as iron sharpens iron. A true God-friend can help keep you sharp in the Spirit, let you know when you are getting too far off track, help you get through and make sense of some of the downswings that can occur in your walk, confirm and help bear witness when you are on the right track, give you pep talks when needed, and help keep you in the game when you start to get too mad and frustrated when things do not go your way.

You each serve to help keep each other **up in the Lord** so that you both can continue to stay on the straight and narrow road that God now has you set up on. You can also help each other out if one starts to be tempted to do something they should not be engaging in. Here is the verse:

[17] *As* iron sharpens iron,
So a man sharpens the countenance of his friend.
Proverbs 27:17

A true God-friend will always be honest and straight forward with you. You cannot help keep each other up and sharp in the Lord unless you are both willing to be totally honest with one another.

Do Not Be Unequally Yoked With Unbelievers

These next seven verses will tell us not to be yoked together with unbelievers, foolish men, dogs, evil workers, those who are disorderly, reckless, contentious and always causing trouble and strife. There is one verse in particular that tells us that **"evil company corrupts good habits."** This verse perfectly shows us what can happen to any of your children if they start hanging out with the wrong type of people.

Here are 7 good verses telling us to stay on our side of the fence, and to stay away from all of the bad apples who have no desire for God or anything that He stands for.

[14] Do not be unequally yoked together with unbelievers. For what fellowship has righteousness with lawlessness? And what communion has light with darkness? [15] And what accord has Christ with Belial? Or what part has a believer with an unbeliever? [16] And what agreement has the temple of God with idols? For you[a] are the temple of the living God. As God has said:
"I will dwell in them
And walk among them.
I will be their God,
And they shall be My people

         2 Corinthians 6:14-16

[20] He who walks with wise *men* will be wise,
But the companion of fools will be destroyed.
         Proverbs 13:20

[6] A scoffer seeks wisdom and does not *find it,*
But knowledge *is* easy to him who understands.
[7] Go from the presence of a foolish man,
When you do not perceive *in him* the lips of knowledge.
         Proverbs 14:6

[2] Beware of dogs, beware of evil workers, beware of the mutilation!
         Philippians 3:2

[6] But we command you, brethren, in the name of our Lord Jesus Christ, that you withdraw from every brother who walks

disorderly and not according to the tradition which he received from us.

2 Thessalonians 3:6

[17] Now I urge you, brethren, note those who cause divisions and offenses, contrary to the doctrine which you learned, and avoid them. [18] For those who are such do not serve our Lord Jesus Christ, but their own belly, and by smooth words and flattering speech deceive the hearts of the simple.

Romans 16:17-18

[33] Do not be deceived: "Evil company corrupts good habits."
[34] Awake to righteousness, and do not sin; for some do not have the knowledge of God. I speak *this* to your shame.

1 Corinthians 15:33-34

All of these verses are giving us major warnings that we are to stay away from all of the bad apples in this life who will do nothing but try and bring us down to their lower way of living in this life. Many Christians have had their lives totally ruined and destroyed as a result of marrying the wrong people or choosing the wrong kinds of friends to hang out with.

Conclusion

Just as God saw fit to create Eve for Adam in the Garden of Eden when He first created the first man – God still places an extremely high value on personal friendships, and He will make sure to bring the right people and the right number of people in your life so you can each help each other out to go farther and fly higher in the Lord.

When Jesus first started to send the 12 apostles out to walk with His anointing, He would always send them out two-by-two.

Once you enter into a real supernatural walk with the Lord, you will go nuts if you do not have someone to share your walk with. There are simply too many good God things that will start to happen in your life, and you will need others to talk with, to vent with, to share with, to learn from one another, and to help keep each other on track.

Chapter 26 Fasting

[17] But you, when you fast, anoint your head and wash your face, [18] so that you do not appear to men to be fasting, but to your Father who *is* in the secret *place;* and your Father who sees in secret will reward you openly.

Matthew 6:17-20

This verse speaks clearly. When God prompted you to do a fast make sure you keep this verse in mind.

Otherwise your fasting might just be for your own personal gain and to show off.

Personally I have found that a short fast of 12 hours works just as well as a 24 hour fast as long as you obeyed God and read the word of God.

I never tell when I am on a personal fast. It is a matter between me and God.

If I fast with my spiritual children for a specific reason, then they, myself and God are the only ones that knows about this.

Chapter 26 Tithe

Some of you are not paying your tithe. Some has never paid a tithe. This is a chapter on what a tithe is and why everyone must pay a tithe.

This chapter is included in this book not because I wanted to but because God directed me to.

God said we should pay 10% of any money that comes into our hands. Why?

⁷ And the LORD God formed man *of* the dust of the ground, and breathed into his nostrils the breath of life; and man became a living being.
Life in God's Garden
⁸ The LORD God planted a garden eastward in Eden, and there He put the man whom He had formed. ⁹ And out of the ground the LORD God made every tree grow that is pleasant to the sight and good for food. The tree of life *was* also in the midst of the garden, and the tree of the knowledge of good and evil.
¹⁰ Now a river went out of Eden to water the garden, and from there it parted and became four riverheads.
Genesis 2:7-10

⁶God put His hand into the earth and carved a square block out of the earth to make man. Not a little dust

---

⁶ Early in *B'reishit* (Genesis 2:7), we discover that God formed *ha-adam afar min ha-adamah,* man from the dust of the earth. A midrash has it that God took the dust from the four corners of the earth so that man would be at home everywhere. Except for the change in the initial vowel sign and the addition of the letter *hei* at the end, *adamah,* earth, soil, ground, is spelled exactly like *adam.* Thus, it is easy to associate *adam* with *adamah.* In his commentary on Genesis, Rabbi Gunther Plaut explains, "Adam is formed from the earth, *adamah,* thus 'earthling.' In

like some of you might think. For many years I've also though that we've been made of a little dust until God showed me.

The earth has got 6 layers. See below.

Top·soil – the upper fertile layer of soil from which plant roots take nutrients.

Hu·mus – a brown or black complex variable material resulting from partial decomposition of plant or animal matter and forming the organic portion of soil.

Eluviation – the transportation of dissolved or suspended material within the soil by the movement of water when rainfall exceeds evaporation.

Regolith – the layer of loose rock particles that covers the bedrock of most land on earth.

Bedrock – the solid rock beneath loose rock particles or soil.

Mineral – a solid homogeneous crystalline chemical element or compound that results from the inorganic processes of nature; broadly : any of various naturally occurring homogeneous substances (as stone, coal, salt, sulfur, sand, petroleum, water, or natural gas) obtained usually from the ground.

---

modern terms, this is an assonance.... Like-sounding words were thought to hint at a special association of concepts. An English equivalent might be: God fashioned a soul from the soil" (*Revised Torah Commentary*, 22).

6 layers of soil + 4 rivers = 10 - This is what makes you

The Tithe Belongs to the Lord
God is responsible for every means that people have to make a living

^{27} John answered and said, "A man can receive nothing unless it has been given to him from heaven.
John 3:27

^{17} Every good gift and every perfect gift is from above, and comes down from the Father of lights, with whom there is no variation or shadow of turning.
James 1:17

Farmers plant God's seeds in His earth and rely upon His rain and sunshine to ripen it to harvest.

Auto worker's use steel, glass, rubber, plastic, oil and gasoline. These are products from God's earth.

Craftsman use their talent or skill to work at a trade that is given by God. God gave you your brain, eyes, ears, mouth, hands, fingers, legs, and feet to use so that you can earn your living.

Even the silver and copper in our coins, and the wood pulp in our paper currency comes from God's earth. It is extremely fair of God to only require a tenth to be returned to Him, since He owns 100% of the universe.

Unfortunately, many Christians misunderstand the idea of tithing. They often think of it as giving a tenth from "their own" property to God. However, in reality it is God that has done the giving to us, and claims the return of only 10% of His own property. Tithing is not taking a tenth of our own money and giving it to God, but it is returning a tenth of what was already His to begin with! The scripture says,

[14] But who *am* I, and who *are* my people,
That we should be able to offer so willingly as this?
For all things *come* from You,
And of Your own we have given You.
1 Chronicles 29:14

God is so generous to us. He gives us the 90% and retains only 10% of what is rightfully His.

Stewards of God's Property

Someone once suggested, "Well, if the tenth already belongs to God, why doesn't He just automatically withhold the tithe and then give us the rest, like SARS/TAX withholds taxes from our wages? That way God won't have to depend on us to pay our tithes."

God has chosen for us to personally return the tithe so that we can demonstrate our stewardship of his property. **Stewardship is the faithful and responsible management of something that belongs to someone else.** Obviously, if God observes that we are irresponsible to return the small percentage that belongs to Him as He has directed, He knows that we can neither be trusted with any greater responsibilities or blessings in the Kingdom of God

[10] He who *is* faithful in *what is* least is faithful also in much; and he who is unjust in *what is* least is unjust also in much.

> [11] Therefore if you have not been faithful in the unrighteous mammon, who will commit to your trust the true *riches?*
>
> **Luke 16:10-11**

Tithing is a test of our stewardship over the property of God, a test of our honesty to return to God what is rightfully His, a test of our obedience to do what He told us to do, and a test of our love and desire to please Him with our lives. Tithing is a demonstration that we believe in God, and that we acknowledge that He is the provider of all material blessings. If you haven't the faith to believe that the tithe belongs to the Lord, neither can you have faith in Him to meet your financial needs. After all, if you don't believe that the tenth is His, you must not believe that the whole earth is His either. Without that confidence in His supremacy, there could be no confidence in His ability to provide our needs.

Most of us realize that robbery is a serious offense in our secular society, and those convicted of this crime can be sentenced too years in jail. But what happens to a person who is guilty of robbing God? The scriptures say that he will be "cursed with a curse"

> [9] You are cursed with a curse,
> For you have robbed Me,
> *Even* this whole nation.
>
> **Malachi 3:9**

What kind of curse is this? From Malachi we see that God's blessing to the tither is to open Heaven's windows and pour out abundant blessings, and to rebuke the devourer (Satan) from destroying their increase and fruitfulness

[10] Bring all the tithes into the storehouse,
That there may be food in My house,
And try Me now in this,"
Says the LORD of hosts,
"If I will not open for you the windows of heaven
And pour out for you *such* blessing
That *there will* not *be room* enough *to receive it.*
[11] "And I will rebuke the devourer for your sakes,
So that he will not destroy the fruit of your ground,
Nor shall the vine fail to bear fruit for you in the field,"
Says the LORD of hosts;

Malachi 3:10-11

In contrast, the non-tither is cursed by having no protection to prevent the devourer from destroying their prosperity, and God cannot shower them with His abundant Heavenly blessings. God cannot bless or protect the prosperity of the person who does not tithe!

This indeed is a curse.

Some claim they can't afford to pay their tithes. But let me ask, "Can you afford to be cursed? Can you afford to not have God's blessings and protection over your finances? Can you afford to be considered a thief or robber of God's property? Or can you afford to be a person who does not obey the Word of God?" The fact is, you cannot afford not to pay your tithes, because this is the principle that God has chosen to bless you! Another person once asked, "Why does God need my tithe?" In answer to this question, He doesn't need your money or anyone else's. Remember, God is the owner of the whole universe and all its wealth. However, He has chosen to use your tithes and offerings for the expenses of maintaining "spiritual meat" in His house

¹⁰ Bring all the tithes into the storehouse,
That there may be food in My house,
And try Me now in this,"
Says the LORD of hosts,
"If I will not open for you the windows of heaven
And pour out for you *such* blessing
That *there will* not *be room* enough *to receive it.*

Malachi 3:10

On the first day of the week you are to bring your tithes and offerings to the "storehouse" where you are spiritually fed.

² On the first *day* of the week let each one of you lay something aside, storing up as he may prosper, that there be no collections when I come.

1 Corinthians 16:2

It is very important that we are faithful in our tithes and offerings, as this is God's method of funding the preaching of His Word and the spreading of the Gospel.

¹³ Do you not know that those who minister the holy things eat *of the things* of the temple, and those who serve at the altar partake of *the offerings of* the altar? ¹⁴ Even so the Lord has commanded that those who preach the gospel should live from the gospel.

1 Corinthians 9:13-14

The Tithe Is Your Land

God is blessed by your tithe as an expression of your love and obedience to Him, yet tithing is primarily for your own benefit so that God can bless you. There is a universal law that God has placed in both the natural and spiritual realms. This is the law of sowing and reaping.

7 Do not be deceived, God is not mocked; for whatever a man sows, that he will also reap.

Galatians 6:7

The tithe is "soil" When you pay your tithe 10% you replace the soil that you are made of.

All farmers understand God's law of sowing and reaping. After a harvest in Bible times, before the farmer would use any of the grain as food for his family or livestock, he would first go through the harvest grain and pick out a percentage that exhibited the best qualities of size, weight, color, and set this aside as seed for the next season's crop planting. This early form of genetic selection helped assure that the next generation of crops would produce higher yields and greater quality.

This illustrates our tithe, why it cannot be the 10% that is left over after we pay everything else. The part that God claims and uses as soil is the first and best 10% of your increase, called the firstfruits.

[9] Honor the LORD with your possessions,
And with the firstfruits of all your increase;
[10] So your barns will be filled with plenty,
And your vats will overflow with new wine.

Proverbs 3:9-10

Do not use the Lord's tithe for anything else! Because if you don't sow, you can't reap.

How We Receive From God

The tithe is God's property that we are required to return to Him, however an "offering & Seed & Donation" is that which we give voluntarily out of our own property after the tithe has been subtracted. As we give our tithes, and give Offerings & Seeds & Donations above our tithe to God, He will continue to bless us and multiply our return in proportion to our investment in Him.

⁶ But this *I say:* He who sows sparingly will also reap sparingly, and he who sows bountifully will also reap bountifully.

2 Corinthians 9:6

I challenge you to become a tither and a giver to God, and "prove" His promise to bless you, just as He invites you to do in…

¹⁰ Bring all the tithes into the storehouse,
That there may be food in My house,
And try Me now in this,"
Says the LORD of hosts,
"If I will not open for you the windows of heaven
And pour out for you *such* blessing
That *there will* not *be room* enough *to receive it.*

Malachi 3:10

Give to God in faith, expecting Him to bless your return.

²⁴ Therefore I say to you, whatever things you ask when you pray, believe that you receive *them,* and you will have *them.*
Mark 11:24

Give cheerfully, expressing joy and confidence in giving to God.

⁷ *So let* each one *give* as he purposes in his heart, not grudgingly or of necessity; for God loves a cheerful giver.
2 Corinthians 9:7

Don't give your tithe with a sad face or have doubt in your heart because then you are not a cheerful giver. The same proportion that you open your faith to give to Him, He will use that same proportion as His measurement to bring blessing back to you!

³⁸ Give, and it will be given to you: good measure, pressed down, shaken together, and running over will be put into your bosom. For with the same measure that you use, it will be measured back to you."
Luke 6:38

When I pay my tithe, I add an extra 10% as a seed. Because the tithe is the soil you need to add a seed this is the seedlings that you plant to grow and because I add an equal 10% my returns from God is 100 Fold.

Light the World Ministries also pay their tithe and a 10% as a seed.

Also keep record of your tithes and seeds, because you can always lift it up to the Lord in touch and trying times and say but I have proof of paying my tithe and

Your Word (the Bible) said that I will be blessed when I do.

PS: Think of the tithe as a ball you throw to God. The ball God is throwing back will always be a bigger one.

References

Berit Kjos - Kjos Ministries

Dr. Dale A. Robbins

Michael Bradley - Bible Knowledge.com

All Bible verses from the New King James Version unless otherwise stated - http://www.biblegateway.com

www.ingramcontent.com/pod-product-compliance
Lightning Source LLC
Chambersburg PA
CBHW050424240426
43661CB00055B/2260